SIDEWAYS IN TIME
Critical Essays
on Alternate History Fiction

Liverpool Science Fiction Texts and Studies, 59

Liverpool Science Fiction Texts and Studies

Editor David Seed, *University of Liverpool*

Editorial Board
Mark Bould, *University of the West of England*
Veronica Hollinger, *Trent University*
Rob Latham, *University of California*
Roger Luckhurst, *Birkbeck College, University of London*
Patrick Parrinder, *University of Reading*
Andy Sawyer, *University of Liverpool*

Recent titles in the series

SIDEWAYS IN TIME

Critical Essays
on Alternate History Fiction

GLYN MORGAN AND
C. PALMER-PATEL

LIVERPOOL UNIVERSITY PRESS

First published 2019 by
Liverpool University Press
4 Cambridge Street
Liverpool
L69 7ZU

British Library Cataloguing-in-Publication data
A British Library CIP record is available

ISBN 978-1-78962-013-9 cased

Typeset by Carnegie Book Production, Lancaster
Printed and bound in Poland by BooksFactory.co.uk

The editors would like to thank their family and friends for their continued support, especially Anna and Toby.

This book is dedicated to our colleagues in the sf academic community, especially those who studied and worked alongside us in 2015.

Contents

Part II. Manipulating the Genre

Foreword

Stephen Baxter

What if you could change the past?

It's an old dream. As far back as 35 BC Livy, a Roman historian, wondered what would have happened if Alexander the Great had not died young.

Someday it may even be possible to change the past, or at least explore alternate realities. Modern scientists speculate that parallel universes might actually exist. Quantum physicists argue that every time you toss a coin, the universe splits into two copies, heads and tails. Some cosmologists believe our universe is just one of many, stacked up like pages in a book. But even if you could, *should* you change the past? Chaos theory tells us that large and unexpected consequences can follow from small actions.

Perhaps someday we will be able to access other timelines, for good or ill. Until then, we can only dream – what if?

The essays in this book explore many aspects of alternate history – but it is important to remember that history is determined by more than human choices and achievements.

The Sidewise Award of 2014, given for the best alternate history fiction of the previous year, featured a tie in its long form section. Of the two (deserved) winners, D. J. Taylor's *The Windsor Faction* (2013) is a subtle alternate history of the early days of the Second World War:

> One notable feature of the last few days of peace was the personal involvement of the King ... He is believed to have despatched a private telegram to the German Chancellor on 28 August – this as German troops were taking up their final positions – reminding him of the ancestral ties that united their two countries. (Taylor 11)

Thanks to the death of Wallis Simpson in 1936 (after complications following surgery for appendicitis), Edward VIII does not abdicate, and as war approaches he is active in trying to avert hostilities: a 'Windsor Faction' gathers, a loose collection of right-wing MPs, writers, and others, who argue against going to war. In the end the Nazis' aggression forces the conflict into being, but a different war from the historical follows.

The second Sidewise winner of 2014 was Bryce Zabel's *Surrounded by Enemies* (2013), in which Kennedy survives the 1963 assassination attempt:

> Millions of Americans and nearly everyone under twenty-five, it seems, remembers the night when the President of the United States appeared on the *Ed Sullivan Show* to greet the Beatles. (Zabel 108)

Ultimately Kennedy becomes obsessed with conspiracies real and imagined ranged against him, and his presidency falls in 1966 when details of his private life are exposed.

These are both fine books and convincing alternate histories – but they deal with relatively familiar and well-explored historical turning points, indeed jonbar hinges explored by the author (an alternate Second World War in *Weaver* (2008), a surviving Kennedy in *Voyage* (1996)). And both these hinges depend on events within the human world, on different choices made by human actors. The destinies of 'great men' are, as so often, the focus: a King, a president.

Yet larger forces shape our destinies. Consider for example Philip Jose Farmer's classic 'Sail On! Sail On!' (1952):

> No, my dear de Salcedo, let's not be ridiculous. Even the ancient Greeks knew the earth was round. Every university in Europe teaches that. And we Rogerians have measured the circumference. (Farmer, 'Sail On!' 88)

We are with Columbus, 'plunging ever deeper into Oceanus in our three cockle-shells', close to the point where the sailors try to insist on turning back. From the beginning there are hints that this is not our universe. Aristotelian physics seems to work in this world – Galileo's famous dropped-cannonball experiment had a different outcome. The crews sail bravely on, '[knowing] for sure that the Indies lie just across the Atlantic'. But then comes a final dawn: 'They had run out of horizon ... Now came the mighty overture; as compelling as the blast of Gabriel's horn was the topple of Oceanus into space' (Farmer, 'Sail On!' 99).

It is hard to imagine a more drastic change in the nature of our world than its being flat. But one can ask at what point this would have made any significant difference to history (in this case Eurasian history, as presumably the Americas do not exist). Aside from the puzzlement of a few astronomers and geographers, a jonbar hinge would presumably only have come as late as 1492, when European ships bravely tried to cross the imagined ocean, or to circumnavigate an imagined globe-world. It is only when we had become explorers on a global scale that we would have perceived such global configurations. But after that history would surely diverge significantly, beginning with a lack of New World gold and silver to finance European imperial ambitions.

The shape of our world – cosmological, geographic, biological – has played a key role in shaping our destiny. And this becomes evident when counterfactuals are considered. If Columbus had failed to raise the money for his transatlantic quest, or had failed in the crossing, surely another of the many contemporary navigators from Portugal or Spain would have made the crossing, sooner rather than later. But it seems inconceivable that an Inca or Aztec 'navigator' would have crossed the other way and 'discovered' Europe. Why should this be so?

Jared Diamond addressed this issue in his epic argument of historical inevitability, *Guns, Germs and Steel* (1997), which was inspired by a simple question asked of Diamond in New Guinea: 'Why is it that you white people developed so much cargo and brought it to New Guinea, but we black people had little cargo of our own?' (14).

Diamond's argument, developed in response to that New Guinea question, is complex, but it boils down to a kind of geographical determinism. The Old World continents had a greater east–west spread than the Americas or Africa. This allowed latitudinal migrations by farming cultures into wide regions with climates suitable for the crop types and herd animals they brought with them – and those crops and animals themselves had offered the proto-farmers a wider domesticable choice than their New World equivalents. This inspired the growth of Eurasian cities and empires, which incubated technological innovations – 'guns' and 'steel' – as well as the crowd diseases, the 'germs' that shattered the New World populations after the Columbian crossing.

The argument remains controversial, but one can see broadly that a subtly different rearrangement of the continents, a matter of trivial differences in the details of tectonic drift in the geological past, could have profoundly altered the course of human history, whatever the choices of human actors in the drama:

> Once the ice had covered continents … Rising seas bit at the coastlines of Northland, the great neck of land that still connected the peninsula called Albia to the Continent. Perhaps that neck would have been severed altogether – if not for the defiance of

> Northland's people, who, tentatively at first, with crude flood-resistant mounds, drainage ditches scratched in the ground, and heaped-up dykes of stone and earth, resisted the ocean's slow assaults ... After two thousand years the farmers' culture reached the shore of the Western Ocean – but here the wave broke. (Baxter, *Northland: Bronze Summer* 2)

My own 'Northland' series (2010–2012) was inspired by recent discoveries in the archaeology of the North Sea. In 8000BC the sea bed, still dry, known as 'Doggerland', was a rich, well-watered plain ideal for human habitation – indeed it was more favourable than the higher lands that surrounded it, in Britain and Denmark. At the time the first farmers were emerging in the Middle East. Perhaps Doggerland, rich and generous, could have hosted a civilization to match the eastern farmers' – but sea levels rose; Doggerland drowned. The books explore a different trajectory for a human civilisation; the 'Northlanders', defying the rising sea, are not farmers, but as hydrological engineers, like the Dutch of later times, they are literate and numerate – and their culture survives the arrival of the easterners' 'farming package'. The North Sea is only thirty metres deep at its shallowest, a puddle that changed north European history.

Even more dramatically, geographical differences could have reshaped the entire human evolutionary story.

The survival of other human species into historical times would surely have had a profound influence on our own development. One thoughtful exploration of this idea is Harry Turtledove's *A Different Flesh* (1988), in which a different sequence of land bridges in the deep past allowed a *Homo erectus* population to reach the Americas, while *Homo sapiens*, as in our history, did not follow until the European explorers. This is not implausible; after all many African mammals such as lions and elephants did manage to cross from the Old World to the New, millions of years before Columbus. Indeed, other primates crossed; the New World monkeys are thought to be descended from African monkeys which crossed a narrower Atlantic on natural rafts.

> 'No churchman I've ever heard of can say for certain whether sims have souls'. Jeremiah doubted it. He thought of sims as nothing more than animals that happened to walk on two legs and have hands. That made them more useful than, say, horses, but not much smarter. (Turtledove n.p.)

The 'sims' hunt in bands and use simple stone tools, but are capable of learning more: for instance, copying humans, they develop a simple sign language and the means of creating fire. And contact with the sims reshapes human history. Their very existence causes academic and spiritual difficulties for the Europeans. Do they have souls, for example? Samuel Pepys, studying chimpanzees and sims brought to London, hits on the notion of evolution two centuries earlier than Darwin in our timeline. Some moral lessons are drawn. The existence of the sims provides a comparison to demonstrate that the differences between human races are relatively trivial, and slavery is questioned earlier.

Unfortunately, this does not save the sims themselves from displacement and exploitation; they are used on plantations, farms, and later in factories and as experimental medical subjects: in this reality the first 'astronaut' was a sim, not a chimp. They can never be free in a human world. Turtledove's handling of the sims and their relationship with humans is deep, but never sentimental, and feels all too plausible: this is surely how we would have treated our cousin hominids, had they survived.

A still more dramatic geographical variation is shown in Turtledove's 'Down in the Bottomlands' (1993), in which a geological divergence six and a half million years ago caused the Mediterranean to be naturally dammed at Gibraltar. The ocean subsequently dried out, leaving a lowland kilometres below average sea level, a place of salt flats and extreme heat where the rivers tumble in sprays off the continental shelf. In reality the Mediterranean did dry out and refill many times, but has remained an ocean throughout the era of human evolution. In Turtledove's fiction, Europe's Neanderthals survived. The dry sea bed and its surrounds are ruled by a Neanderthal nation – but this is threatened by a nation of *Homo sapiens* which plans to use nuclear weapons to blow the Gibraltar natural dam.

The survival of Neanderthals, our closest hominid cousins, has in fact become a much-loved trope:

> I am laughing, laughing, laughing. Just because you're a freak of nature, a monstrosity whose bones all went wrong in the womb, you've dreamed up this fantastic myth about being descended from the Neanderthals. (Farmer, 'The Alley Man' 15)

Philip Jose Farmer's memorable 'The Alley Man' (1959), strictly speaking a secret rather than an alternate history, is about Old Man, a 'ragpicker' with a peculiar physique, who survives in Illinois alleys. Could the Old Man really be the last true-blood Neanderthal, as he claims? He speaks of battles lost long ago by the 'Real Folk' against the incoming 'Falser Folk', and fifty thousand years of ancestors surviving on trash heaps and back alleys. Or perhaps Old Man is merely a victim of 'acromegaly' and has concocted this legend from comic books and TV shows. 'Just think a it ... fifty thousand years behint me ... older'n Adam and Eve by far ... last a the Paleys ...' (53) You long for it to be true.

If such hominids had survived, these fictions advise us, our souls would have been coarsened by our complicity in the eternal subjugation of one intelligent, self-aware species by another.

More dramatic divergences yet can be imagined. What if we shared our world, not with Neanderthals, but with dinosaurs?

> 65 million years ago ... a meteor six miles in diameter hit the Earth ... The age of the dinosaurs was over ... But what if that meteor had not fallen? What would our world be like today? (Harrison, 'Foreword', *West of Eden* n.p.)

In Harry Harrison's thrilling *West of Eden* sequence (1984–1988), the dinosaur-killer meteorite never fell, and the dinosaurs lived on. By the present day the Old World is dominated by the Yilanè, a breed of intelligent bipedal dinosaur descended from marine reptiles called mososaurs. The Yilanè are intricately depicted by Harrison, with assistance from advice from evolutionary biologist Jack Cohen. Their technology is biological – cities are like huge trees grown from single seeds – and their ancient culture is rigidly stratified. But now a cooling climate forces the Yilanè to seek footholds in North America – where they come into contact with a humanoid species descended from New World primates who call themselves the Tanu, Ice Age nomads who are themselves forced to migrate south. The contact is soured by instinctive mutual repulsion, mammals against reptiles; there is slaughter on both sides. The Yilanè are barely able to recognize the humanoids as intelligent at all. In the series' subsequent books (1986, 1988) the long battle between Yilanè and human continues, but perhaps there is hope of eventual reconciliation: '[It will] not always be a Yilanè world' ('Envoi', *Return to Eden* n.p.).

Perhaps this is too big a dislocation to be recognized as an authentic alternate history; if the dinosaur killer had missed, it seems likely that in reality nothing like humans would have evolved at all, and perhaps Harrison's books should be regarded as science fantasy. But the scenario does illustrate the role that cosmic chance plays in our existence. The slightest deflection of one not-very-large space rock would have changed the course of not just our own destiny but that of Earth's biosphere.

Earth's very formation, however, a matter of collisions of planetesimals in the chaotic violence of the early solar system, was itself a matter of chance, and the outcome could have been very different.

In Harry Turtledove's alternate history novel *A World of Difference* (1990), planetary formation was different from our reality, so that there is what astronomers would now call a 'super-Earth' in our solar system in place of Mars. The new planet, Minerva, is more or less Earth-like, but bigger, and colder; ice caps reach down halfway to the equator. Intelligent Minervans, built on a six-spoked radial plan, are cold-adapted, and make buildings and tools of ice and stone.

As with other apparently dramatic changes in our backdrop, all this makes little difference on Earth until the twentieth century, when astronomers become aware of water and oxygen on the planet – and, in 1976, a Viking lander on Minerva is destroyed by a tool-wielding alien, caught on camera. In the 1980s, Soviet and US ships race to be the first to land on Minerva. The cooperation of astronauts and cosmonauts in halting a war on Minerva may presage a more peaceful age on Earth – but in this case Minervan history has surely been altered far more profoundly than the human.

It is even possible to speculate about our fate in a different frame of physics. What if we had evolved in an alternate universe structured around Aristotelian cosmology? I've already referenced something of this sort in 'Sail On! Sail On!' above. So too in my short story 'No Longer Touch The Earth' (1993), an immobile Earth is surrounded by spheres, concentric and transparent. Remarkably, even this might have made no difference to our history until we began to mount planetary-scale explorations: no difference, until Amundsen and Scott reach the South Pole to find a huge, turning crystalline Axis.

In *Celestial Matters* (1996) Richard Garfinkle makes a more extensive exploration of an Aristotelian world. In AD 400, in the Greek-led Delian League, scientists tinker with combinations of the four elements, earth, air, fire, and water, and brave crews pilot craft to the celestial globes, which revolve around the Earth on crystal spheres. Now there is an outrageous plan to fly to the sun to steal its celestial fire for war-making. The book is an entertaining and logically rigorous vision of a different cosmos, and a parable of mankind's predisposition to militarize science, in our universe as in Garfinkle's.

> It seemed possible … that he was nearing the Byzantine empire, coming towards Constantinople from the north and west. Sitting slumped before his nightly bonfire, he wondered if Constantinople would be dead too. (Robinson, *The Years of Rice and Salt* 18–19)

Kim Stanley Robinson's *The Years of Rice and Salt* (2002) is a conscious exploration of a historical adjustment of the grandness of scale discussed in this paper.

In a take on the 'germs' element of Diamond's 'guns, germs, and steel' argument (1997), Robinson's book is an epic of a different biological history. He imagined the fourteenth-century Black Death wiping out 99% of Europe's population, rather than one-third, thus removing Europeans from the historical scene before the Renaissance and the age of discovery: Columbus never existed, nor did Galileo. Robinson's saga spans the centuries, with history driven by non-European cultures. Europe is repopulated by Muslim explorers, the native peoples of the Americas resist invaders from Europe and China, and in a different twenty-first century a long war is fought between the Chinese and Islamic states. Robinson focuses mainly on the lives of 'ordinary' people, as opposed to the 'great men' of history whose choices have been overwhelmed, in this story, by nothing more than the blind working-out of a minor variation of the pathology of bubonic plague.

Alternate histories dealing with choices made by humans will always offer counterfactual insights into the way those choices were made. Yet all our history takes place against a backdrop of large-scale, chance events: the 'choices' of Mother Nature, on a climatic, biological, geographic, even cosmological scale. A sub-genre of alternate histories which explores different outcomes of these 'choices' gives us a glimpse of the string of cosmic coincidences which has led us to being the kind of creatures we are, in the familiar world around us. For it need not have been so.

References

Baxter, Stephen. 'No Longer Touch the Earth'. *Interzone*, no. 72, June 1993. Online. Accessed 6 March 2017.
—. *Northland: Bronze Summer*. Gollancz, 2011.
—. *Northland: Iron Winter*. Gollancz, 2012.
—. *Northland: Stone Spring*. Gollancz, 2010.
—. *Time's Tapestry: Weaver*. Gollancz, 2008.
—. *Voyage*. HarperCollins, 1996.
Diamond, Jared. *Guns, Germs and Steel*. 1997. Vintage, 2005.
Farmer, Philip Jose. 'The Alley Man'. 1959. *The Alley God*. Sidgwick & Jackson, 1970.
—. 'Sail On! Sail On!' 1952. *The Best of Philip Jose Farmer*. Subterranean, 2006.
Garfinkle, Richard. *Celestial Matters*. Tor Books, 1996.
Harrison, Harry. *West of Eden*. 1984. Gollancz, 2011. E-book.

—. *Winter in Eden*. 1986. Gollancz, 2013. E-book.

—. *Return to Eden*. 1988. Gollancz, 2011. E-book.

Robinson. Kim Stanley. *The Years of Rice and Salt*. HarperCollins, 2002.

Taylor, D. J. *The Windsor Faction*. Chatto & Windus, 2013.

Turtledove, Harry. *A Different Flesh*. 1988. Gollancz, 2013. E-book.

—. 'Down in the Bottomlands'. *Analog Science and Science Fiction*, January 1993. Online. Accessed 6 March 2017.

—. *A World of Difference*. 1990. Hodder & Stoughton, 1999.

Zabel, Bryce. *Surrounded by Enemies*. Mill City Press, 2013.

Introduction

Glyn Morgan and C. Palmer-Patel

I think you're saying, sir, that – well as there must be any number of futures, there must have been any number of pasts besides those written down in our histories. And – and it would follow that there are any number of what you might call 'presents'.

Murray Leinster, 'Sidewise in Time' (262)

Murray Leinster's iconic short story 'Sidewise in Time', first published in the American magazine *Astounding* in 1934, is often cited as the point at which the alternate history narrative first enters science fiction as a plot device. It is not a conventional alternate history as we now recognize them, but it is nonetheless significant for demonstrating to fans and writers of speculative fiction (sf), particularly American science fiction (at that time undergoing its crucial metamorphosis in the Golden Age of the sf magazines), that speculation need not restrain itself to 'what if' stories predicated on questions of science and technology, but that it may also encompass historical questions. In recognition of this important position within the field, the awards presented annually for best alternate history fiction are named the Sidewise Awards.

As the above quotation from 'Sidewise in Time' suggests, what alternate history really represents is nothing less than an unravelling of our linear and singular notions of history, an infinite fracturing of time into infinite pasts, presents, and futures. Alternate history then is not just about history; it is very much also about the present and the future. Indeed, as we shall see throughout the following chapters, the alternate history texts which are the most compelling works of fiction are those which use the alternate world of their creation to alter the reader's perceptions of their own history, present, and potential futures. Beyond mere allegory, the best alternate histories offer an avenue of critique and provocation which exceeds the capacities of their nearest genre neighbours (historical fiction, science fiction, or fantasy).

11

This is one of the reasons why it would be a mistake to categorize alternate history as purely a sub-genre of science fiction. Whilst much of the familiar iconography of science fiction can find its roots in the pre-genre literature, alternate history narratives have not only a separate genesis but an independent literary history. Conventional claims for the oldest recorded alternate history narrative in Western literature are generally attributed to the Roman writer Livy who speculates in the ninth book of his *Ab Urbe Condita* (circa 25 BCE) on the possibility of Alexander the Great forging an Empire in the West. Similarly, isolated thought experiments can be found throughout literary history, such as Joanot Martorell's *Tirant lo Blanch*, a chivalric romance published in Valencia in 1490 which rewrites history to save the Byzantine Empire by writing a history in which Constantinople never falls. In his chapter in this collection, Adam Roberts suggests Samuel Gott's *Nova Solyma, the Ideal City; or Jerusalem Regained* (1648) as a candidate for the earliest sustained alternate history. Katherine Gallagher, in her recent study of the subject, begins her history of counterfactual thought with the philosophical works of Gottfried Wilhelm von Leibniz who proposed in his *Theodicée* (1710) that at every turning point in history God guides our reality to the best long-term possibility, illustrating his point with a speculative discourse about the rape of Lucretia and the founding of the Roman Republic. However, a broad consensus, and the subject of Roberts's chapter, posits Louis-Napoléon Geoffroy-Château's *Napoléon et la conquête du monde*, published in France in 1836, as the first alternate history novel. There are numerous publications, in both English and French, between Geoffroy-Château's and Leinster's short story, but the most significant development in alternate history literature over this time is the blossoming of the form as a subject for essays and historical debate. Isaac D'Israeli wrote the first such piece in English, his 'Of a History of Events Which Have Not Happened' appearing as a chapter in his *Curiosities of Literature* (1824). The most important early publication of this type, however, was J. C. Squire's *If It Had Happened Otherwise* (1931) which included essays by Hillaire Belloc, G. K. Chesterton, and Winston Churchill, amongst others. Such essays become sufficiently commonplace that historian E. H. Carr can rail against them in his 1961 *What is History?*:

> What I may call the 'might-have-been' school of thought – or rather emotion. [...] one can always play a parlour game with the might-have-beens of history. But they have nothing to do with determinism [...]. Nor have they anything to do with history. (96–97)

What Carr calls the 'might-have-been' school of thought is now better recognized as counterfactual writing, and if anything they have become even more common since Carr's critique: Niall Ferguson's *Virtual History: Alternatives and Counterfactuals* (1997), Robert Cowley's *What If?* (1999), Andrew Roberts's *What Might Have Been* (2005), Duncan Brack's *President Gore ...: and Other Things That Never Happened* (2006), and Gavriel D. Rosenfeld's *What Ifs of Jewish History* (2017) are just some of the more recent collections continuing Squire's format.

These counterfactual essays, which can be referred to as *belles-lettres* (Hellekson, *The Alternate History* 454), differ from alternate history fiction in both their style and intention. Counterfactuals are normally presented as thought experiments with a pedagogical purpose though it's worth noting that the validity of that pedagogy is disputed by some such as historian Richard J. Evans who argues that 'long-range counterfactual speculations are unconvincing and unnecessary for the historian because they elide too many links in the proposed causative chain after the initial altered event' (174), and besides, 'Counterfactuals are ironical because, ultimately, they always cast more light on the present than on the past' (176). Indeed, 'most historians and social scientists, if they have considered counterfactuals at all', writes Geoffrey Hawthorn on this issue, 'have done so only nervously, in asides' (4). Regardless, it is important to distinguish counterfactuals as kindred, but separate from alternate history fiction; not because as Niall Ferguson has written 'of course Hollywood and science fiction are not academically respectable', but because the two forms are narratologically distinct (Ferguson, *Virtual History* 3). They do, however, demonstrate the wide-reaching and extensive record of alternative history as a thought experiment, as a tool with which to analyze the past. That said, as Ferguson's snide remark indicates, whilst literary scholars have an appreciation for the counterfactual, the relationship rarely works both ways and (with the exception of Rosenfeld, whose *The World Hitler Never Made* (2005) is a detailed survey of Nazism in alternate Second World Wars) the historians mentioned above have given little, if any, serious consideration to the worth of alternate history fictions as cultural artefacts through which to consider the past.

Since 'Sidewise in Time' was published, the alternate history has become a staple of science fiction and fantasy storytelling, sometimes incorporating time travel, magic, or trans-dimensional portals as a means of explaining the alternate world. Meanwhile, the popular-reception of quantum mechanics, from Schrodinger's cat in the 1930s to the 'many-worlds' interpretation of quantum mechanics first proposed by Hugh Everett III in 1957, has allowed the concept to wrap itself in the glamour of scientific credibility, or at least controversy. Alongside the many sf writers who have produced alternate history fiction (not least Stephen Baxter and Adam Roberts who both contribute non-fiction pieces to this volume), further evidence of its unique status within the genres of speculative fiction can be seen in the ready reception of the form by writers within the literary mainstream including Nobel Laureates (Kazuo Ishiguro), Booker Prize winners (Kingsley Amis and John Banville), Pulitzer Prize winners (Michael Chabon and Philip Roth), and recipients of the Walter Scott Prize for historical fiction (Kate Atkinson), amongst many others.

There are no other speculative fiction genres or tropes which have been so readily adopted by the cultural mainstream. This is particularly true of television and serial drama, as Karen Hellekson demonstrates in her chapter at the end of this book. Television is a particularly interesting case because of the breadth of alternate history's acceptance into otherwise non-sf narratives. For example, the characters in American sitcom *Friends* (1994–2004) do not make contact with extra-terrestrial life, nor are they involved in a government conspiracy, time travel, or a nuclear holocaust; they do however have episodes which imagine *what if* key decisions in their lives had been made differently, presenting alternate versions of themselves ('The One That Could Have Been, part 1 & 2'). In addition to science fiction programming where we might expect to find them (seemingly every show from *Buffy the Vampire Slayer* to *Star Trek* features episodes which play with the idea), similar alternate history episodes can be found in *The Fresh Prince of Bel-Air*, *Scrubs*, *Frasier*, and *The Simpsons* (sitcoms seem to have a particular affinity for the genre), as well as detective dramas *NCIS* and *Bones*, amongst others. That many of these television shows likely draw their lineage down from Frank Capra's *It's a Wonderful Life* (1946), itself shows the extended lineage of the alternate history genre and its complex relationship with popular culture, independent to that of science fiction and fantasy.

Yet, despite crossing easily out of the conventional sf sphere (or, perhaps, precisely because it refuses to sit neatly within it) alternate history has attracted surprisingly little scholarship. Against this backdrop, the *Sideways in Time* conference, held over two days at the University of Liverpool in 2015, generated interest from scholars with a wide range of academic and literary backgrounds. This collection presents essays which build upon some of the papers presented there and expand those conversations further. It is our hope, as both conference organizers and as editors, that this collection can help to expand a pioneering body of research on a neglected area of literature, allowing other researchers and students to explore this complex genre.

Of course, this collection of essays does not appear in a scholarly vacuum and a number of key critical works on alternate history have emerged in the twenty-first century. These include Karen Hellekson's *The Alternate History: Refiguring Historical Time* (2001) which is approaching canonical status within the genre. Hellekson builds on sub-divisions in alternate history texts proposed by William Joseph Collins to suggest her own categories for the fictions based on their divergence points. These are:

> (1) The nexus story, which includes time-travel-time-policing stories and battle stories; (2) The true alternate history, which may include alternate histories that posit different physical laws; and (3) The parallel worlds story. Nexus stories occur at the moment of the break. The true alternate history occurs after the break, sometimes a long time after. And the parallel world story implies that there was no break – that all events that could have occurred did occur. (*The Alternate History* 5)

So, Isaac Asimov's *The End of Eternity* (1955) and Harry Turtledove's *The Guns of the South* (1992) are examples of nexus stories, whilst Ward Moore's *Bring the Jubilee* (1955) and Keith Roberts's *Pavane* (1966) are true alternate histories and Frederick Pohl's *The Coming of the Quantum Cats* (1986) is a good example of the parallel world story. Hellekson chooses these categories because she sees 'the alternate history as querying historical concerns about time, including the notation of sequence that is so integral to the concept of time' (5).

More recently, significant studies have been conducted by other scholars. Kathleen Singles, *Alternate History: Playing with Contingency and Necessity* (2013) compares alternate history to postmodernist historical fiction, science fiction, and counterfactual history. Of particular note is the way Singles draws on German-language research into historical fiction as well as English-language novels, films, and other texts as yet not translated into English from their original German. She provides numerous case studies from these works, in each case using Philip K. Dick's *The Man in the High Castle* as a baseline to determine the extent to which each work conforms to – or deviates from – generic conventions, describing Dick's novel as 'paradigmatic of alternate histories in terms of its simplified view of history, use of a point of divergence, and the paradox of necessity/determinism versus contingency/free will' (148).

All alternate histories, Singles argues, demonstrate a tension between contingency and necessity: they pose 'what if' questions yet this attitude is rarely perpetrated throughout the fiction and thus there is a constant theme of free will versus determinism.

Another of the most recent monographs on the topic of alternate history is by another of the contributors to this collection. Derek J. Thiess's *Relativism, Alternate History, and the Forgetful Reader: Reading Science Fiction and Historiography* (2014) examines alternate history through the lens of postmodern historiography, in particular the revelations that relativism has on our understanding of the past and how we interpret (and reinterpret) it. Starting from the philosophical position that history as written is no more truthful about the past than fiction, Thiess interrogates various alternate history and secret history texts, as well as works of more mundane historiography, to expose the aspects of history that have been obscured and the motivations for forgetting about them.

Finally, whilst we were compiling this volume Catherine Gallagher released her study, *Telling It Like It Wasn't: The Counterfactual Imagination in History and Fiction* (2018). Alternate history is an easy companion for the school of New Historicism, of which Gallagher is amongst the most preeminent scholars, and this holds true in *Telling It Like It Wasn't*. Whilst the majority of the study is of texts speculating about a Confederate victory in the American Civil War, or an occupied Britain in the Second World War, some of the most fascinating contributions to wider alternate history scholarship come in its earlier chapters. For example, Gallagher presents Gottfried Leibniz's eighteenth-century theological work *Theodicy* (1710), as the beginning of the history of counterfactual thought then tracing a route through theological debate, philosophical counterpoint, and critical military history before being picked up by the early French novelists like Geoffroy-Château. In another interesting variation, Gallagher also draws a distinction between texts of three types: the non-fiction 'counterfactual histories' and remaining narrative forms split into two categories: the 'alternate history' and the 'alternate history novel', the distinction being that the alternate history describes 'one continuous sequence of departures from the historical record [...] drawing the dramatis personae exclusively from the historical record', whilst alternate history novels invent 'not only the alternative-historical trajectories but also fictional characters' (3).

Hopefully these recent monographs represent the beginnings of a change in attitude towards alternate history and counterfactual narratives more widely. Certainly, they represent vital corrections to the scholarly neglect in this area, something which this book seeks to further remedy. As detailed above, alternate history narratives have a long history, but it is in the twenty-first century that we are beginning to realize their true importance. Contemporary alternate history demonstrates an awareness of historical narrative's inextricable connection to our society and how this can be fascinating and enlightening, but it can also be dangerous and easily exploitable. As the chapters in this volume show, however, these connections are not static and indeed the relationships between history, alternate history, and reader are constantly evolving.

For example, Philip Roth's *The Plot Against America* was a compelling and powerful analysis of fascism in the United States when it was published in 2004. Roth considers the novel to be about the past, an analysis of the possibilities which existed, 'that in the 30's there were many seeds for [fascism] happening [in America], but it didn't' (Roth, 'The Story Behind "The Plot Against America"'). Yet numerous critics see the novel as an obvious allegory for post-9/11 America with 'references to George W. Bush's America [that] are impossible to miss' (Brownstein, 'Fight or Flight'). What neither the author nor contemporary critics could predict was that the novel would only increase in relevance, its demonstration of the ways fascism could rise to power through legitimate routes of American legislature becoming if anything more powerful in the era of the alt-right and President Trump.[1]

Roth's novel centres on the presidential campaign, and subsequent premiership, of Charles Lindbergh in 1940. Running as an America First Republican, Lindbergh keeps the United States out of the war in Europe and makes overtures of friendship and support to Hitler's Germany. It highlights the fragility of American democracy to populist politics, especially at a time of global uncertainty, and counters popular mythology of American exceptionalism (the notion that 'it can't happen here'). It is not unique in these outcomes, and writers of alternate history from the 1930s to the present day have similarly problematized these issues. What imbues Roth's novel with its true power is not the alternate history of the United States' president, but the more intimate narrative of an alternate history of Philip Roth. Born in 1933, the same as the author, young Philip experiences an America twisted by fear and anti-Semitic hatred. Through Philip, Roth demonstrated the human cost of far-right and fascist politics and ideology, creating a proxy with

---

[1] Incidentally, Roth told *The New Yorker* that, if anything, he finds the election of Trump harder to believe than the fictional world of *The Plot Against America*, remarking that 'Lindbergh, despite his Nazi sympathies and racist proclivities, was a great aviation hero [...]. He had character and he had substance [...]. Trump is just a con artist. The relevant book about Trump's American forebear is Herman Melville's "The Confidence-Man"' (Thurman, 'Philip Roth e-mails on Trump').

whom readers can empathize and giving the politics of the novel a real emotional heft. Most importantly, it's a novel which could only be written as an alternate history.

Whilst an exceptional novel, Roth's *The Plot Against America* is nonetheless a fairly typical alternate history. Like most alternate history novels, it focuses on a well-known historical moment: the Second World War (the most common category of alternate history, except in the United States where it is held to second place by the American Civil War). Similarly, its alternate reality is driven by the changed biographies of significant figures from history, not only Lindbergh and those around him, but Roosevelt too. Indeed, it is Roosevelt who emerges as the linchpin in American history of this time. As the novel suggests it's the absence of Roosevelt's leadership at this crucial juncture, rather than Lindbergh's ascendency, which allows the rise of an American fascist state. Similarly, Roosevelt is reinstalled at the novel's conclusion and America's historical course is duly corrected to something similar to our own, further underlining his significance.

By imbuing Roosevelt and Lindbergh with such capacity to change the course of history, *The Plot Against America* can be viewed as a text which supports a Carlylian view of history. Thomas Carlyle's conception of the 'History of the World' as 'the Biography of Great Men' (*On Heroes* 17), is borne out by narratives which centre on such individuals, or singular events to which they contribute, or which contribute to their rise or fall such as iconic battles or military campaigns. This is problematic for several reasons, first and foremost being that even in altering the historical record, such alternate histories are implicit in propping up conventional historical narratives, narratives which are predominantly white, heterosexual, and (as Carlyle's phrase implies) male. Some authors, however, resist this model of history and write alternate history fiction which suggest a more structuralist view of history, one in which large social, political, cultural, and technological forces develop over the centuries and are not easily redirected by individuals. Stephen Fry's *Making History* (1996) is one example of this narrative which deals with the same historical period as Roth's novel. In Fry's novel Hitler is never born, but rather than thus preventing the rise of fascism in Germany and a Second World War, a different dictator rises to the peak of political power and unlike Hitler, prone to emotional and irrational outbursts, this new Fuhrer is more coldly rational and more politically adept, particularly in the international arena. The alternate history in *Making History* is thus a world in which the development of fascism in Europe and the march to war are driven less by the 'greatness' of a Hitler (or even a Stalin, Roosevelt, or Churchill), and more by unresolved grievances from the First World War, mushrooming financial and social inequality, and the development of new technological, philosophical, and cultural innovations. It would be naïve to claim that all alternate history fiction can be reduced to its compliance with a given model of history (neither Roth nor Fry's novels play out completely faithfully to either Carlylian or Structuralist models), yet the divide between people and processes is nonetheless a frequent factor in the creation of an alternate historical setting. Alongside questions of free will versus determinism, the reinforcing or undermining of 'great men' models of history is just one of the central debates being conducted by scholars of alternate history, but also between the texts themselves, exemplifying the manner in which alternate history narratives engage with analyses of history and historical narratives as well.

It is also worth recognizing the terminology of the genre is itself a subject of extended debate. The phenomenon of the historical counter-factual is discussed above, and we've tried to present the rationale for considering such pieces as separate but crucially and closely related to alternate history fiction. Yet the term 'alternate history' is itself not universally accepted. The more grammatically correct (at least in British-English) 'alternative history' is preferred by some, however this term is already employed by scholars to refer to new historical perspectives which differ from the mainstream such as Susan Neiman's, *Evil in Modern Thought: An Alternative History of Philosophy* (2002), Matthew Brown's *From Frontiers to Football: An Alternative History of Latin America Since 1800* (2010), or Steven Moore's two volume *The Novel: An Alternative History* (2010; 2013). As such, 'alternate' is preferable when discussing fiction partly because of the term's already fixed roots in popular and scholarly understandings of the medium, particularly in the United States, but also to avoid confusion with these historical alternatives. Similarly, for clarity's sake we also avoided using the acronym form 'ah', despite the generally accepted use of speculative/science fiction's sf in contemporary criticism.

With regards to other possible terminology, we've disregarded the term 'allohistory' because of its infrequent usage, as we have 'parahistory' which has failed to gain traction since being coined by German scholar Joerg Helbig. The term 'uchronia' stems from Charles Bernard Renouvier's 1876 French novel *Uchronie (l'utopie dans l'histoire), esquisse historique apocryphe du développement de la civilisation européenne tel qu'il n'a pas été, tel qu'il aurait pu être* [*Uchronia (Utopia in History), an Apocryphal Sketch of the Development of European Civilization Not as It Was But as It Might Have Been*], which depicts a history in which Avidius Cassius succeeds Marcus Aurelius as Roman Emperor. Yet whilst this

term has the benefit of historical long-life, its connections with the genre
of utopia (replacing the *topos* of place for a *chronos* of time), indicate a
specific type of alternate history which incorporates a wistful longing for
a better or idealized world which is incompatible with most twentieth
and twenty-first-century alternate history fiction. Nonetheless, in his
chapter in this collection, Adam Roberts discusses a genuine historical
uchronie, whilst Andrew M. Butler adapts 'uchronia' more purposefully
for contemporary texts.

Another related body of texts and terminology is that of the 'secret
history'. Secret history narratives are an off-shoot of true alternate
histories, combining the 'what if' question of alternate history with
conspiracy theory. Secret history narratives distinguish themselves
from alternate histories by depicting events which, whilst counter to
established historical fact, do not impact our recorded history due to
the hidden (secret) nature of the events. A famous twenty-first-century
example is Dan Brown's *The Da Vinci Code* (2003) which offers an
alternate history of Christianity and the Church, but because of the
conspiracy surrounding the truth, history is not altered. Brown's novel
feeds on conspiracy theory (and, Ouroboros-like, itself feeds them), while
maintaining a veneer of plausibility. The novel asserts itself as lifting
the veil on history's narrative to reveal the previously unknown truth
beneath: that the Church is built upon the 'greatest cover-up in human
history' (*Da Vinci Code* 249). Given their relationship with conspiracy
fiction, which is always anti-establishment in nature, secret history
narratives tend towards fast-paced thrillers with establishment figures
as antagonists. There are, of course, exceptions to the realist secret
history from within sf: Neil Gaiman's 'A Midsummer Night's Dream'
(1990), an award-winning nineteenth issue of the *Sandman* comic book
series, shows William Shakespeare giving the inaugural performance
of his own *A Midsummer Night's Dream* on a grassy hill to an audience
of fairy-folk and elves; whilst the television mini-series *Ascension* (2014)
posits a secret facility in the United States simulating a generational
spacecraft, the inhabitants of which (descended from America's best and
brightest) are secretly responsible for numerous technological advances
such as MRI machines.

Finally, a special place in this family of literatures is reserved for what
can best be described as alternate futures: narratives which proposed a
vision of the future, the date of which has now passed into our own
pasts. Essentially retroactive alternate histories, George Orwell's *Nineteen
Eighty-Four* (1949) and Arthur C. Clarke's *2001: A Space Odyssey* (1968)
can both be considered in this category, along with the broad sweep
of sf which predicted a future for humanity living on other planets

before the end of the twentieth century. Such works were written to extrapolate a possible future, and they vary in the extent to which they describe the specific roadmap to their vision, but as history inevitably catches up to them, and events transpire differently, re-reading them as a form of alternate history allows the texts to retain a relevance they may otherwise lose. Indeed, through the prism of alternate history, these alternate futures, can potentially become more significant for scholarship than they were as oracles of what was to come.

Other terminologies worth exploring here refer to a mechanism of the alternate history: the moment at which the historical narrative separates from our own timeline. In some science fiction scholarship this is referred to as the 'Jonbar Hinge', a reference to Jack Williamson's short story 'The Legion of Time' (1938) in which the seemingly negligible actions of the child John Barr ultimately lead to the creation of one of two empires. However, the usefulness of the term can now be called into question given that the relevance of Williamson's story to the rapidly growing and evolving canon of alternate history fiction has significantly diminished, not least because it roots the scholarship of the genre in the study of science fiction when, as we have already seen, alternate history spans a wider field of literature. As such, scholars have sought alternative terminology. Finding the Jonbar Hinge to be 'confusing and unwieldly', Hellekson refers to a nexus point, borrowing the term from author Poul Anderson who employs it in many of his novels (*The Alternate History* 6). In most cases this book uses 'point of divergence' in reference to this moment, adhering to the trend of moving away from Jonbar as a reference, whilst also acknowledging the acronym POD used as a shorthand by the alternate history fan community.

Similarly, fans and scholars of alternate history have come up with myriad terms with which to refer to the real world in which we live in, in order to distinguish it from the alternate/counterfactual timeline. Again, the online community favour an acronym (OTL to refer to the 'original' or 'our' timeline), and elsewhere references can be found to the Zero World, baseline, primary history, prime timeline or universe, or simply 'our history' which perhaps has the accidental effect of embracing groups within a history they feel doesn't represent them. This book adopts the usage 'our timeline' in most instances which, as with the point of divergence, has been selected to favour clarity above all else.

~

In compiling this collection, we have separated the chapters into two categories. The first, entitled 'Points of Divergence', focus on specific texts or text clusters, offering close readings of those texts and allowing us to look on them with new eyes. In doing so, these essays widen our appreciation of alternate history's own history as a genre, its scope, and its range both in terms of its capacity to approach many different historical periods and cultures, but also to deliver new understandings of history, society, and culture from authors and creators of different backgrounds and periods. The second section, 'Manipulating the Genre', takes the alternate history genre as it is presented in part one and expands it, stretching it, subverting it, and redefining it. The second part of this collection show us that alternate history is a still-developing genre that cannot be easily quantified or described, and that readings of alternate history texts can in turn present us with analytical tools to consider other texts and scenarios beyond the genre.

We are delighted that this book opens with a foreword from award-winning science fiction and alternate history author Stephen Baxter. Baxter is both a former winner and now a judge of the Sidewise Award for Alternate History, the only individual to thus far have a claim to both titles. As such he has a unique perspective on alternate history and so his foreword takes the form of a sweeping survey of the genre, showcasing the inherent potential of this type of writing, and the range of ideas and histories open to authors, not just human but geological, even cosmic in scale.

The first chapter in the 'Points of Divergence' section is by Adam Roberts. Like Baxter he is both a writer of alternate history fiction and a scholar of it. Roberts is also a professor of nineteenth-century literature and so brings a specialist understanding of the period into his investigation of one of the earliest of alternate history novels: Geoffroy-Château's *Napoléon et al conquête du monde* (1841). In doing so he explores how alternate history fiction is influenced by the author's own conception of historical events, their 'historicity' and the manner in which that is made available to a readership, and the implications of 'altering not just the material but the *spiritual* facts of history'. Roberts acknowledges the distinctive literary history of alternate history fiction, giving credence to it being considered as kindred but separate to wider sf. However, at the same time he demonstrates that both alternate history and sf have shown a historic tendency to rely on the stories of 'great men' rather than a more Tolstoyan approach to grand narratives. Certainly, the question of individual agency versus the 'great man' theory of history is one which has been with alternate history from the beginning and is thus echoed through many of the chapters which follow.

From Roberts' look at some of the earliest moments of alternate history fiction, the rest of the section skips forwards to some of the most recent and exciting, presenting texts from the twenty-first century with contemporary concerns. Chris Pak's chapter examines Kim Stanley Robinson's *The Years of Rice and Salt* (2002) in order to discuss the global implications of alternate history. In a novel which erases European culture from history, thanks to an even more devastating Black Death in the fourteenth-century, Pak examines the textual strategies Robinson deploys and the manner in which alternate history can 'account for silences and omissions'. In the absence of white-European culture on a global scale, Robinson's multi-generational novel can explore suppressed voices and marginalized cultures now brought to the forefront. In Robinson's novel Chinese and Islamic 'great men' rise from the pages of history to replace the European leaders, thinkers, and inventors, yet the very interchangeability of these significant figures with our own history is itself an indicator that history may summon greatness rather than greatness altering history. Pak shows how Robinson's novel exposes the artificiality of historical narratives, the selectiveness of them, and the extent to which white-European (and later, American) dominated narratives have contributed to a monologic history in constant need of revision and re-examination.

Where Pak presents an alternate history text which uses the form to highlights gaps and moments of erasure in the mainstream historical narrative, the next chapter refocuses the lens of history precisely upon some of those narratives. As we've already noted, the body of texts surrounding alternate histories of the Second World War is massive. However, the clear majority of these texts concern themselves with the European theatre of war and Nazi Germany, which reflects the predominantly British-European-American origins of most of their creators. Jonathan Rayner's chapter presents a range of Japanese science fiction films and anime from 2005–2013 and considers Japanese engagement with their wartime history. In particular, he focuses in on the cultural fascination with the battleship *Yamato*, and the problematic relationship this then perpetuates as an ostensibly pacifist nation is caught by the allure of a warship. Rayner's chapter presents a summary of these unusual texts, which include alternate histories, time travel narratives, and science fiction adventures, many completely unknown to Western audiences, and ultimately challenges our understanding of postwar reception of the Second World War by discussing how these films 'render the past a contestable and re-interpretable space'.

Contesting and re-interpreting space is central to the next chapter, written by Brian Baker, who like Pak and Rayner uses alternate history texts to question and examine existing historical narratives, in this case the history of our near-contemporary era of space exploration. Baker presents the *Apollo Quarter* (2012–2016), a series of texts by British science fiction author Ian Sales, which reimagines NASA's early decades and the Apollo programme. In doing so the narratives explore the conceptual promise of the Golden Age of rocketry, and science fiction staples such as moon bases and expeditions to Mars feature, yet these tropes are secondary compared to Sales' evolving critique of the patriarchal constructs which embody NASA's history and science fiction itself. Baker demonstrates how Sales is able to use the formal apparatuses of the alternate history and the parallel world narrative to bring these 'unresolvable tensions into relief', to highlight fundamental issues of gender inequality, including tensions within masculinity itself. Where Pak and Rayner's chapters challenge the overwhelmingly white narrative of popular history, Baker's speaks to its predominantly male nature, and the particular variety of male most often pushed to the forefront.

Rounding out the first part of this book is Anna McFarlane's reading of Lavie Tidhar's *Osama: A Novel* (2011). Tidhar's novel centres on the 11 September attacks, and it is from a text which deals with such an emotionally charged recent trauma that McFarlane develops a reading of alternate history as a form of emotional historiography. She writes, 'rather than write a traditional alternate history, *Osama* uses the genre as a discourse to express the affect of the post 9/11 atmosphere'. Tidhar's novel blends alternate history with detective fiction, with humour, with shades of Philip K. Dick's *The Man in the High Castle* (1962), and tones of steampunk. Like much of Tidhar's work *Osama* confounds categorization and genre expectations, yet as McFarlane shows it is thus an exceptionally apt novel through which to examine the status of history (and thus, alternate history) in the twenty-first century. However, because of *Osama*'s complex genre-bending nature, McFarlane's chapter is also the perfect bridging point to draw to a close the first section of this collection and lead us into the second.

Each of these chapters demonstrates the manner in which alternate history engages with historical narratives, either conscripting or rejecting a Carlylian model of 'great' history, affirming or denying preconceptions of Anglo-European hegemony, and attempting to redistribute spheres of narratological power (from west to east, from male to female) by literally rewriting the historical narrative. They demonstrate that although the style in which novels and fiction are written, and the specific concerns of that fiction, have changed in the century-and-a-half since *Napoléon et al conquête du monde*, the fundamental form of the genre was in place almost from the very beginning and that it persists and can be found in narratives being produced in the twenty-first century. The next section however demonstrates that although this is true, alternate history is still very much open to expansion and alteration, and that our definitions of the genre itself can still be challenged, altered, and updated.

The latter half of the collection, 'Manipulating the Genre', focuses on texts which stand apart from many of the conventions demonstrated in the preceding chapters. Whilst the texts of the first section use alternate history to challenge historical narratives, the texts analyzed in this section take a metatextual leap and challenge the conventions of alternate history whilst continuing to problematize historical narratology.

Many alternate histories, including many of those considered in this introduction, and in the first part of this book, have a focus on the macro: they take their point of departure and sketch out the sweep of history for nations, empires, and civilizations, dealing in major battles and figures who are heavily laden in history ('great' or otherwise). Molly Cobb's chapter takes us towards the micro, exploring the role of the individual, time as a social force, and the subjective experience of the historical moment in the work of American science fiction author Alfred Bester. Cobb's reading of Bester's short fiction challenges the notion of history in alternate history, seeking alterity and counterfactualism in our individual perceptions of the world, our psychology, and our identity. For Bester, time is a social force susceptible to the perception of the individual. The historical context of Bester's work is crucial coming as it does in the early years of America's postwar existence when individualism, particularly creative or social individualism, fell so frequently under the scrutiny of McCarthyist politics. Despite a continued fascination with time travel, Bester did not see history as something an individual could alter, even if they could control their own individual time, and so the stories Cobb analyzes are particularly fascinating as being distortions, almost anti-, alternate histories.

The following two chapters further problematize history as the narrative foundation of alternate history by examining texts which thread a fine line between alternate and secret history or conspiracy fiction. The first of these chapters is by Derek Thiess who argues that there is an implicit link between the construction of historical narratives and religion. Thus, the apocryphal becomes alternate. Thiess centres his argument around Spanish science fiction writer Juan Miguel Aguilera's *La locura de Dios* [*The Madness of God*] (1998), a text little known to English-speaking readers, but one which perfectly demonstrates history as a process of storytelling conducted in order to make sense of certain events. In this case, those events have simply been suppressed; a cosmic secret which has implications not only for the church, but for the history of life on Earth. Thiess uses Aguilera's novel to demonstrate that grand Carlylian forces may indeed shape history, but they might not be the forces we know about or expect.

Chloe Germaine Buckley's chapter, which follows Thiess's, takes the notion of secret or apocryphal history to another level by examining a text which takes its primary narrative not as history (or not as history alone) but the continuity of another text. Germaine Buckley examines the mixing of weird fiction archetypes from the cosmic-horror mythology of H. P. Lovecraft with the rational detective stories of Conan Doyle's Sherlock Holmes. In creating these mash-ups the authors of such tales, exemplified by the collection *Shadows Over Baker Street*, are creating not only an alternate Victorian London, but also an alternate Sherlock Holmes, one who must grapple with challenges that exceed rationalism by their very nature. Germaine Buckley's chapter therefore expands our concept of alternate history to encompass other texts of alterity.

Andrew M. Butler extends this line of thought with his chapter on John Wyndham's short story 'Random Quest' (1962). Reviving the term uchronia, Butler presents a lesser known element of Wyndham's work, the 'time-schism love stories' and suggests that their manipulation of time and alternate worlds presents a different type of alternate history, one which eschews the political and militaristic foundations of the vast majority of alternate history, and instead focuses on the intimate, the romantic, and the domestic. Furthermore, building on Germaine Buckley's expansion of our ideas of alternate history's boundaries as a genre, Butler examines filming adaptations of 'Random Quest' such as *Quest for Love* (1962) and argues that adaptation itself is a form of alternate history storytelling, creating a new narrative which branches from its primary source based on the creative decisions and alterations which occur.

Finally, the last chapter in this collection extends Butler's examination of alternate histories outside of the printed text. Alternate history scholar Karen Hellekson revisits *Alternate History: Refiguring Historical Time* which, as mentioned earlier, remains a seminal text in the study of alternate history narratives. The monograph, however, focused upon literary texts and thus Hellekson argues in this chapter that the categorizations which she developed there differ in regard to other mediums, particularly televisual narratives. Hellekson asserts that while the written texts are centred around revising history, televisual narratives are concerned with the individual and individual agency. Televisual alternate history is just one facet of the hyperactive growth which the genre has experienced in the late twentieth and early twenty-first century, as alternate history narratives have flourished in other media alongside their conventionally printed forebears. Whilst restricting her focus to these televisual narratives, Hellekson's chapter concludes the collection with an examination of the state of the alternate history genre and questions what has made it so popular in more recent years, providing a launchpad for further investigation.

~

Each of the chapters in this section takes the ideas of alternate history, which by now should be familiar, and spins them out into new areas whether those be individualistic or intimate narratives, secret histories and alternative narratives, or other media. They demonstrate that whilst the printed text, and particularly the novel, remain the primary home of alternate history it is not limited to the page, and the scope for the way the genre can be presented is in fact far vaster than most existing scholarship has begun to grasp. The chapters of the second half of this collection allow us to return to those of the first, further deepening our appreciation for Roberts's contrasting dualism of Tolstoy versus Geoffroy-Château, for the historical narratives submerged under the generally white, Euro-American, male norm, and for the fragility of historical 'knowledge'.

This then is the overriding aim of this collection, to expand and strengthen discussion about alternate history narratives as a subject worthy of serious academic consideration and to demonstrate not only that the genre is vital and vitally alive, but that it is also capable of sustaining varied and serious discussion but a range of authors with a range of approaches, styles, and interests. This collection is not comprehensive in its presentation of the different aspects of the genre or the possibilities for its study, nor was that ever the aim, such a collection would be unwieldly and prohibitive. Rather, this collection represents the latest words in a conversation which is only just reaching the ears of the academy; it aims to bring more voices into that conversation and encourage its proliferation. We hope that this collection will be welcomed as an important addition to a growing body of work on the study of alternate history narratives, and that its chapters are found to be as useful and fascinating as we found them.

References

Brownstein, Gabriel. 'Fight or Flight'. *The Village Voice*. 2004. Accessed 7 February 2016. <http://www.villagevoice.com/arts/fight-or-flight-7139189>

Carlyle, Thomas. *On Heroes, Hero-Worship and the Heroic in History*. Adelaide University Press, 2010.

Carr, E. H. *What Is History?* Penguin, 1968.

Chapman, Edgar L. 'Introduction: Three Stages of Alternate History Fiction and the "Metaphysical If"'. *Classic and Iconoclastic Alternate History Science Fiction*. Eds. Edgar L. Chapman and Carl B. Yoke. Edwin Mellen Press, 2003, pp. 1–28.

Evans, Richard J. *Altered Pasts: Counterfactuals in History*. Little Brown, 2014.

Ferguson, Niall. 'Virtual History: Towards a "Chaotic" Theory of the Past'. *Virtual Histories: Alternatives and Counterfactuals*. Ed. Niall Ferguson. Picador, 1997, pp. 1–90.

Fry, Stephen. *Making History*. Hutchinson, 1996.

Gallagher, Catherine. *Telling It Like It Wasn't: The Counterfactual Imagination in History and Fiction*. Chicago University Press, 2018.

—. 'War, Counterfactual History, and Alternate-History Novels'. *Field Day Review*, vol. 3, 2007, pp. 52–65.

Hawthorn, Geoffrey. *Plausible Worlds: Possibility and Understanding in History and the Social Sciences*. Cambridge University Press, 1991.

Hellekson, Karen. 'Alternate History'. *The Routledge Companion to Science Fiction*. Eds. Mark Bould, Andrew M. Butler, Adam Roberts, and Sherryl Vint. Routledge, 2009, pp. 453–457.

—. *The Alternate History: Refiguring Historical Time*. Kent State University Press, 2001.

Leinster, Murray. 'Sidewise in Time', *The Mammoth Book of Classic Science Fiction: Short Novels of the 1930s*. Eds. Isaac Asimov, Martin H. Greenberg, and Charles G. Waugh. Robinson, 1988, pp. 241–289.

Mitrovich, Matt. 'Warping History: An Overview of Fans and Creators of Alternate History in the Internet Age'. *Sideways in Time: Alternate History and Counterfactual Narratives Conference*. 'Sideways in Time Schedule'. 7 March 2015. Accessed 15 September 2017. Abstract. <https://sideway-sintime.wordpress.com/>

Roth, Philip. 'The Story Behind "The Plot Against America."' *New York Times*. 19 September 2004. Accessed 7 February 2015. <http://www.nytimes.com/2004/09/19/books/review/19ROTHL.html>

Singles, Kathleen. *Alternate Histories: Playing with Contingency and Necessity*. Walter de Gruyter, 2013.

Thiess, Derek J. *Relativism, Alternate History, and the Forgetful Reader: Reading Science Fiction and Historiography*, Lexington, 2015.

Thurman, Judith. 'Philip Roth e-mails on Trump'. *The New Yorker*. 30 January 2017. Accessed 20 June 2017. <https://www.newyorker.com/magazine/2017/01/30/philip-roth-e-mails-on-trump>

Part I

Points of Divergence

Napoleon as Dynamite

Geoffroy's Napoléon Apocryphe and Science Fiction as Alternate History

Adam Roberts

Louis-Napoléon Geoffroy[1] is usually credited as the author of the first 'alternate history'. Karen Hellekson asserts confidently that 'the alternate history did not exist in Western literature until 1836', the 'year that saw the first novel-length alternate history, Louis-Napoléon Geoffroy-Château's *Napoléon et la conquête du monde 1812–32*' (*Alternate History* 13), and Paul K. Alkon describes Geoffroy's novel as 'the first uchronia of alternate history' (*Origins of Futuristic Fiction* 146). This belief connects with a larger thesis, to which many scholars of science fiction subscribe, that the late eighteenth-century flourish of political revolutions across Europe and America, into which we may bracket the effectively global Napoleonic wars to which they gave rise, reconfigured the logic of the genre; that, as Darko Suvin puts it, 'around 1800, space loses its monopoly upon the location of estrangement and the alternative horizons shift from space to time' (*Positions and Suppositions in Science Fiction* 89). Revolution, the argument runs, challenged the older preconceptions about history as such, undid perceived inevitabilities and opened the door to imagined alterities. Out of this rupture emerged, inter alia, alternate history as a new sub-genre, fully formed in Geoffroy's novel, as abruptly as Athena bursting from the forehead of Jove. It is an argument unlikely to be disturbed by the observation that, in fact, there were many earlier-published novels with good claims to be alternate histories, going back to the middle of the seventeenth century.[2]

---

[1] He changed his name from Geoffroy to Geoffroy-Château late in life, but for purposes of discussion I'm going to stick with the earlier, simpler form.

[2] As I go on to argue in this paper, mere chronological precedence has little bearing on the history of alternate history as a sub-genre; but for the sake of completeness I will here note my preferred candidate for 'first alternate-history novel'. This is Samuel Gott's *Nova Solyma, the Ideal City; or Jerusalem Regained* (1648) based on the notion that in the year 1600 the Jews of the world had received a divine vision that converted them en masse to

So instead of trying to unseat Geoffroy from his position of absolute priority, this chapter will start with the observation that there is a reason why his name stands, conventionally, at the origin point of alternate history. Something about Geoffroy's particular approach proved influential in subsequent iterations of the mode, sometimes at second-hand; and this fact has had profound consequences for how history as such is portrayed in science fiction. And indeed we need not look far to see what this is: the ideological valence of his subject, the way Napoleon blasts through the obstacle of 'actual' history by sheer force of military, political, and persona charisma. Geoffroy was a man who hero-worshipped Napoleon (he changed his first name from Louis to Louis-Napoléon in homage, for instance), and the whole of his novel makes quite plain his investment in a 'great man' model of history. This, combined with a second formal innovation – that is the way Geoffroy worked *systematically* at his premise – decided the terms of this novel, thereby shaping the template that alternate history as sub-genre went on to follow.

Geoffroy's novel, originally published as *Napoléon et la conquête du monde* ['Napoleon and the Conquest of the World'] in 1836 and revised in 1841 as *Napoléon apocryphe* ['Apocryphal Napoleon'] identifies its point of divergence in Napoleon's successful invasion of Russia in 1812. Having subdued the Russians, the emperor moves quickly to conquer the English in 1814, followed, in short order, by the entire rest of the world. This triumph propels humanity into a new golden age of technological advance, peace, and prosperity.

I want to start by picking out several episodes in the novel indicative of the way Geoffroy conceives of history as such. The first is the facility with which Napoleon conquers the United States. Revolution has so weakened this nation that it simply collapses:

> Depuis plus de vingt années, L'Amérique, cette terre sans passé, sans races, sans patries, qui, pour remplacer ses enfants égorgés, avait mendié à L'Europe son trop plein de peuples et à L'Afrique le marché de ses douleurs; cette terre qui, sans avoir eu de

Christianity. In Gott's timeline, these redeemed Jews then seized Jerusalem and remade it as a Christian utopia. The novel is both a detailed account of this alt-historical city and also a response to the specifics of the English Civil War, in which Puritan-Parliamentarian Gott was involved. In other words, *Nova Solyma* is one reaction to the imaginative space the upheavals of that devastating war opened for reimagining social possibility. My *History of Science Fiction* (Palgrave 2006; 2nd edition 2016) discusses another half a dozen alt-historical works published before Geoffroy.

jeunesse, était arrivée à la décrépitude au milieu de révolutions innombrables, l'Amérique se dissolvait, et tendait à une ruine complète. (Geoffroy 415)[3]

[For more than two decades, America, this land without past, without races, without countries, has had to replace its own murdered children by going begging to Europe for its excess population and in trade with Africa at the market of its miseries; this land that, without ever having been young, had arrived at decrepitude in the midst of endless revolutions – America was dissolving, heading for complete ruin.]

For Geoffroy's novel, America can only be saved from disaster by the intervention of Napoleon: 'Napoléon seul pouvait sauver l'Amérique [...] [d]ans tous les cas, il n'y'avait plus de salut pour elle en dehors de la monarchie napoléonienne' [Only Napoleon could save America [...] whatever else was true, there was no salvation for that country except under Napoleonic Rule]. It is worth noting that America has no larger role in the narrative of *Napoleon apocryphe*; its conquest is a sidebar on the way to global supremacy. It is invoked here as an example of history itself as a kind of short-circuit: America a country with no history of its own, a land that has passed directly from 'le jeunesse' [youth] to 'la décrépitude' [decrepitude] without any intervening historical narrative at all. Geoffroy's United States subsists, vampire-like, by devouring the children of Europe and the slave labour of Africa. In such a situation there is no intrinsic historical evolution or even revolution that can address the problems, because there is no history out of which evo- or revolution can emerge. Only Napoleon himself can offer a remedy for the catastrophe of the extra-historical. In other words, Geoffroy's Napoleon embodies a sort of 'solution' to and therefore *for* history itself.

This early imagining of America as, in effect, a place where history has been botched or chaotically circumvented raises key questions. We might want to argue that the USA 'possesses' history in two contradictory ways at once: it has both *too little* history to be properly grounded (since it is a 'new' or only potential nation, especially only a few decades after the Declaration of Independence) and *too much* history, as the dead hand of the old world is carried through by its settlers. There's a third American history too, of course, one perfectly invisible to Geoffroy in

---

[3] All quotations from Geoffroy's novel are from the revised edition, *Napoleon apocryphe. Histoire de la conquete du monde et de la monarchie universelle* (Paris: Chez Paulin 1841). Translations into English are my own.

the 1830s, the history of its aboriginal inhabitants, but this is a history inassimilable to the model of the Old World, since it is nether bookish, nor linear, not Whiggish, neither Herodotean nor Thucydidean. The 'new world' and 'old world' versions of history are both, in different ways, these latter things, and it is precisely these latter modes of history that Geoffroy's novel wholly circumvents, by positing historical alterity – his world-conquering Napoleon – as the only possible stability. What interests me here is the extent to which this historical problematic has fed through to the genre of alternate history writing today. America (we could say) 'has' more history now than once it did, and a great deal of alt-historical writing has explored American settings – a Confederate victory in the Civil War as a point of divergence, for example, is frankly a cliché of the genre nowadays.[4] Nonetheless, if we look at the most celebrated examples of this kind of writing, we find a similar pseudo-Geoffroyan suspicion of American history. In Murray Leinster's celebrated short story 'Sidewise in Time' (1934), competing alternate history timelines have generated a kind of crazy-paving chaos out of America (resulting in a chaos not a million miles away from Geoffroy's failed state). Even in Ward Moore's splendid novel *Bring the Jubilee* (1953), the richly imagined alternate North America (in which the Confederacy won the Civil War) exists only for the novel's time-travelling historian protagonist to revert history back to *our* timeline. More recently, and more Geoffroyan in a way, is a novel like Felix Gilman's *Half-Made World* (2010). To quote Abigail Nussbaum:

> Gilman builds a secondary world in which everything from our history of American Western expansion is present and yet different. Instead of the original, Eastern colonies of the United States we have nations with names like Koenigswald and Juddua. Instead of the Appalachians and their Cumberland Pass we have the Opals and their pass at the town of White Rock. [...] Alongside these parallels, however, there is one unique trait, the literalized metaphor at the center of the duology's world. The further one travels to the West in Gilman's alternate America, the less solid, the less made, the world becomes. The laws of nature break down and give way to magic, and at the furthest reaches of the West, 'Sea, sky, land, day,

---

[4] Robert B Schmunk's comprehensive database of alt-historical novels www. uchronia.net declares on its main page that 'the two most common themes in alternate history are 'What if the Nazis won World War II?' and 'What if the Confederacy won the American Civil War?' [consulted November 2016].

night, [are] indistinguishable, not yet separated. ... creation begins, or maybe hasn't happened yet'. That creation occurs in response to human settlement, which solidifies and finally normalizes the half-made world, but the meeting between human fears and desires and the in-flux world's magic has unexpected results. It gives rise to the Line and Gun, not just metaphors for capitalism and lawlessness run amok, but manifestations of it with minds of their own, who can conscript and enslave humans to their purpose. (Nussbaum n.p.)

This articulates something important about history itself, or more precisely about history under the aegis of the American experience (necessarily an important experience, in the development of science fiction). Nussbaum is surely correct that one of the weaknesses of Gilman's book and its sequel is a kind of blindness to 'the Folk', the Native American equivalents in the novels: they are outside European conceptions of history, and therefore out of history altogether.

In the timeline of *Napoléon apocryphe*, 1827 is the year global military conquest is accomplished, and 'Universal Monarchy' established:

La monarchie universelle! Combien ont prononcé ces mots qui ne comprenaient pas l'idée qu'ils renferment. Combien le sont balbutiées et répétées froidement ces paroles: enfants, hommes, pédants et rois, qui ne savaient ce que c'était que la monarchie universelle, pas plus que l'infini et que Dieu, dont à chaque instant leurs bouches murmurent les noms. (Geoffroy 412)

[Universal monarchy! How many have uttered those words without understanding them? How often are they stammered out, coldly repeated by children as by men, by pedants and kinds, who had no more idea of their meaning than they did of 'infinity' or 'God', words their mouths were constantly murmuring.]

Geoffroy thinks of Napoleon as Napoleon thought of himself: as a man elevated above the common herd, looking down upon the ideological and political lowlands of the world. And considerably more space is devoted, in *Napoléon apocryphe*, to the discourses of the legal and social settlement than is given to descriptions of war. For instance, Geoffroy lists all the articles of the new Napoleonic world order:

Art. 1. *Les continents, les îles et les mers qui couvrent la surface du globe composent la monarchie universelle.* [Universal Monarchy comprises all the continents, islands and seas of the world]

Art. 2. *Le christianisme est la seule religion de la terre.* [Christianity is the sole world religion]

Art. 3. *La monarchie universelle réside en moi et dans ma race à perpétuité.* [Universal Monarchy resides in me and my descendants in perpetuity]

Art. 4. *Le siége de la monarchie universelle est à Paris, capitale de la terre.* [The seat of Universal Monarchy is Paris, capital city of the world]

Art. 5. *La terre est divisée en quatre parties: L'Europe; L'Asie à laquelle sont réunies les îles de l'Océania; l'Afrique et l'Amérique.* [The world is divided into four portions: Europe; Asia including the Pacific islands; Africa and America.]

Art. 6. *Les quatre parties de la terre sont subdivisées en royaumes.* [The world's four portions are subdivided into kingdoms.]

Art. 7. *La France conserve seule le nom d'empire.* [France reserves to herself the title 'Empire']

Art. 8. *La guerre est désormais interdite aux rois et aux peuples.* [War is henceforth forbidden between kings and peoples]

Art. 9. *L'esclavage est détruit.* [Slavery is abolished]

Art. 10. *Les rois de la terre sont, sous notre souveraineté, chargés en ce qui les concerné de l'exécution du présent décret.* [The kings of the earth are, under our sovereignty, charged with the execution of this decree] Donné à Paris, ce 4 juillet 1827. NAPOLEON. (Geoffroy 414)

We might be forgiven for finding a sharp irony in that ninth article, announcing the abolition of slavery, since both the specific and the cumulative nature of all the others amount to distilled essence of totalitarianism, slavishly subordinating all the world's people to Napoleon as *dirigeant* or *commandant*, leader or general. Article 1 and Article 3 are unambiguous. Paris is made capital of the world and Christianity decreed as the only world religion.

The day-and-month are significant too: Geoffroy is appropriating America's 'Independence Day' in order to overwrite US exceptionalism with his own vision of French metahistory. Everyone seems blithely accepting of Christianity as the sole global religion, including all the Jews, with one single exception:

Samuel Manassès, rabbin de Strasbourg, protesta avec la plus grande violence contre la décision de ses frères, et, dans un moment d'exaltation, il s'écria: 'a que le Christ signale donc sa vérité et sa puissance! Pour moi, fidèle à la loi de mes pères, je le blasphème hautement, et je défie le dieu des chrétiens!' (Geoffroy 435)

[Samuel Manassas, a Strasbourg Rabbi, protested violently against the decision of his brothers, and in a moment of exaltation he cried out: 'oh that Christ should thus signal his truth and power! For myself, faithful to the law of my fathers, I blaspheme strongly against him, and I defy the Christian God!']

But this protest goes nowhere: stubborn Manassas, touched by 'le doigt de Dieu' [the finger of God], has a seizure, falls to the ground and dies there and then. 'Cette circonstance extraordinaire', Geoffroy adds blandly, 'porta le dernier coup à la religion juive, elle expira cette année avec le culte et les constitutions de Moïse'. [This extraordinary event delivered the final blow to the Jewish religion, which died that same year, along with the whole cult and constitution of Moses.]

The Jews (Geoffroy calls them 'cette nation mystère', literally 'this mysterious nation'), of course, stand for the opposite sort of 'historical' force to the Americans. They embody not too little but *too much* history; the antique law that must be overcome for the ahistorical, alt-historical Napoleonic utopia to come into being. But if overcoming too little history is a simple matter of military conquest, overcoming too much requires this extraordinary (in several senses) divine intervention.

French is made the universal language; everybody is happy and at peace. Of course 'l'empereur conserva son immense armée' [retains, that is, his enormous army], although there seems to be no enemy against which it can be sent into battle. But the army is the externalization of Napoleon's history-altering charisma, and so naturally this novel cannot imagine it being disbanded. The emperor draws up a plan to eliminate all other races by selective breeding over seven generations ('arriver à la suite de quelques générations à une unité de race et de couleur'; to arrive at a unified race and colour) and he makes great strides in science, including the invention of superfast trains ('des voitures qui volaient avec la rapidité de la foudre sur les routes en fer') and a fleet of airships, or 'ballons aérostatiques' powered by 'les forces magnétiques avec l'électricité' [magnetic and electrical forces]. Geoffroy mentions some more eccentric inventions as well: pliable soft-glass ('le verre, si résistant et si friable, s'amollit sous les doigts de la chimie, il se plia comme une cire assouplie'; [glass, formerly so brilliant and fragile, softens under the fingers of chemistry and becomes a pliable as wax]). A new planet is discovered, and named 'la planète de Vulcain', providing an unspoken but implied arena into which Napoleon can continue his military–imperial expansion. The unspoken logic of the novel seems to be that once history has been so forcefully reshaped, all other aspects of reality become similarly malleable. So, for instance: under World-Emperor Napoleon actual mathematical impossibilities are accomplished, including: 'une merveilleuse inutilité, long-temps crue impossible, la quadrature du cercle, fut découverte dans des circonstances singulières' [one marvellous though useless thing, long thought impossible, was accomplished in the most singular circumstances: squaring the circle]. These literal impossibilities, mixed in with the various mere improbabilities, speak to the contradiction the novel acknowledges without making explicit. Napoleon becomes a kind of transcendental signifier, a magic finger capable of altering not just the material but the *spiritual* facts of history.

One way to frame the distinctive version of history elaborated, via its alterity, in Geoffroy's novel is to contrast it with another, rather more famous literary representation of Napoleon from the nineteenth century: Tolstoy's Война и миръ (*War and Peace* 1869). This immense novel advances a particular agenda in the way it dramatizes Napoleon. Tolstoy sees him as a man radically self-deluded about the power he has to shape events, an individual who continually over-estimated his ability to change history as such. This is a moral hammered home by the second, interminable portion of the novel's epilogue, a lengthy essay on history as such, laying out Tolstoy's objections to the 'Great Man Theory' of historical change. For Tolstoy, all historical events are inevitably the result of millions of smaller events, and history as such is driven by the immense numbers of ordinary individuals that constitute humanity itself. The comparison he makes is with calculus, and the (then) recently discovered ability of mathematicians to sum infinitesimals. His argument in turn expresses a fundamental logic of individual human life, which is determined by an inverse relationship between necessity and free will, necessity for Tolstoy being defined by reason and therefore explicable to historical analysis, where free will is 'consciousness' and therefore inherently unpredictable. In other words, Tolstoy is the great *anti*-alternate-historian. He thinks it doesn't matter what any one individual does, no matter how mighty s/he might be in the conventional scheme of things. History is 'like a deaf person who is in the habit of answering questions that no one has put to them', Tolstoy famously insists.

> If the purpose of history is to give a description of the movement of
> humanity and of the peoples, the first question – in the absence of
> a reply to which all the rest will be incomprehensible – is: what is
> the power that moves peoples? To this, modern history laboriously
> replies either that Napoleon was a great genius, or that Louis XIV
> was very proud, or that certain writers wrote certain books. All
> that may be so and mankind is ready to agree with it, but it is not
> what was asked. (Tolstoy, trans. George Gibian 1045)

What Napoleon, Louis XIV, or any other individual does or doesn't do
is irrelevant. The real business of history is located elsewhere.

Alternate history as a mode is Geoffroyan rather than Tolstoyan in
this sense. It is the deaf sub-genre that can only think of history as a
succession of 'great' (that is, significant) individuals, of moments around
which everything might hinge. We could say that alternate history
necessarily styles history as fundamentally fragile; or we might prefer to
put the emphasis the other way about and argue that it styles 'man' as
possessing the sublime power to bend history and society around him.
For Tolstoy one man, even one battle in which hundreds of thousands
die, like Borodino, is not enough to overcome the immense inertia of
history as such. Napoleon thinks he has won the Battle of Borodino,
because he held the field, the Russians retreated and he is able to occupy
Moscow. But the novel shows that Napoleon is wrong, and it is precisely
this error that Geoffroy makes in his novel. History doesn't work that
way, according to Tolstoy.

The striking thing is how often science fiction follows Geoffroy, and
how very rarely it proves itself Tolstoyan. Indeed this, to speak a little
more widely, is the impetus Romanticism gave to the whole of the
burgeoning mode we now call science fiction, relocating its Sublime
from a collectivist to an individualist epiphany, styling the cosmos a
backdrop to the drama of the exemplary self. The last man, the tragic
or exalted figure on the mountain-top, the brilliant monster shunned
by society, the Poe-hero revelling in his something ghastly intensities,
Napoleon turning to an alternate history to manifest his global destiny:
these become the new icons of genre.

'History' in science fiction very often devolves upon great individuals,
and very rarely manifests any Tolstoyan suspicions. Some of the
most acclaimed alt-history tropes have become subgenres, or perhaps
sub-subgenres, in their own right: 'Hitler Wins' being the most
populous.[5] In many cases, as with Geoffroy's novel, a 'great man', much

---

[5] John Clute, Peter Nicholls and David Langford's *Encyclopedia of Science Fiction*

more rarely a 'great woman', overpowers the adventitious or circum-
stantial obstacles of 'real' history to rewrite the historical narrative. If
the 'great man' does not actively force history around his lines of force,
then the removal of the 'great man' effects that change by, as it were,
default. The altered timeline in Keith Roberts's celebrated *Pavane* (1968)
branches from our world when Queen Elizabeth is assassinated; and
Stephen King's *11/22/63* (2011) spins various alt-historical possibilities
out of the assassination, or otherwise, of John F. Kennedy.

The terms of such debate as there are lie elsewhere: as, for instance,
in the stand-off between positivist and what we would now call 'chaos
theory' models of historical progression. I can best explain what I mean,
here, by bringing in two of the genre's most famous dramatizations
of long-term historical development: Isaac Asimov's Foundation books
(the stories comprising the original trilogy of Foundation novels were
published 1942–1950, with various later titles added to the sequence
1982–1993) and Frank Hebert's Dune books (Herbert published six
Dune novels 1965–1985; his son and other writers have published a
great many more since his death). Asimov's text is predicated on the
notion that history can be completely mapped, comprehended with
such precision that perfectly accurate predictions can be made, over the
longest term. Asimov called this imaginary discipline 'psychohistory',
and it is a pure importation of Comtean ideas of positivism into science
fiction. Asimov objective correlative for this understanding of history
is the encyclopaedia – the cover-story of his 'Foundation', that they
are collating the *Encyclopedia Galactica* (when in fact they are working
behind the scenes to manipulate galactic history to ameliorate the
fall of the empire) speaks to the tacit model of history in the novels.
History for Asimov is a large quantity of data to be sorted, classified,
arranged, and thereby mastered. When Frank Herbert wrote the first
of his Dune novels in the 1960s he was reacting specifically against
Asimov's version of 'history'. In place of the notion of history as
an orderly assemblage of known and mastered facts, Herbert posits
history as a sandstorm, through the eddies and whorls of which – in
a memorable scene in the first novel – the hero Paul Atreides must
pilot a flying 'ornithopter' in order to escape death at the hands of
his enemies. Paul acquires future-vision, and in some respects this
prophetic power does grant him accurate precognition. But in other
regards he is as blind about the future as he becomes, literally, in the
world in *Dune Messiah*. Herbert's model of history anticipates chaos

(3rd ed., sfe3.org, consulted November 2016) has an entire entry on 'Hitler
Wins', and discusses more than seventy discrete novels and stories.

theory: it is a storm, not the regimented *omnium gatherum* of Asimov's Foundation.

And yet, despite this fundamental difference in conceptions of what historical progress actually is, both writers in fact bend their respective versions of history to 'great men'. The broader narrative of Asimov's original Foundation trilogy posits history as, in effect, the struggle between two powerful men: Hari Seldon, the inventor of 'psychohistory' and therefore the tamer of history as such, and 'the Mule', a mutant dictator unforeseeable by psychohistory – because that discipline deals only with the collective, and not with individuals – and therefore able to upset Seldon's predicted path. This struggle is resolved with a twist, whereby it is revealed that Seldon has anticipated the Mule's disruption and planned to counter it with a secret second Foundation. And in Dune, the stormwinds of history are harnessed by Paul Atreides, an individual who combines the roles of political dictator and religious messiah. Later in the sequence, and especially in *God Emperor of Dune* (1981), Herbert interrogated the logic of fascism implicit in this vision to some extent, but in doing so he more deeply embeds the sense that history is malleable in the hands of the powerful: in that novel, Duke Leto II has mutated into an immortal sandworm-human hybrid, powerful enough in effect to force history to a full stop for 3,500 years.

The invented in-text histories of science fiction often follow this logic. All the shenanigans and pseudo-political folderol of George Lucas's *Star Wars* movies exist as iterations of the in-family dynamic of one group of supernaturally powerful and forceful people. Heinlein's elaborate future history is, as we might expect, construed around the figure of the great man, with this wrinkle: that the great man is always a version of the patriarch, Heinlein, himself. I could, if I had space, spool out a great many similar examples.

This is not to suggest that the situation is entirely monolithic. There are of course examples, and influential ones, of sf history rendered in Tolstoyan terms. Olaf Stapledon's novels would be one important example; Kim Stanley Robinson's future histories another. But even in these instances, history is as much defined by its breaks as its continuities. It is just that the breaks are not caused by a single great man. In Stapledon's *Last and First Men* (1930) eighteen distinct species of men follow, one after the other, the passage from one to the other being marked by a variety of catastrophes – war, plague and the like; and in Robinson's future history, environmental collapse punctuates and drives the momentum of the historical process.

It's tempting to see this as the paradigmatically sciencefictional model of history: it is prone to sudden rupture. It can be forced. And sf, broadly speaking, valorizes the force that busts through the obstacle, the superweapon, the superhero, the straight line to goal. This is as much a feature of sf culture as plot and story – it is, in other words, as much about form as content. Not for nothing are the Star Wars films, *Avatar* and *Terminator* called 'blockbusters'. It's not that continuity is disregarded. On the contrary, sf fans are very often heavily invested in continuity, figured in terms of the coherence of world-building and the consistency of in-story metanarratives, the so-called 'canon' of text-to-text links and structures. Yet even that continuity is conceptualized around a sort of sanctified breach, a meta point of divergence to which any given congeries of storylines can return: the retcon. Any given version of DC Comics' superhero trans-dimensional apocalypse 'Crisis on Infinite Earths' construes a new continuity precisely via a rupture, or 'crisis'.

What's significant about this is the way it exists centrally in the rhetoric of *any* kind of historiography. Fredric Jameson proposes the relationship as a dialectic that is also a quasi-Kantian antinomy (that doubled strategy is surely one of the most characteristic conceptual strategies of late Jameson). And although the following passage is not 'about' science fiction, Jameson is (of course) a major critic of the genre, and what he says here crystallizes the larger argument I'm advancing here. He is trying to find a way of talking meaningfully about 'the modern' or 'modernity', of separating (that is) this period from the larger flow.

> What we have tried to isolate is a dialectic of break and the period, which is itself a moment of some wider dialectic of continuity and rupture (or in other words of Identity and Difference). For the latter process is dialectical in that it cannot be arrested and 'solved' in and for itself, but generates ever new forms and categories … The choice between continuity and rupture is something like an absolute historiographic beginning, that cannot be justified by the nature of the historical material or evidence, since it organizes all such material and evidence in the first place. (Jameson, *A Singular Modernity* 23)

This brings us back to the starting point of the present essay. It does not matter that scholars can unearth any number of alternate histories that predate Geoffroy's novel. *Napoléon apocryphe* is both an example of generic continuity, and a rupture in that continuity – a new thing, a sub-generic novum, the first alternate history novel – because that is precisely the dialectic that defines the start of this new strand of histori-ography (we might call it alternate historiography). Napoleon himself becomes simultaneously the transcendental signifier of history as such *and* of the supersession of all history.

If the 'rupture' in conventional history is usually styled as the significant event or individual, the 'rupture' in history as discourse must be the point of divergence, the site where *history itself* is broken into two (or in some alternate historical fantasies, myriad, perhaps infinite) pieces. If history itself is the province of historians and historical novelists, this larger frame belongs to sf. And insofar as we chose to identify sf as the modern mode par excellence, Jameson's reading of the historical dialectic seems peculiarly relevant:

> I am tempted to argue that the present cannot feel itself to be a historical period in its own right without this gaze from the future, which seals it off and expels it as powerfully from time to come as it was able to do with its own immediate precedents. (Jameson 26)

It is precisely in this manner that sf mediates its textual commitment to a possible future with its necessary engagement with the present day and the now; and out of this tension, or rupture, the specificities of sciencefictional disclosure spring.

Clearly, this is to move the terms of the debate self-reflexively, from in-text specifics to the genre as such. But that's a move not only licensed by, but fundamentally implicit in, the logic of the mode. It goes beyond that smaller group of texts classically pigeonholed as 'alt-history' in order to make the case that *all* sf follows this logic. The 'alt-' prefix is doing the work that in traditional attempts at definitions of sf has been done by terms and phrases like 'novum', 'structural fabulation', and so on.

There are various ways in which this applies, but I'm going to focus on one of them: the way sf narratives of in-text history run in parallel to 'actual' history, and more specifically what happens when the two lines cross. So, for example: it is conventional for critics to argue that Orwell's *Nineteen Eighty-Four* (1949) is not, despite its title, set in a notional version of 1984 – writing as he was in 1948, Orwell merely reversed the last two digits of the year to provide the title.[6] The novel might be set hundreds, perhaps thousands of years into a stagnant future, since the Party has complete control over the narratives of history. But this has always struck me as a strangely oblique, almost perverse way of reading the novel's title. Why not take it at its word, as it were? Orwell's novel is, after all, set in a recognizably postwar British world of

---

[6] See for instance Irving Howe, *Orwell's Nineteen Eighty-Four: Text, Sources, Criticism* (Harcourt Brace Jovanovich, 1982).

hardship, rationing, and social exhaustion; his title posits a future close enough for that mood to have persevered, even as it extrapolates quite profound structural changes to actual British society. One suspects the main reason why such a common-sense reading might strike people as unappealing is that the actual 1984 came and went and nothing like Orwell's nightmare came to pass. But this relies upon a *naïf* sense of what science fiction does. 'Extrapolation into the future' is manifestly not the same thing as 'prophesy'. Far from marking the point at which Orwell 'got it wrong', the passage of '1984' from future-possibility through present actuality into past represents something crucially important about the genre. In a nutshell this is the way reality is continually catching-up with the speculations of genre. It leads to a far-reaching question. Pulp sf writers of the 1930s wrote stories set on the shores of warm Venusian oceans. American and Russian probes in the 1960s demonstrated that Venus is actually dry, punishingly hot, and utterly barren. What was a possibility in the 1930s becomes an impossibility in the 1960s. Where does that leave the work? If we choose to apply rigid standards of observational scientific accuracy to science fiction, then it leaves these earlier texts in the dustbin of history. But we need not be so procrustean. As the introduction to this volume argues, we might posit such 'failed' extrapolations as inhabiting a branched-off alternate version of the possibilities of history – might, that is, read Orwell's *Nineteen Eighty-Four* as an instance of exotic alt-history rather than a failed prediction of any actual 1984. This is one way of noting that history is an ongoing process, and that anticipations of a specific future will inevitably, eventually, be overtaken by actual historical process. That is, in fact, the Tolstoyan model of history as a flow of supraindividual forces, and not the Geoffroyan fantasy of a point of stoppage to history as such, embodied in his 'Great Man'.

If we look at science fiction this way, its own history becomes a delta of branching paths that deviate from the baseline history (which we might call 'classic' or 'core' genre). The entire genre formally enacts alt-historical patterns. Napoleon's dynamitic example shatters the discursive monologism of the scientific paradigm, and frees the genre. 'C'est une des lois fatales de l'humanité', Geoffroy declares ringingly at the beginning of his novel, 'que rien n'y atteigne le but' (Geoffroy 10). [It is one of the fatal laws of humanity that nothing accomplishes its object.] 'Loi terrible!' he adds, as if his fictional elaboration of Napoleon finally achieving his object can undo the terribleness. In fact the reverse is accomplished in this novel, and its many successors. Science fiction, and even history itself, is shattered into myriad branching possibilities. Apocryphal indeed.

References

Alkon, Paul. *Origins of Futuristic Fiction*. University of Georgia Press, 1987.

Clute, John, Peter Nicholls, and David Langford. *Encyclopedia of Science Fiction*. 3rd ed. Accessed November 2016. <sfe3.org>

Geoffroy, Louis-Napoleon. *Napoleon apocryphe. Histoire de la conquete du monde et de la monarchie universelle*. Chez Paulin, 1841.

Hellekson, Karen. *The Alternate History: Refiguring Historical Time*. Kent State University Press, 2001.

Howe, Irving. *Orwell's Nineteen Eighty-Four: Text, Sources, Criticism*. Harcourt Brace Jovanovich, 1982.

Jameson, Fredric. *A Singular Modernity*. Verso, 2002.

Nussbaum, Abigail. 'On the Meeting of Epic Fantasy and Western in Felix Gilman's Half-Made World Duology', *Crooked Timber*, 9 May 2013. Accessed November 2016. <https://goo.gl/8899GX>

Roberts, Adam. *History of Science Fiction*. Palgrave, 2006.

Suvin, Darko. *Positions and Suppositions in Science Fiction*. Macmillan, 1988.

Tolstoy, Leo. *War and Peace*. 1869. Trans. George Gibian. 2nd ed. Norton Critical Edition, 1996.

'It Is One Story'

Writing a Global Alternate History in Kim Stanley Robinson's The Years of Rice and Salt

Chris Pak

Kim Stanley Robinson's *The Years of Rice and Salt* (2002) depicts a world that might have developed had European civilizations been eradicated by the Black Death. Scenes set in the bardo, an intermediate state between death and rebirth in Tibetan Buddhism, introduce a narrative frame for reflecting on the language games relating to history that are portrayed in the text.[1] In this chapter, I examine the ways in which the alternate history is used to present history and the development of societies in the context of an absent Europe, and in the absence of the concept of Europe as historically constructed in our timeline. Analyzing the use of textual strategies such as the narrative cohesion generated through the reincarnation of focal characters, I consider what it means to tell stories about history by investigating how the text represents several non-European civilizations, and by examining what these portrayals say about the relationship of history to the formation of stories about cultural identity and the future. These non-European civilizations include the Chinese and Arabic societies that are portrayed in the novel across a period of over 680 years.

This analysis will begin by considering a scholarly dispute over interpretations of the metaphysical significance of reincarnation for

---

[1] In *Philosophical Investigations*, Wittgenstein describes language games as a category encompassing multiple communicative utterances and/or actions, and he calls 'the whole [of natural language], consisting of language and the actions into which it is woven, the "language-game"' (5). Alternate histories engage in communicative acts specific to their form and their narratives' relationship to history, and call upon their readers to acknowledge potential realities alternative to our timeline. Such language games include allusions to the history of our timeline, extrapolation and speculation that make salient aspects of society, culture and history that might otherwise have remained unremarked, hidden or difficult to disentangle from the history or our timeline.

the cosmology of Robinson's alternate history in order to highlight the differences in various readers' orientation to the text. Emphasis on plausibility and representations of reincarnation and the bardo as evidence of a 'true' reality results in a different interpretation when compared to a treatment of the text according to what the historian Gavriel Rosenfeld describes in his 2002 article, 'Why Do We Ask "What If?" Reflections on the Function of Alternate History', as a 'document of memory', for which he argues the alternate history is well suited (90). Rosenfeld argues thus:

> Ironically, alternate histories lend themselves very well to being studied as documents of memory for the same reason that historians have dismissed them as useless for the study of history – namely, their fundamental subjectivity. (Rosenfeld 93)

The fundamental subjectivity of alternate histories – the narrowing of perspective necessary to the presentation of a fictional account that is situated through one or multiple characters – allows these fictional texts to be analyzed for the ways in which they present the memory of history. As Robinson's narrative begins as an alternate history preoccupied with the past and ends as a science fictional narrative that gestures toward a future of hope, in this chapter I likewise consider the importance of the relationship between the memory of the past and the imagination of the future for telling stories about civilizations. Ultimately, I show how *The Years of Rice and Salt* portrays the actors who make up the story of history, how this history is itself characterized and what repercussions these explorations have for reading the stories that make up the history of our timeline. If, as one of the characters suggests, individuals are 'a thread in a tapestry that has unrolled for centuries before us, and will unroll for centuries after us', then, as I will show in this chapter, alternate histories help us to explore the multiple configurations of that loom and to assess the possibilities inherent in that fabric for an extension into the future (Robinson 663).

Unlike many of the alternate timelines that have occupied thought in alternate history, counterfactual history, and science fiction scholarship, Robinson's alternate history is based on demographic trends and not on war and its aftermath. This statistical basis sets the scene for a narrative that unfolds across a period of over 680 years, from the fifteenth to the late twenty-first centuries, where the story of the expansion of non-European civilizations and the concomitant shifts in science, religion, culture, geopolitics, and social justice are played out. As Stephen Baxter explains in the foreword to this volume, Robinson draws on

Jared Diamond's analysis of the factors that influence the development of societies in his popular environmental history, *Guns, Germs and Steel: The Fates of Human Societies*, to imagine how a traumatic biological event that refigures the environments made available to Earth's remaining civilizations might lead to an alternative configuration of power and geopolitics. Plagues, and more specifically the Black Death, as the historian Geoffrey Hawthorn argues in 'Plague and Fertility in Modern Europe', is one of the most significant aspects of a biological regime in Europe that 'marked the limit between the possible and the impossible' (39). Alternate histories engage in language games that interrogate that space between the imagination of the possible and impossible.

The Years of Rice and Salt is divided into ten books, each of which centres on a cast of characters living in different societies throughout this span of time. Readers are given a sense of these civilizations' development through the experiences of these characters, whose struggle with authority in various guises is both a part of – and sometimes directly contributes to propel – the social changes depicted in each epoch. Both an alternate history and an epic narrative, Robinson transforms the epic's fascination with questions of historicity and the nation by portraying the inter-relationships of multiple national cultures to develop a global narrative of human history. Patrick Parrinder argues in 'Science Fiction as Truncated Epic' that sf is a form of 'truncated epic' that is concerned with 'future or alternate history' and the fate of 'whole societies or of the human race, its collaterals or descendants' (93). Responding to the re-figurations of epic form throughout its history, Adeline Johns-Putra describes in *The History of the Epic* how epic undergoes 'an accumulation of definitions, a piling on, as it were, of different meanings from different points in the epic's history' that point to 'an intriguing moment in its development and, second, a reflection of that development; that is, a reflection of past moments' (10). Robinson's epic speaks to this history by transforming a range of epic tropes to reflect on past moments both in human history and in the development of the narratives that frame those histories.

Paul Merchant writes in *The Epic* (1971) that it 'is a still developing and expanding form' (viii) characterized by 'the large scale of each work, and its all-inclusiveness' (71). This association of 'scale', 'mass', or 'weight' (4) is complemented by two features drawn from Mary McCarthy's definition of epic in 1968 as 'surpassing the dimensions of realism' and Ezra Pound's 1961 definition as 'a poem including history' (1). These two dimensions are poles, what Merchant calls '[t]he double relation of epic, to history on the one hand and to everyday reality on the other', which highlight the social function of epic as chronicle and story (2). These two features in turn open lines of enquiry into '[t]he sophisticated relationship of the poet to his material, his awareness of historical perspective' (2). Robinson draws from the parallel projects of the epic and the alternate history as documents of memory, thus illustrating Johns-Putra's contention in *The History of the Epic* that the epic is 'a game of inter-textuality' (58).

In order to provide coherence across the vast span of time depicted in *The Years of Rice and Salt*, and to connect the macro-level portrayal of the growth of each society to the micro-level biographies of the characters, scenes set in the bardo establish reincarnation as a cosmological frame for connecting the lives of each set of characters. The device that Robinson adopts to signal this continuity to the reader – the use of the same initial for the name of each reincarnated individual – is an attempt to bridge the disconnection between each cast of characters. Thus, the literary critic Gib Prettyman explains in his 2011 article 'Critical Utopia as Critical History: Apocalypse and Enlightenment in Kim Stanley Robinson's *The Years of Rice and Salt*':

> Character 'B', Bold and his later selves, is the bodhisattva, typically emphasizing compassion and spiritual insight; character 'K' is kinetic and impetuous, intent always on justice; character 'I' is inductive and investigative, often a scientist; character 'S' is self-indulgent, often in a position of power. (Prettyman 350)

These characters are destined to cross paths throughout their multiple lives by virtue of their membership in a 'jati', a cohort of individuals who are reincarnated as a group. This use of reincarnation has received criticism from scholars such as Farah Mendlesohn, who argues that the scenes set in the bardo 'do not belong in this book [...] because the structure of *The Years of Rice and Salt* is ostensibly polysemic, that being the baseline of all alternate histories, while the scenes in the bardo insist on the Truth' (25). The capacity for alternate histories to promote multiple interpretations is based on its resistance to a deterministic historical truth that cannot entertain the alterity of difference.

The alternate history is thus a polysemic form that invites multiple meanings and historical interpretation. *The Years of Rice and Salt* compounds this formal polysemy with a cultural polysemy conveyed by direct representation. Religious explanations of time are one element of a culture's narrative about their place in the world and in history, and are predicated – at least for Abrahamic traditions – on a teleological progression toward an apocalypse of a sort that presents itself as an exclusive truth. Thus, Mendlesohn explains, given that Christianity is excised from Robinson's history, 'the presentation of one of the remaining interpretations as a universal truth seems inappropriate and oddly evangelical' (25). Yet Keith Brooke observes that at one point, 'Robinson reminds us that there is a narrator to these tales, that this is an artifice, an act of storytelling' and that 'the "truth" of the extrapolation is relative and it's embedded in the narrator's world view, highlighting how blind we are to all the comparable assumptions made in more conventional western narratives'. An additional perspectival polysemy is thus joined to the other ways in which the text represents multiplicity. So, while Douglas Barbour points out that each of the books is, in his words, 'narrated in a manner proper to its time and place', Prettyman explains that:

> [J]ust as earlier the details of the bardo matched the cultural expectations of the souls who entered, when the inductive and anthropogenic expectation takes root the novel no longer gives us explicit glimpses of the bardo or of the gods at work. (Prettyman 352)

One of the strategies that Robinson uses in the text involves priming the reader to a hypersensitivity to interpretation that, while offering the possibility of closure through this religious theme, ultimately renders it ambiguous and opens it up to alterity.

I present this dispute over interpretations of the metaphysical significance of reincarnation for the cosmology portrayed in *The Years of Rice and Salt* so as to highlight the differences in these readers' orientation to the text. Reading the scenes set in the bardo as encompassing the 'true' metaphysical reality of the novel's world can result in overlooking the interpretative ambiguity of the text's portrayal of reincarnation and enlightenment. Documents of memory focus on the ways a text responds to the present, rather than to the past or the future: Rosenfeld argues that 'nearly all alternate histories explore the past instrumentally with an eye towards larger present-day agendas' (93). A good case can be made for an extension of this principle to sf. One aspect of the alternate history is its capacity to engage in language games that highlight classic science fictional operations, such as extrapolation, analogical thinking, estrangement, and the tendency to refract or project the present into the past or future. Enlightenment, which Prettyman regards as a collective utopian break from history, is in many ways the obverse of the apocalypse. Following Fredric Jameson, Prettyman argues that enlightenment 'works on the level of subjectivity and the individual' (339) to represent an 'asymptotic approach of a decisive break with the familiar narratives of history and utopia that paradoxically helps to generate empowering historical perceptions and utopian representations' (346). The approach of this decisive utopian break is an ongoing process that itself becomes subject to being transformed into story, and which is capable of generating further narratives about history and the future. Arguably, as implied by its characterization as asymptotic, the approach of this utopian break is always deferred; rather, its importance as a narrative subject and principle that provides foundations for the development of further narratives of empowerment and emancipation suggests that the imagination of the future is a utopian intervention.

One of the strategies for which Robinson uses the alternate history is to highlight aspects of world history that, while not unknown, certainly have little circulation in popular Anglo-American contexts and discourse. As the critic of utopia, Phillip E. Wegner, argues in 'Learning to Live in History: Alternate Historicities and the 1990s in *The Years of Rice and Salt*':

> [P]erhaps the greatest achievement of the novel [...] is the way it works to teach its audience, in a true Brechtian fashion, to think and hence to live in history in new ways, to overcome the sense of paralysis and inaction that have been considered characteristic of postmodernism and to actively take control of our destiny once more. (Wegner 99)

Thus, this pedagogic element of the text begins with Book One, 'Awake to Emptiness', and Bold's travels with the Mongol emperor Temur on his attempted conquest, not of China (as was the case in our timeline), but of the Franks and Magyars. This decision, one of the first bifurcations of history after the novel's portrayal of a European extinction caused by the Black Death, depends on the toss of a coin and leads the Khan to journey to the West and to the lands of those wiped out by the Plague. The contingency involved in his choice of target is duplicated shortly thereafter: Temur is struck by lightning before reaching his destination, in contrast to his death by illness on his way to China in our timeline. Bold's speculation that '[m]aybe China would have been worse' thus reinforces for the reader the implication that destiny imposes limits on historical alterity (Robinson 17).

This opening, however, allows the book to explore through Bold's capture and enslavement both the empty lands of the plague-stricken Europe and the booming Indian Ocean trade in the fourteenth and fifteenth centuries, along with the primarily East African slave trade that had existed there since the second century, itself conducted between cities and nations along the coast of the Indian Ocean. These trade routes, comparable to the Silk Road in terms of their significance for cultural exchange, were not accessible to Europe in the fourteenth and fifteenth centuries. The reader is introduced to the vast treasure ships of the Chinese mariner and diplomat Zheng He during one of his famous diplomatic and trade expeditions amongst the societies of Asia, Persia, Arabia, and East Africa – although this narrative appears to conflate, as Mark Rosa notes, the third, fourth and fifth of Zheng He's seven voyages (2004).

Ma He, later renamed Zheng He, was a Muslim in the Mongol occupied Yunnan province who was taken as a boy after the Ming captured the region in 1381–1382. He was castrated and became a eunuch and favourite of the third Ming Emperor, Ming Taizhong (Supreme Ancestor), or the Yongle (Perpetual Happiness) Emperor as he is known by his era name. In one scene, Bold witnesses the reception of Zheng He's fleet into Calicut (or Kozhikode) in the Indian state of Kerala, and 'all those people in their colours waving their arms overhead in awe' (35). Zheng He's fleet comprised from 100–300 ships, compared to the three or four of Christopher Columbus' and Vasco da Gama's expeditions, fifty of which were treasure ships that were up to five times as large as other ships that had been constructed up until that time. The spectacle of these vast ships draws on the technological sublime and leads one character, Kyu, to insist that '[t]hese Chinese will conquer the whole world' (35).

Historian John Keay compares the incontrovertible evidence of China's technological and political superiority at this moment of history to the American space launch programme, and explains that these voyages 'seemed to herald a new age of commodious travel, bulk transport and unchallenged maritime security' (381). Indeed, the purpose of these expeditions, as Keay explains, was to 'promote and extend that vital cosmic harmony throughout "All under Heaven"' – a reference to the mandate of heaven that legitimized Imperial rule in China (22). When da Gama reached the Indian Ocean in 1498, Keay reports that his favourable reception was, according to one of da Gama's Portuguese companions, due to the positive legacy of contact with Chinese navigators and traders. This story helps to shape our understanding of trade and cultural contact during this period of our timeline. Yet China's Indian Ocean trade contracted, and Keay offers an account of the ramifications of this change to Chinese expansionist policy during this period:

No permanent overseas representation or settlement had resulted from these contacts; rather than seek ways to make the voyages pay for themselves, the Ming emperors had discontinued them. Chinese empire would remain restricted to China and its immediate neighbours. A fifth of the world's population would advance no claim to a fifth of the world's cultivable surface area. (Keay 23)

These depictions thus challenge preconceived notions of technological progress as linked to an unerring expansion of territory and power and underscores the cultural polyphony and the scope of intercultural exchanges in the Medieval and Early Modern world. Economic accumulation and geographic expansion is not an inevitable outcome of the growth to dominance of a civilization. The contraction of the Chinese involvement in the Indian Ocean trade had little to do with a clash between civilizations, but with an internal political struggle that found expression in protest over the lavish state expenditure required to support the Chinese government's fleet.

As the narrative approaches our contemporary period and reaches beyond it, real world historical figures recede from the narrative while climatic and geological events remain. The alternate history as a document of memory helps to explain the persistent shadow of our contemporary history as a backdrop for the history of the narrative's civilizations. The text's focus on the development of science and social justice finds a correlative in the jati's long approach toward enlightenment, but it also speaks of a utopian desire for enlightenment in this world. Thus, Robinson's portrayal of scientific and technological development, as Mendlesohn has pointed out, implausibly recapitulates such developments in our timeline (25). On another level, the sixty-six year Long War between the Islamic Nations and China that begins in 1914 collapses the First World War, the Second World War, and the Cold War into a single event. It is as if Robinson needed to ensure a complementarity between the two timelines, which belies the difference one might expect of an alternate history that diverged from the historical in the fifteenth century. This suggests that the conditions for war in the twentieth century were laid before the fifteenth, and that it is somehow an inherent aspect of the way in which civilizations interact as a consequence of expansion. Notably, the political intransigence of the two sides and the absorption of each nation's economy in the war effort leads to an extended conflict that ultimately delays the development of nuclear weaponry. The Long War can be interpreted as a symbol that translates the experience of conflict in our timeline into an expression of the failure of the project of enlightenment. Indeed, the characters we follow through the conflict begin to doubt their existence and imagine the interminable nightmare of war as the bardo itself. The severity and length of the war correlates with the cultural significance of the World Wars, the bombing of Hiroshima and Nagasaki, and the shadow of the Cold War.

Book Nine, 'Nsara', is set in what in our timeline would be modern-day France. It takes place after the Long War in the eponymous Muslim city in Firanja, or what would be Europe in our timeline. At this late stage of the narrative, the Islamic Nations have lost the Long War to China and their allies (primarily Travancore, or India, the centre for the industrial revolution in this narrative). The loss of the war weighs heavily on this culture, but it is here that the project of emancipation set out in earlier periods of the narrative is taken up by feminist Muslim scholars and students. This echoes the earlier Muslim diaspora to al-Andulas (Spain in our timeline) in Book Two, 'The Haj in the Heart', led by the Sultan Mawji Darya and the proto-feminist Sultana Katima. In one significant conversation, several of the characters engage in counterfactual speculation regarding the absent Europeans, who remain a shadow in the minds of those in the narrative's timeline – one character says that '[t]hey are our jinns' (Robinson 661). Budur, the main focal character and a student of history and archaeology, asks a historian of Frankish music whether he ever speculates about the absent Europeans. The historian's reply is indicative of how speculation about history is subject to ambiguity and resists deterministic interpretation:

> 'All the time. I think they were just like us. They fought a lot. They had monasteries and madressas, and water-powered machinery. Their ships were small, but they could sail into the wind. They might have taken control of the seas before anyone else'.
> 'Not a chance', said Tahar. 'Compared to Chinese ships they were no more than dhows. Come now, Tristan, you know that'. (Robinson 660)

This discussion of counterfactual history highlights the assumptions that underlie the extrapolation of history: assumptions regarding techno-logical capability and linguistic and geopolitical fragmentation. For instance, one character notes that '[t]hey [Europe] had ten or fifteen languages, thirty or forty principalities, isn't that right? [...] They were too fractured to conquer anyone else' (661). Cultural sophistication, too, is considered: in response to one character's view that the Europeans believed themselves to be God's chosen people, another responds that '[p]rimitives often think that', leading Tristan to reiterate, '[a]s I say, they were just like us' (661). This scene overturns contemporary discourses in our timeline regarding the relative or absolute primitiveness of non-European cultures that informs orientalist discourse, and it also undermines assumptions that contemporary civilization has discarded traits that they disavow as primitive.[2] These contemporary discourses are inherited from nineteenth-century colonial-anthropological discourses that the critics Michael Hardt and Antonio Negri explain 'presented non-European subjects and cultures as undeveloped versions of Europeans and their civilization: they were signs of primitiveness that represented stages on the road to European civilization' (126). One character refutes the implication that European cultures of the past were similar to their contemporary Nsaran culture, preferring instead a perspective that emphasizes the differences between them. In many ways they were different but in other important ways there are similarities that are often elided. The difficulty of entertaining counterfactual histories, however, highlights the difficulties involved in disentangling these assumptions from demography:

> 'You can say anything you like about them, it doesn't matter. You can say they would have been enslaved like the Africans, or made slaves of the rest of us, or brought a golden age, or waged wars worse than the Long War ...'
> People shook their heads at all these impossibilities. (Robinson 661)

Several of the characters subscribe to race-based physiological arguments, ostensibly supported by scientific examination, which reprises racist discourses so familiar in our timeline. As the scepticism of the characters makes clear, these impossibilities, so hard to entertain when thought of within the confines of another history, highlight for the reader the far broader scope of possibility that these counterfactual speculations offer for thought about the history of our timeline.

The continued European presence in the history of the text is for the Firanjas an opportunity to project their own stories about history that express their fears and desires regarding civilization and social justice: '[t]hey're the blank on the map, the ruins underfoot, the empty mirror. The clouds in the sky that look like tigers' (Robinson 662). Conversely, these fictional civilizations and the stories of the characters who guide us through their worlds are cloud-shaped tigers against which the

---

[2] See Edward Said, *Orientalism* (1979) and *Culture and Imperialism* (1994); Michael Hardt and Antonio Negri, *Multitude: War and Democracy in the Age of Empire* (2004), pp. 121–122, 125, and *Empire* (2000), p. 126; and John Rieder *Colonialism and the Emergence of Science Fiction* (2008), p. 5.

desires, hopes, fears, and guilt regarding our contemporary history can be projected. In this way, the text works as a document of history that tells us more about contemporary Anglo-American perspectives on history and culture. Robinson uses the alternate history in order to explore how these assumptions might be decoupled from counterfactual speculation. Nevertheless, as has been acknowledged above, Robinson fails to do this fully for some assumptions – with regard to science and the course of history, for example – while the representation of some cultures – those situated in the African continent, for example – remain neglected. Nevertheless, the fact that such a work raises debate over the specifics of historical influence and widens consideration of history to include cultures that have been marginalized is valuable for the way in which it encourages reflection on the stories that we accept as making up the history of our timeline.

During the conversation on counterfactual history that is discussed above, Kirana explains that 'we don't know if history is sensitive, and for want of a nail a civilization was lost, or if our mightiest acts are as petals on a flood, or something in between, or both at once' (Robinson 662). The question, central to the epic form, as to whether individual human agency is capable of having an effect on events – in accordance with popular conceptions of the butterfly effect – or whether destiny is in some senses fixed – as the death of Temur in Book One implies – is central to Kirana's complaint that the utility of counterfactuals for speculation on history cannot be predicated on any capacity for definitively establishing any one story as factual.[3] Adam Roberts describes these two competing explanations in terms of a stand-off between positivist conceptions of historical progress and models of historical progression based on chaos theory in his chapter in this book. Within the confines of the text, agency is clearly effective in helping to shape the course of history, although these achievements are only infrequently the result of individual choice. Book Four, 'The Alchemist', and Book Five, 'Warp and Weft', perhaps exemplify the exceptions, being the

---

[3] The butterfly effect is a popular term that references the oftentimes unpredictable cascades that occur in non-linear dynamic feedback systems. The Lorenz attractor models the values toward which dynamic feedback systems trend. When visualized through digital means, it is described as resembling a Mobius strip, the logical sign for infinity or the two wings of a butterfly. The butterfly effect refers specifically to a popular narrative that describes a hypothetical butterfly whose flapping wings are able to affect dramatically scaled-up events, such as storms in distant parts of the Earth, thus reflecting the notion that dynamic feedback systems are highly sensitive to initial conditions.

closest to 'Great Men' histories in their focus on the contributions to a civilization of specific male characters.[4] Matt Hills argues that 'sf's use of counterfactuals is hence one way in which it can destabilize ontological perspectives and compel readers to see the "real" historical world in different, perhaps more critical ways' (437). Fundamentally, fictional alternate histories, in contrast to non-fictional counterfactual history, are constructed for different purposes, but both appeal to an individual's curiosity: 'people enjoyed contemplating the what might have been' (Robinson 663). For the historian Kirana, however, she wonders whether 'it would be better just to focus on the future [...] as a project to be enacted. Ever since the Travancori enlightenment we have had a sense of the future as something we make' (Robinson 663). This utopian outlook toward the future is a sentiment that Robinson explores at length throughout his oeuvre, and which he portrays in terms of a utopia of process toward which societies approach asymptotically. That the creation of the future is a structural process made up of the contributions of multiple agencies speaks to Robinson's preoccupation with environmentalism, sustainability, and social justice, which likewise depend on processes oriented toward the construction of alternative futures.

This sense of the future as being malleable and open to being shaped by individual and collective agency becomes increasingly urgent throughout Books Nine and Ten. On the morning that Budur is asked to lead a group of blind soldiers to protest a military coup, she hears a cleric reciting a poem:

> Past and future all mixed together
> Let those trapped birds out the window!
> What then remains? The stories you no longer
> Believe. You had better believe them.
> While you live they carry the meaning
> When you die they carry the meaning
> To those who come after they carry the meaning
> You had better believe in them.

---

[4] 'The Alchemist' tells the story of Khalid in seventeenth-century Samarkand, who develops a scientific method involving systematic experimentation and the verification of received knowledge. 'Warp and Weft' tells the story of the arrival of a Japanese samurai to the New World after Japan is conquered by China. This protagonist, named 'From West' by the Iroquois, helps to inspire the organization of the North American tribes into the confederacy known as the Hodenosaunee League, and teaches them how to manufacture guns to resist future Chinese invasions.

In Rumi's story he saw all the worlds
As one, and that one, Love, he called to and knew,
Not Muslim or Jew or Hindu or Buddhist,
Only a Friend, a breath breathing human,
Telling his boddhisatva story. The bardo
Waits for us to make it real. (Robinson 696)

The protest expands until Nsara is overwhelmed by a popular movement composed of women, the poor, and the dispossessed, which successfully overturns the coup. This poem by the Nsaran poet Ghaleb, killed on the last day of the Long War, begins with reflections on death and the bardo. The past and the future are confused in this image of time as caged birds: they resemble one another insofar as the future simply repeals the past, as the preceding discussion about Kirana's reflection on the absent Europeans exemplifies. When these categories no longer function as a rigid guide for action in the present, a space opens for stories to take shape and to shape the world. It is, however, the intermixture of the past and the future which provides the ground for the formation of these stories. Nevertheless, they have an agency of their own and are capable of transferring meaning between contemporaries and to future generations. It is by reflecting on the past and the future, but also by moving beyond these conceptions of time to create stories that do not simply re-inscribe history onto the future, that individuals and collectives are able to make an impact on history and to the shaping of the future. The poem establishes a complementarity between the abstract and the multiple and the singular and specific; it reduces the many to one and positions exchange between individuals as symbolically embodying possibility through the image of Rumi's view of a multiplicity of worlds that reflect each other. Belief, too, occupies a complex relationship toward the past and future as it is a belief in stories, regardless of their veridical power or factual accuracy, which allows meaning to be invested in the images of the future that the characters in the narrative strive to realize or avoid.

The bardo according to this poet's conception re-orients us toward the present and toward the poem, itself a text about the power of stories. The story of the bardo in *The Years of Rice and Salt* and the poet's exploration of the power of stories and the necessity of belief are themselves language games. Wegner argues that, '[w]hen it is most successful, the alternate history confronts us with the dizzying prospect that "what is" is in fact surrounded by an infinity of possible other worlds, other collective destinies whose lack of substantiality is simply a matter of accident' (100). The poem cited above provides a key to reading the scenes from the bardo as themselves stories that symbolize an iterative approach towards maximizing rights and freedoms for all. In this view, *The Years of Rice and Salt* is a complex document of memory that outlines a vision of emancipation awaiting realization. The poet's reflection on Rumi's notion of a multiplicity of worlds both alludes to the cultural multiplicity portrayed in the narrative, but more fundamentally to the multiplicity of historical narratives that the alternate history invites. These multiplicities are combined in the image of the bodhisattva's story, which collapses the religious and philosophical concept of the 'many' into the 'one' as reflections of one another. This poem thus recalls the title of this article, 'It Is One Story', and implies that world history and culture is a composite narrative constructed through an ongoing series of dialogues and language games.

The importance of stories for extending the individual's sphere of influence beyond the limited timescale of a single lifespan is an important area of enquiry in the last of the books, aptly titled 'The First Years' to reflect the ongoing struggle to shape the future. Taking place in China, the protagonist of this story, Bao Xinhua, speculates on the nature of reincarnation and the future with his students and reflects that 'consciousness gets reincarnated another way, when the people of the future remember us, and use our language, and unconsciously model their lives on ours, living out some recombination of our values and habits. We live on in the way future people think and talk' (Robinson 751). Thus, the behaviours, habits, values and languages that are inherited in the future are in part constitutive of that future, and are circulated and made meaningful by being told as epic stories. These narratives function as documents of memory that help to guide the development of societies in the future. In the face of one student's frustration with this explanation of reincarnation, Bao suggests that '[r]eincarnation is a story we tell; then in the end it's the story itself that is the reincarnation' (Robinson 753).

The Years of Rice and Salt uses the alternate history to reflect on how the stories that are told about culture and society motivate social change. In doing so, it explores the ways in which history can be re-imagined to account for silences and omissions that result in the formation of a monologic version of history that marginalizes many social and cultural groups. While novels such as John Jakes' *Black in Time* (1970), S. M. Stirling's *The Peshawar Lancers* (2003) and Bernardine Evaristo's *Blonde Roots* (2009), engage in similar projects, this approach is unusual for alternate histories, which are more often concerned with the histories of European and American nations, particularly with alternate histories of the Second World War and the American Civil

War.[5] By expanding the pool of available stories, Robinson challenges this approach to history and storytelling. The bardo as represented in the text is itself a symbol of a collective approach toward greater social justice, one that is reflexive and builds upon the activity of predecessors who have shaped the stories that future generations receive. Thus, the multiple stories that circulate throughout the long period of time depicted in the novel are parts of a single epic narrative insofar as they are retrospectively incorporated into an account of history which provides a basis for a vision of the future to strive toward. This view of the multiple stories throughout history as belonging to a single global narrative is itself a story advanced by the text that seeks to make meaningful the actions of individuals and collectives when working toward realizing a vision of the future.

References

Barbour, Douglas. 'Warmly Humane Touches in Disaster Tale'. *Edmonton Journal*. 27 June 2004. Retrieved from Lexis Nexis database.

Brooke, Keith. '*The Years of Rice and Salt* by Kim Stanley Robinson'. *Infinity Plus*, 2002. Accessed 1 June 2016. <www.infinityplus.co.uk/nonfiction/riceandsalt.htm>

Diamond, Jared. *Guns, Germs, and Steel: The Fates of Human Societies*. Norton, 1999.

Evaristo, Barnardine. *Blonde Roots*. Penguin, 2009.

Hardt, Michael and Antonio Negri. *Empire*. Harvard University Press, 2000.

—. *Multitude: War and Democracy in the Age of Empire*. Penguin, 2004.

Hawthorn, Geoffrey. 'Plague and Fertility in Modern Europe'. *Plausible Worlds: Possibility and Understanding in History and the Social Sciences*. Cambridge University Press, 2012, pp. 39–80.

Hills, Matt. 'Time, Possible Worlds, and Counterfactuals'. *The Routledge Companion to Science Fiction*. Eds. Mark Bould, Andrew Butler, Adam Roberts, and Sherryl Vint. Routledge, 2009, pp. 433–441.

Jakes, John. *Black in Time*. Paperback Library, 1970.

Johns-Putra, Adeline. *The History of the Epic*. Palgrave, 2006.

Keay, John. *China: A History*. Basic Books, 2009.

---

[5] In Jakes' *Black in Time*, the novel's protagonist attempts to preserve history from transformation by two antagonists who struggle to create a future dominated by white supremacists on the one hand, and the African Songhay Empire on the other. Stirling's *The Peshawar Lancers* features a devastating meteor shower that changes the course of world history in 1878. Evaristo's *Blonde Roots* speculates on a trans-Atlantic slave trade in which Europeans are enslaved by Africans.

Mendlesohn, Farah. 'The Years of Rice and Salt'. SFRA Review, vol. 257, 2002, pp. 24–27.

Merchant, Paul. The Epic. Methuen, 1971.

Moore, Ward. Bring the Jubilee. Millennium, 2001.

Parrinder, Patrick. 'Science Fiction as Truncated Epic'. Bridges to Science Fiction. Eds. George E. Slusser, George R. Guffey, and Mark Rose. Southern Illinois University Press, 1980, pp. 91–106.

Prettyman, Gib. 'Critical Utopia as Critical History: Apocalypse and Enlightenment in Kim Stanley Robinson's The Years of Rice and Salt'. Extrapolation, vol. 52, no. 3, 2011, pp. 338–364.

Rieder, John. Colonialism and the Emergence of Science Fiction. Wesleyan University Press, 2008.

Robinson, Kim Stanley. The Years of Rice and Salt. Bantam, 2003.

Rosa, Mark. 'Timeline for The Years of Rice and Salt by Kim Stanley Robinson', OOcities. 2004. Accessed 1 June 2016. <http://www.oocities.org/heiankyo794/timeline.html>

Rosenfeld, Gavriel. 'Why Do We Ask What If: Reflections on the Function of Alternate History'. History and Theory, vol. 41, no. 4, 2002, pp. 90–103.

Said, Edward. Culture and Imperialism. Vintage, 1994.

—. Orientalism. Vintage, 1979.

Stirling, S. M. The Peshawar Lancers. Penguin, 2002.

Wegner, Phillip E. 'Learning to Live in History: Alternate Historicities and the 1990s in The Years of Rice and Salt'. In Kim Stanley Robinson Maps the Unimaginable. Ed. William J. Burling. McFarland, 2009, pp. 98–112.

Wittgenstein, Ludwig. Philosophical Investigations. Trans. G. E. M. Anscombe. Basil Blackwell, 1986.

Forever Being *Yamato*
Alternate Pacific War Histories in Japanese Film and Anime

Jonathan Rayner

The constructed identity of the postwar Japanese is inherently unbalanced, reflecting the yet unresolved nature of their past. It would not be an exaggeration to say that the single most important problem of 'postwar' Japan is this inability to come to terms, once and for all, with the pre-1945 past (Shimazu 116).

Since 2000, a series of mainstream Japanese feature films have addressed the subject of the Pacific War and lavished long running times and high production values on the representation of this destructive and controversial conflict. These films can be seen within a wider international context in which the Second World War has re-emerged as a spectacular and popular cinematic preoccupation, but while these Japanese examples are comparable to and often visually resemble Hollywood precedents such as *Saving Private Ryan* (Steven Spielberg, 1998) or *Pearl Harbor* (Michael Bay, 2001), their national context makes their specific depictions of history divisive and problematic. Films such as *Men of the Yamato* (Sato Junya, 2005), *Sea Without Exit* (Kiyoshi Sasabe, 2006), *For Those We Love* (Taku Shinjo, 2007), *Admiral Isoroku Yamamoto* (Izuru Narushima, 2011) and *The Eternal Zero* (Takashi Yamazaki, 2013) evince an uneasy balance between lamentation for the destruction of the war, denial or evasion of Japanese responsibility for the conflict, and a celebration of self-sacrifice in the past in the creation of Japan's future peace and prosperity. The vexed status of Japan's war history, in political debate and in education, renders the recent past a contestable and re-interpretable space. The problematic and ambiguous treatment of war history in contemporary Japan (by turns pacifist and ruminative, conservative and deterministic, and inconsistent and paradoxical) which these films exhibit and exemplify is also found in films and animated series which carry their reinterpretation of the past further into active rewriting, creating divergent, alternative histories of the conflict.

Surveying these recent films foregrounds one of the most stereo-typical and controversial aspects of Japan's conduct of the war in the Pacific: knowing and willing self-sacrifice by Japanese soldiers, sailors, and airmen to the imperial cause. In portraying the readiness of Japan's young men to die for the nation, the films express and encourage admiration for their heroism and selflessness, while treating the military authorities commanding them, the nation for which they died, and the postwar Japan their deaths delivered in equivocal or outrightly ambiguous terms. For example, *Admiral Isoroku Yamamoto* was released to coincide with the seventieth anniversary of the Japanese Navy's raid on Pearl Harbor, where Michael Bay's *Pearl Harbor* marked the sixtieth anniversary of this event from the American side. This film biography of Yamamoto cements rather than questions the admiral's continuing iconic status as the mastermind of the attack, as a patriot reluctant to go to war, as a moderate within an aggressive Army-led Japanese establishment, and as a martyr and prophetic hero killed in the service of his country. This stands in contrast to the reappraisals of Western commentators such as Robert Lowe which repudiate Yamamoto's hallowed status (Lowe 83). *Sea without Exit*, *For Those We Love* and *The Eternal Zero* offer even more sympathetic portrayals of self-sacrifice in the cause of the war, and even more strident assertions of the unyielding national necessity of such actions. The fact that the screenwriter and executive producer of *For Those We Love* was the controversial author and right-wing politician Ishihara Shintaro underlines the provocative appropriation, rather than simple evocation, of national history in which such films indulge (see Aoki). Thus these films straddle and complicate the categories of war history, war cinema, and alternate history.

These highly popular, yet problematic film texts stand as marked re-interpretations or revisions of history redolent of the divisive, ongoing debates inside Japan on the facts as much as the significance of the past. The contestable nature of history is indicative of political polari-zation in the ways in which the conflict in the Pacific in particular is interpreted. Postwar generations and governments have struggled to reconcile awareness of Japanese wartime suffering (for example under allied blockade and bombing attacks, including the nuclear raids on Hiroshima and Nagasaki) with acknowledgement of Japanese militarism and imperial expansion as the causes of the war in the first place:

> The Japanese are frequently accused of 'failing to address the past' or of 'denial', 'ignorance' and 'amnesia' concerning the war. These conclusions are often based on assertions that 'Japanese children do not learn about the war in school' or the 'state-centred' thinking

that because the Japanese government has failed to adequately address war issues in the eyes of most outside Japan, the Japanese people fail to address the past too. The reality, however, is that debate over how to address war responsibility issues has ensured that war history remains highly contested in Japan and Japanese people have been unable to settle on a dominant narrative of the conflict. (Seaton 54)

Compromises in coming to terms with Japan's militaristic past are focused by the circumstances of its explicitly pacifist present. Specifically, Article 9 of the postwar Japanese constitution allows armed forces for defensive purposes only, and outlaws the use of military force for the purposes of aggression. Indeed, hard-line left-wing elements in Japan have asserted that a strict interpretation of Article 9 should prevent Japan from possessing armed forces at all. Debates about Japan's military present almost inevitable provoke highly divisive debate on the interpretation of the country's military past, as epitomized by the controversies surrounding the academic career of historian Ienaga Saburo (Ienaga, *Japan's Past* 147). The rapid expansion of Japan's armed forces (especially its navy, now referred to as the 'Maritime Self Defence Force') and calls for the dispatching of Japanese forces overseas (for example in support of their American allies during the 1990s and since 9/11) have been highly controversial (Woolley 30–34). At the same time, Japan's commitment to defence and stated espousal of pacifism have been criticized by an America treaty bound to guarantee the country's security. From its role in Japan's relinquishment of the right to use its forces overseas, to its constant pressure on Japan to rebuild its armed forces during the Korean War, to its mixed signals of cooperation and competition as Japan became an economic world power, America's lack of clarity in its posture toward Japan during the postwar period has been the source of ambiguity and confusion within Japan over its own position in the world (Fisch 61–62).

Reinterpretation of Japan's imperial, military past has been linked inextricably with the reappraisal and renegotiation of Article 9 and its significance for a Japanese postwar national identity (Ienaga, 'Glorification of War' 119–120). Contemporarily, academic disputes over the interpretation of Japan's history have escalated into court cases in which scholarly freedom, the impartiality of history text books in the country's classrooms, and international relations with regional neighbours have been at stake (see Ienaga, *Japan's Past*; Jeans 183–193). The significance of this historically and culturally specific range of debatable pasts and divisive presents distinguishes the retrospective films produced in Japan since end of the Second World War. These re-readings and rewritings of history encompass representations in war and fantasy genres, and also span (and often conflate) the categorizations of alternate history narratives in their navigation of problematic pasts (Hellekson 5–6). In this nationally specific context, alternate history has moved from peripheral, hypothetic debate to didactic, institutionalized re-inscription.

The ambivalent current of patriotic celebration and national mourning reaches an apotheosis in the three-hour epic *Men of the Yamato*. (The title is also translatable as *The Men's Yamato*). This film adopts a flashback structure to recreate the final mission of the Imperial Japanese Navy in the Second World War, the last sortie of the super-battleship *Yamato* to the island of Okinawa in what was in effect the largest kamikaze mission of the war. There was no hope of return or success, and the *Yamato* was sunk with heavy loss of life. This feature film brings together many problematic threads in the ownership and interpretation of Japan's war history. While it is based on a novel by Henmi Jun, it also draws inspiration from the autobiographical account of Yoshida Mitsuru which was subject to censorship (for its alleged nationalistic and militaristic sentiments) in postwar, American-controlled Japan (Yoshida xxix–xxxi). Footage of the wreck (from an underwater expedition funded by the national newspaper the *Asahi Shimbun*), including images of the prominent Imperial Chrysanthemum crest on its bow, are integrated in the film, as are scenes of exhibits in the Kure Naval Museum dedicated to the ship. This concentration upon the *Yamato* reflects its overwhelming national and cultural significance, as a symbol of the navy and country. The name *Yamato* is a poetic appellation for the country and nation, comparable to terms and ship names like Albion or Britannia or Columbia in the UK or United States (Evans and Peattie 378). The word is also contained within the phrase 'yamato damashi-i' referring to the national soul or spirit, communal values, and explicitly martial virtues of Japan enshrined in shared tradition and belief (Perry 317).

The film's flashback construction is crucial to this espousal and inculcation of the values and virtues of the past. In its narrative an old fisherman, a survivor of the *Yamato*, sails out to the site of the wreck at the behest of a young woman on the sixtieth anniversary of its sinking. It is subsequently revealed that she is one of many orphaned children raised by another survivor, a senior enlisted man who saved many young crewmembers and whom the fisherman had believed had perished when the ship sank. The journey to the wreck site precipitates a series of traumatic flashbacks, in which the old fisherman relives the wartime past and relates his story and the fate of the ship to the young woman and his teenage deck hand. During their trip, the old man even seems to see *Yamato* sailing towards them out of the mist, magically restored to her 1945 glory. This CGI-recreation of the *Yamato*, complemented by an enormous 600-million yen set constructed for the film, can be seen to parallel the 70 ft model of the ship which occupies pride of place in the Kure Naval Museum (Takekawa). When they finally reach the wreck site, the three travellers symbolically salute the *Yamato* and her crew, in a scene which combines memory, commemoration and memorialization in 'the perfect image of three generations coming to respect the sacrifice made by the sailors' (Condry).

The respectful and forcible link to the past made by the film sits uncomfortably alongside some melodramatic scenes set in 1945 of the young sailors bidding farewell to a home to which they are resolved to return, and anachronistic speeches given by the ship's officers in which Japan's defeat, and their sacrifice, are deemed to be inevitable and necessary for the country to survive and progress. Here the film appears to transgress its own flashback logic (and to follow and paraphrase Yoshida's memoir) to ascribe future knowledge to prescient characters placed aboard the doomed ship in the historical past, who conceive of themselves as 'harbingers' of a new nation (Yoshida 40).

Ironically, this implied transporting of the *Yamato*, and the ideology it personifies, into a future its sacrifice has facilitated, had already been accomplished in highly symbolic fashion in manga form, and in a succession of animated films and television series in *Space Battleship Yamato*. Made in the 1970s and exported to the West in modified form as *Star Blazers*, *Space Battleship Yamato* records the voyages and adventures of a massive spaceship, built from the remains of the Second World War battleship, which defends Earth from alien invaders in the distant future. With its representation of the planet Earth and its (Japanese) human population suffering devastating nuclear attacks from hostile aliens, *Space Battleship Yamato* has been interpreted as an allegory of Japan's experience of American bombing in the Second World War, which valorizes a redeemed Japanese military and propagates 'master narratives of noble failure and national victimhood' (Ashbaugh 345). In order to defeat the superior extra-terrestrial forces, the rejuvenated *Yamato* must be expended as before in a self-sacrificial mission. Heroically (and illogically), in the series *Yamato* is repeatedly resurrected and destroyed in last-ditch suicidal missions in order to safeguard the planet's and humanity's future (Ashbaugh 330). The ship's apparently unending sacrificial duty is indicated by the title of the 1980 entry in this series, *Be Forever Yamato*. The popularity of this franchise and the pervasive recognition of its reincarnation of the *Yamato* can be gauged from the production of a big budget, live-action version of the narrative in 2010.

However, the national icon of the *Yamato* also features widely in other examples of Japanese alternate history fiction exploring the country's war in Asia and the role of this symbolic and ideologically-laden ship (see Penney 48). In addition, the transformational encounter between Japan's revered past (embodied by the national icon of the battleship) and its potential future represented in *Space Battleship Yamato* is also played out in other films and anime series, which foreground, assert, and challenge the history, ethos, role, and identity of the country's military in science fiction and fantasy narratives.

While it might represent a well-known example in the West, the convergence of science fiction, national history, and exploration of enduring notions of martial spirit, sacrifice, and military duty in *Space Battleship Yamato* is by no means unique. A recent trilogy of science fiction films from novels by the same author confront aspects of Japanese history and its traditions of militarism in past and present in similar alternate histories of the 'nexus' or 'parallel world' types (Hellekson 5–6). In *Lorelei, the Witch of the Pacific Ocean* (Higuchi Shinji, 2005), a German super-submarine handed over to the Imperial Japanese Navy in the last days of the Second World War is ordered to prevent the dropping of a third atomic bomb on Tokyo. The submarine has a top-secret sonar system which relies on the telepathic abilities of a teenage Japanese girl whose powers are the result of experiments in a Nazi concentration camp. The submarine's mission is compromised when it emerges that ultra-nationalist elements in the Japanese Navy actually desire and plan for the third bomb to hit Tokyo, to ensure the eradication of the Japan that has lost the war and the creation of a new, pure state. Again, the conflagration and willing sacrifice of the nation in defeat is deemed necessary for a future of progress and an untainted national identity.

The violent creation of an alternate future out of an altered past is also seen in another film in the trilogy *Samurai Commando Mission 1549* (Tezuka Masaki, 2005). In this story, a group of modern-day soldiers from Japan's Self Defence Force are transported back in time to the Middle Ages. As might be expected in a time travel story, an army officer from the present gets left behind in the past, assumes the identity of a samurai warlord, and hatches a plan to alter Japan's history so that militarism and samurai values predominate. The film's defining image is a meeting between different generations of the Japanese military: one bent on conquest and aggression and wedded to notions of loyal self-sacrifice, the other tasked only with defence, but inevitably sharing principles of sacrifice in their loyalty and duty to present-day Japan.

The manga and fantasy television series *Gate* (2015) provides a similarly redemptive depiction of the Japanese Ground Self Defence

Force. In this science fiction/fantasy narrative, Japanese soldiers repel an attack upon Tokyo launched through an inter-dimensional portal. In a highly problematic amalgam of allegorized imperial expansion and defensive military operations in the present day, Japan's armed forces then travel through the gateway in order to demand reparations for this aggressive action, but eventually colonize and bring order to the fantasy realm (replete with dragons and magical beings) which they discover. Notably, within *Gate*'s portrayal of the twenty-first century world confronting an unknown, adversarial but resource-rich culture, Japan's powerful but paternalistic intervention in the resulting global crisis is favourably compared to the acquisitive, destructive, neo-imperialist machinations of the United States and Russia.

The third film in the trilogy *Aegis* (Sakamoto Junji, 2005) portrays a terrorist threat to modern Japan which tests the country's international allegiances and requires the intervention of the Maritime Self Defence Force, specifically the newest Japanese warships equipped with the American-supplied Aegis defence system. While this film is more concerned with contemporary, rather than historical militaristic sentiments inside Japan, its connection of threats to national security to American military cooperation and American technology evokes comparison with the manga and adapted science fiction animated series *Zipang* (2004–2005), set aboard a similar, albeit fictional ship of the Maritime Self Defence Force.

The narrative of *Zipang* (a combination of the familiar 'nexus' and 'battle story' alternate history models) centres on a twenty-first-century Japanese warship, the destroyer *Mirai*, which gets caught in a storm while en route to Pearl Harbor to join in naval exercises with the US Navy (Hellekson 7). Emerging from the squall, the crew finds the ship has been transported back through time to the Second World War. This *Twilight Zone*-like scenario closely resembles the plot of the American science fiction film *The Final Countdown* (Don Taylor, 1980) in which a modern US Navy ship time travels to the eve of the attack on Pearl Harbor. While in that example the American sailors debate their responsibility to defend America in the past and the present, in *Zipang* the Japanese sailors are presented with the dilemma of aiding their historical countrymen, by attacking their allies of the present day. Again, this paradox invokes the relevance of the postwar Japanese constitution, and Article 9's prohibition of war for aggressive purposes: *Mirai* pointedly belongs to the Maritime Self Defence Force, not the Imperial Navy. The sailors of the *Mirai* possess a superiority of knowledge granted by their historical understanding of the Pacific conflict, and a moral superiority in their dedication to defending Japan and saving lives rather than taking them, but they also possess immeasurably superior firepower for the 1940s, and must decide how, and if, the capabilities of their ship should be used. Since they know the coming events, they could try to end the war and avoid Japan's destruction. Yet they also suspect that they should avoid involvement in the conflict, in order to ensure that their stream of history remains unchanged. However, an acute awareness of their duty also demands that if they and their country are in danger they must fight, and perhaps protect and serve Japan best by winning the war.

Mirai is introduced in the television series as a potent symbol of modern Japan (her name means 'Future'), a powerful and technologically advanced warship. With a degree of inevitability, when she is transported through time, *Mirai* encounters a parallel national symbol from the past: the battleship *Yamato*. As in *Men of the Yamato*, the battleship and the past she represents appear to emerge from the dark and the fog. Indeed, it is the very sight of the *Yamato* surrounded by the Japanese fleet heading for the Battle of Midway, which convinces the sailors of the *Mirai* that they have actually arrived in mid-1942. In the manga version of this meeting, the Chrysanthemum Imperial crest on *Yamato*'s bow is especially prominent. Thereafter, while events rapidly overtake the *Mirai* and the modern sailors are forced to fight to defend themselves in the middle of the Pacific War's decisive battles, the *Yamato* takes a leading role in the unfolding narrative. In a moment marked by reverential awe, when a member of *Mirai*'s crew visits the *Yamato*, he meets the commander-in-chief, Admiral Yamamoto himself.

One of the *Mirai*'s first humanitarian acts, and the one with the far-reaching consequences, is the rescue of a downed Imperial Navy pilot. This officer, Lieutenant Commander Kusaka, is taken aboard the ship and given medical treatment. Kusaka quickly learns that the *Mirai* is from the future and while the twenty-first-century sailors wonder how they should intervene in the imminent battle for the island of Guadalcanal, he accesses the ship's databases and comes to understand his country's fate in the current war. In comparison with the indecisiveness of the *Mirai*'s crewmembers, Kusaka knows at once where his duty lies and what he must do to save Japan. Kusaka flies to the Japanese Navy base at Truk, for meetings with Japanese naval commanders. He reveals the facts behind the sudden appearance of the *Mirai* amidst the Midway task force, shares the knowledge he has gained about Japan's inevitable and crushing defeat, and proposes a new strategy, with which Japan can win.

As the *Mirai* gains the attention of the American military and is herself attacked by US Navy submarines and aircraft, Kusaka sets his plans in motion, organizing the departure of a massive Japanese naval

force to Guadalcanal which, armed with the knowledge of *Mirai*'s history
files, will be able to decisively defeat the Americans on the island and
compel the United States to make peace. A small group of *Mirai*'s sailors
land on the island and use a display of the destroyer's high technology
weapons to try to persuade the Americans to withdraw without loss of
life. However, Kusaka radios their leader (from the *Yamato*) to explain
his vision for a new Japan: not the defeated and transformed country
which *Mirai* represents, nor the militaristic and short-sighted country
which launched the Pacific War against the Western powers, but a new
'ideal' country and empire based on conquest of the Asian mainland
which he describes in terms redolent of national divinity and destiny:

> It is not the Great Japanese Empire, which thoughtlessly threw and
> trapped herself into a state of war. Nor is it the post-war Japan, who
> yielded to an unconditional surrender and is burdened with shame.
> It is a country which spans these two eras ... An independent island
> nation, full of power ... a new country that no Japanese has ever
> experienced: Zipang. (Kaiji)

This is explicitly an oceanic empire, deriving its identity as well as its
resources from the conquest of China. Although this rhetoric obviously
coincides with Japanese expansionist policies of the 1930s and 1940s, its
proclamation is remarkable in a twenty-first-century text, in a context of
troubled regional relationships rooted in perceptions of historical conflict,
and economic transformation in the form of Japan's post-1990s decline
and China's emergence as an industrial and military superpower. Most
significantly perhaps, Kusaka is proposing (and it seems, creating) an
alternate history, as events in 1942 since *Mirai*'s arrival do appear to
diverge from the historical record. This is made clear at this moment
as the *Yamato*, in reality kept away from the fighting at Guadalcanal,
approaches the island to deliver a shattering bombardment on the US
marines ashore. This marks a moment of historiographic revisionism,
as key historical readings of the Pacific War have noted the inactivity
of the super-battleship at critical moments in the conflict and hypoth-
esized the potential effects of its intervention in the crucial Guadalcanal
campaign (see Peattie and Evans 379). However, *Mirai* herself intercedes
to overturn the *Yamato*'s intervention, using its advanced missile system
to shoot down the battleship's shells in flight and so save the American
soldiers on the island.

The complex associations of this plot twist are worth careful consideration: the *Mirai* uses a missile defence system, the Aegis radar, to defend
America and circumvent the objectives of one or more incarnations of

Imperial Japan. Aegis itself is an American system, shared with the Maritime Self Defence Force for its newest vessels for interoperability between the allies, and specifically as part of the ongoing development of ballistic missile defences for Europe and Asia. Japan's Aegis-equipped ships are tasked explicitly with defending the Home Islands from anticipated ballistic missile attacks, from North Korea and possibly China. Consequently, *Mirai*'s intervention in shooting down *Yamato*'s shells may be read as a trumping of Japan's offensive imperial militarism with the defensive technologies and allegiances of the present day: a benediction of the modern form which Japan's armed forces take in distinction from their manifestations in the past. However, after the events around Guadalcanal, while accepted history seems to continue to play out in some of *Zipang*'s plotlines, it is noticeable that the *Yamato*, and Kusaka's vision, remain intact and it is the *Mirai* herself who becomes an inactive, controversial symbol of the Navy when she 'returns' to her home port in Yokosuka. The series and the manga on which it was based end inconclusively, with the *Mirai* in danger as elements within the Imperial Navy consider the warship and crew from the future to be unreliable and insubordinate. While the *Mirai*'s sailors are reluctant to participate in the war and instead commit themselves to aiding their country after its inevitable defeat, it becomes obvious from the divergences from documented history they have observed since their arrival in 1942 that this, in any case, is not, or no longer, 'their' past after all, but a vexed parallel world. Without a pure and pre-existent historical script to follow, the *Mirai*'s crewmembers must respond individually and conscientiously to their duty-driven dilemma.

The visions or versions of the Pacific War past which these examples of film, manga and animation propagate are challenges to ready interpretations and simple syntheses, and are redolent of passionate political and historical disagreements within contemporary Japan:

> It is careless to write about 'the Japanese' view of the war, when the struggle over museums, textbooks, the flag, the national anthem, the emperor, and whether Japanese government officials should visit the Yasukuni Shrine reveal, above all, a divided Japan. (Jeans 194)

Commentators on contemporary Japan such as Shimazu Naoko and Mizuno Hiromi have drawn stark contrasts between the deliberate or disingenuous amnesia displayed in official circles and establishment statements on the Pacific War, and the frequent and repeated revisionist representations of the conflict, evincing both left and right-wing, pacifist and militarist biases, and proposing parallel or alternate histories, broadcast within Japanese popular culture (see Shimazu; Mizuno). This phenomenon has been labelled a genre of 'war fantasy', a term which belies the diversity and seriousness of historical and cultural debate within such uniquely Japanese texts, but which also acknowledges their peculiar propensity to create a 'discursive space open enough' to represent sundry and dissonant views, where 'the clichés of established genres can easily become the foundation for parody and criticism' (Penney 44). In this respect, the continuing and apparently accelerating production of war films and war fantasy narratives in contemporary Japan appears to speak to a concentrated re-engagement with the Second World War as a subject, with a concomitant reappraisal as much as reiteration of what that conflict was and is assumed to mean:

> War fantasy has presented a diverse array of images of war [...] In contrast to government silence and ambiguity and the oft cited 'victim's view', Japanese popular works have taken a 'victim-izer's view' as well, utilizing it to present anti-war messages to readers. These patterns of expression have shaped some of the most important works of the war fantasy genre, presenting a critical view of organized violence, not simply 'war as entertainment', to Japanese audiences. (Penney 51)

Despite Penney's assertion of the oppositional potential of these texts, their resemblance to conservative Western war genre precedents and their inclusions of spectacles of combat and military hardware makes their ideological positioning difficult. Since the appearance of *Zipang*, several more recent manga sequences, derived animated series, and spin-off films have extended and further complicated the fantasy rewriting of the Second World War. *Strike Witches* (2008–2015) posits an alternate history of the Second World War and follows the adventures of magically empowered teenage girls who assume the guises and names of fighter aces in battles against alien invaders. Notably, the war against the extra-terrestrials means that in this parallel universe the European phase of the conflict is either curtailed or never takes place. Nonetheless, battleship *Yamato* still makes an appearance in this narrative. In *Girls Und Panzer* (2012), members of girls' academies engage in a sporting competition based on Second World War armoured combat. Teams use vintage tanks of various nationalities in games imparting leadership skills and inculcating team spirit. In both of these series, the person-alities, uniforms, insignia, and equipment of Allied and Axis nations are appropriated and re-used, either in alliances against common alien adversaries or in friendly rivalry.

More recently, *Kantai Collection* a.k.a. *Fleet Girls* (2015) merges some of these concepts with the awareness of naval tradition displayed by *Zipang*, in a plot-line in which an alien invasion is opposed by an all-female academy of students endowed with the names, weapons, and personalities of Imperial Navy warships. This series' narrative is difficult to situate within the categories of alternate history, yet its assertive invocation of parallels between its fantasy and documented history (for example when the girl named after the destroyer *Kisaragi* lost in 1942 off Wake Island, is 'sunk' in a battle at 'W Island') mean that its allusions to the past are inclusive and affirmative for informed viewers, and intentionally alerting and educational for uninformed ones. In appearing to restage and refight the Second World War against uncontroversial enemies, or even to reuse the fetishized hardware of the conflict in entirely harmless and edifying contests, these fantasy narratives emphasize the history of the war as much as they appear to obfuscate its underlying, abhorrent realities.

Perhaps even more troublingly, the popularity and pervasiveness of manga-derived militaristic imagery has prompted its incorporation into public relations and recruitment material for the Self Defence Forces (see Brummer). However, these most recent manga and animations can also be seen to be recapitulating representations of the Second World War provided by earlier postwar Japanese popular texts. In emphasizing the youthfulness of pilots and portraying their under-dog, defensive missions rather than any offensive action, manga of the 1950s and 1960s similarly obscured and sanitized aspects of Japan's war history (see Nakar 64, 68). In this transmutation of the still recognizable history of the war, and the substantive repositioning and revaluation of Japan's part within it, Thomas Schnellbächer describes these recent fantasies as serving as 'purification rituals' as much as popular entertainments, for a youthful (Japanese) audience widely considered to lack a full spectrum of national, historical knowledge (Schnellbächer 393; Condry).

Several consistencies yoke together the examples examined here, not least of which is the heightened emphases upon military and naval iconography, artefacts, and fetishized hardware, which contribute to the perception of warfare and war film as uncritical entertainment. In this respect, the submarine *Lorelei*, the destroyer *Mirai* and above all the battleship *Yamato* are naval symbols which embody and articulate national ideals, and which are enmeshed in discourses desiring the re-examination and rewriting of Japan's military history. These discourses are not simply left or right-wing, traditionalist or progressive, militarist or pacifist, but represent a 'fusing' of numerous threads and versions of nationalism (see Takekawa). Augmenting their alternate-ness, ambiguity and evasion characterize these texts' stances on Japan's imperial history and naval traditions: for example, in their lamenting of loss of life in war while simultaneously championing suicide and martyrdom, and in condemning the militaristic wartime Japan which squandered a youthful generation while celebrating the peaceful and progressive Japan created by its creeds of self-sacrifice. *Mirai*'s community of sailors incarnates modern Japan, and yet it sails under the same flag, and in essence belongs to the same country, as the Imperial Navy men of 1942. Their principled sacrifice, in continuing to fight for Japan (or an idea of or an ideal Japan) links them ideologically as well as imagistically to their forebears. In episodes of *Zipang*, the frequent and ultimately intractable debates about the proper course of action for Japan's two navies and their men, and the meanings and consequences of past and future deeds, are inevitably paralleled textually and comparable ideologically. That they suffer doubts, express ambivalence, and search for the correct response to history, in fact underlines their striking representativeness of the wider, contemporary Japan at personal, societal, and cultural levels, where 'debates about national identity are intimately connected with a transnational imaginary, and not simply a national ambivalence' (Condry).

The three symbolic names which permeate *Zipang* – *Mirai*, the mature future, *Yamato* the past of naval and national tradition, and Zipang, the imagined regional, imperial destiny – are at once contradictory and complementary principles, communal values and dissensions in ultimately insoluble dilemmas within the national imaginary. Together they form a type of politico–military double-think, a specific form of culturally determined cognitive dissonance which ranges across the national and wartime history, and which gives rise to fertile and illustrative alternatives to that history: 'alternative history, then, does not change the past as we know it, but changes our understanding about the past we know' (Easterbrook 489). In the struggle to redeem the nation's armed services, condemned for past aggression, through assumption of a uniquely defensive role, in the difficulty of military characters incarnating a high principle of pacifism, and in the unfeasibility of crafting a historical representation palatable to all political constituencies, the *Yamato* and its alternate histories provide a recurrent, if not consistent iconography and narrativization for the projection of Japan's past, as Mizuno Hiromi observes:

> As the battleship *Yamato*'s enduring presence in the postwar anime illustrates, the historical context is not simply 'the background' of the text but is a crucial aspect of the text. Analyzing desires,

their ambiguity, and complexity that variously configure this intertwined text-context relation helps us read these anime works not as a history of anime but as a history of Japan, and not as an embodiment or a representation of some unchanging 'authentic' Japanese culture [...] but as a site of a constant construction of national identity. (Mizuno 121)

The apparently accelerating production of alternate histories in contemporary Japan appears to reflect on ongoing and obsessive engagement with and renegotiation of the significance of the past, and to contribute to and modify a conflicted present. This is not simply what Ian Burama has labelled 'seeing history through the eyes of identity', but an emphatic re-inscription of identity via the rewriting of history (Burama 122).

References

Aoki, Mizuho. 'Controversial to the End, Shintaro Ishihara Bows out of Politics'. *The Japan Times* 16 December 2014. Online. 22 May 2016. <http://www.japantimes.co.jp/news/2014/12/16/national/politics-diplomacy/ishihara-bows-wants-war-china-compares-hashimoto-young-hitler/#.V0GnIulFCP9>

Ashbaugh, William. 'Contesting Traumatic War Narratives: *Space Battleship Yamato* and *Mobile Suit Gundam*'. *Imag(in)ing the War in Japan: Representing and Responding to Trauma in Postwar Literature and Film*. Eds. D. Stahl and M. Williams. Brill, 2010, pp. 327–353.

Brummer, Matthew. 'Japan – The Manga Military: How Japan's "Creative Industry Complex" is Using Manga to Shape Public Perceptions'. *The Diplomat* 19 January 2016. Online. 23 March 2016. <http://thediplomat.com/2016/01/japans-creative-industrial-complex/>

Burama, Ian. *The Wages of Guilt*. Jonathan Cape, 1994.

Condry, Ian. 'Youth, Intimacy and Blood: Media and Nationalism in Contemporary Japan'. *Japan Focus* 8 April 2007. Online. Accessed 1 June 2010. <http://japanfocus.org/-Ian-Condry/2403>

Easterbrook, Neil. 'Alternate Presents: The Ambivalent Historicism of Pattern Recognition'. *Science Fiction Studies*, vol. 33, no. 3, 2006, pp. 483–504.

Evans, David C. and Mark R. Peattie. *Kaigun: Strategy, Tactics and Technology of the Imperial Japanese Navy 1887–1941*. USNI Press, 1997.

Fisch, Michael. 'Nation, War, and Japan's Future in the Science Fiction Anime Film *Patlabor II*'. *Science Fiction Studies*, vol. 27, no. 1, 2000, pp. 49–68.

Hellekson, Karen. *The Alternate History: Refiguring Historical Time*. Kent State University Press, 2001.

Ienaga, Saburo. 'The Glorification of War in Japanese Education'. *International Security*, vol. 18, no. 3, 1993–1994, pp. 113–133.

—. *Japan's Past, Japan's Future: One Historian's Odyssey*. Trans. Richard H. Minear. Rowman and Littlefield, 2001.

Jeans, Roger B. 'Victims or Victimizers? Museums, Textbooks and the War Debate in Contemporary Japan'. *Journal of Military History*, vol. 69, no. 1, 2005, pp. 149–195.

Kaiji, Kawaguchi. 'The Ideal Country', *Zipang*. Trans. Ralph McCarthy. Kodansha, 2012, pp. 88–90.

Lowe, Robert. 'The Height of Folly: The Battles of the Coral Sea and Midway'. *The Pacific War Companion*. Ed. Daniel Marston. Osprey, 2005, pp. 79–97.

Mizuno, Hiromi. 'When Pacifist Japan Fights: Historicizing Desires in Anime'. *Mechademia*, vol. 2, 2007, pp. 103–123.

Nakar, Eldad. 'Memories of Pilots and Planes: World War II in Japanese "Manga" 1957–1967'. *Social Science Japan Journal*, vol. 6, no. 1, 2003, pp. 57–76.

Penney, Matthew. 'War Fantasy and Reality: War as Entertainment and Counter-narratives in Japanese Popular Culture'. *Japanese Studies*, vol. 27, no. 1, 2007, pp. 35–52.

Perry, John Curtis. 'Great Britain and the Emergence of Japan as a Naval Power'. *Monumenta Nipponica* vol. 21, no. 3/4, 1966, pp. 305–321.

Schnellbächer, Thomas. 'Has the Empire Sunk Yet? The Pacific in Japanese Science Fiction'. *Science Fiction Studies* 29.3 (2002): 382–396. Print.

Seaton, Philip. '"Do You Really Want to Know What Your Uncle Did?" Coming to Terms with Relatives' War Actions in Japan', *Oral History*, vol. 34, no. 1, 2006, pp. 53–60.

Shimazu, Naoko. 'Popular Representations of the Past: The Case of Postwar Japan'. *Journal of Contemporary History* vol. 38, no. 1, 2003, pp. 101–116.

Takekawa, Shunichi. 'Fusing Nationalisms in Post-war Japan: the Battleship *Yamato* and Popular Culture'. *Electronic Journal of Contemporary Japanese Studies*, vol. 3, no. 12, 2012.

Woolley, Peter J. *Japan's Navy: Politics and Paradox 1971–2000*. Lynne Reinner, 2000.

Yoshida, Mitsuru. *Requiem for Battleship Yamato*. USNI Press, 1985.

Filmography

Admiral Isoroku Yamamoto (Izuru Narushima, 2011)
Aegis (Sakamoto Junji, 2005)
Be Forever Yamato (Masuda Toshio, 1980)
The Eternal Zero (Takashi Yamazaki, 2013)
The Final Countdown (Don Taylor, 1980)
For Those We Love (Taku Shinjo, 2007)
Lorelei, the Witch of the Pacific Ocean (Higuchi Shinji, 2005)
Men of the Yamato (Sato Junya, 2005)
Pearl Harbor (Michael Bay, 2001)
Samurai Commando Mission 1549 (Tezuka Masaki, 2005)

Saving Private Ryan (Steven Spielberg, 1998)
Sea Without Exit (Kiyoshi Sasabe, 2006)
Space Battleship Yamato (Yamazaki Takashi, 2010)

Anime Television Series

Gate (Kyogoku Takahiko, 2015)
Girls Und Panzer (Mizushima Tsutomu, 2012)
Kantai Collection a.k.a. *Fleet Girls* (Kusakawa Keizo, 2015)
Space Battleship Yamato (Matsumoto Leiji, 1974–1975)
Strike Witches (Takamura Kazuhiro, 2008)
Zipang (Furuhashi Kasuhiro, 2004–2005)

'Her Dreams Receding'
Gender, Astronauts, and Alternate Space Ages in Ian Sales' Apollo Quartet

Brian Baker

In this chapter, I will consider a sequence of alternate history science fictions by the contemporary British sf author Ian Sales. These novellas, titled the 'Apollo Quartet', re-imagine the NASA space programme of the 1950s, 1960s and 1970s to critique the ideological and gender codings of what Dale Carter called the 'American Rocket State' of the decades following the Second World War. Carter, in his book *The Final Frontier*, suggested that not only did the NASA space programme and its male astronauts articulate a peculiarly 'American pioneering tradition' and masculine heroism, they 'embodied a nation, a social system, a whole way of life. Their mission would make manifest America's destiny; their achievements would universalize the American Century' (159).

In the second decade of the twenty-first century, Sales returns to this historical moment to interrogate its particular mode of spectacular geopolitical strategy, where the Space Race was part of the Cold War, a technical and ideological supplement to the Arms Race: '"To insure Peace and freedom", Kennedy told the voters a month before the [1960] election, "we must be first"', Carter notes (154). Sales' fictions reveal the belligerent, violent practicalities of space 'exploration', inextricably bound up with the Cold War, and also the systemic exclusions and blinkered thinking of NASA's technocratic project. For us, in the twenty-first century, the heroic images of the Saturn V rocket launch or of Aldrin (and reflected in his visor, Armstrong) standing on the Moon tend to mask the rather less heroic realities: thus I will begin with NASA's implication in both utopian dreaming and nostalgia. Sales is sophisticated enough, however, to allow those tensions, between a longing for the heroic spectacularism of Apollo and a critique of its foundational principles and operation, to form the very fabric of his fictions.

In his book on Apollo, *Moondust: In Search of the Men Who Fell to Earth* (2005), Andrew Smith characterizes the programme in terms of spectacle and theatre:

Apollo was a performance, pure and simple. JFK wanted something to capture the global imagination, and to excite his own people, and he found it. But he didn't create the idea, the fantasy was already there, independent of the Cold War, and there's no question that Kennedy knew he was tapping into something far deeper and more primal than an urge to humiliate the Soviet Union. All those space novels and sci-fi movies and articles in *Colliers* and *Space Cadet* magazines sat at the top of a pyramid of human dreaming that stretched back thousands of years. Apollo may have been driven by the Cold War, but it was an emanation of American popular culture at that moment in time. It occurred to me that, in the end, it was *theatre* – the most mind-blowing theatre ever created. (297)

As an emanation of 'cultural dreaming', there is something utopian about Apollo, something to do with enacting an idea of the future which in indissoluble from science fiction itself. Constance Penley, in *NASA/TREK* (1997), wrote that at the time of writing 'NASA remain[ed] a repository for utopian dreaming' (15). That there has been a relative paucity of science fiction texts that deal directly with Apollo indicates that it offers little symbolic capital upon which the sf writer can draw, because Apollo was science fiction already, of a particular kind: a heroic, spectacular adventure narrative which both echoed the themes and ideas of early twentieth-century pulp sf and anticipated the cinematic imagination of post-*Star Wars* spectacle sf. As Penley wrote in *NASA/TREK*, 'NASA has already put itself in the terrain of fiction, folklore, myth and popular culture; NASA *is* fiction, folklore, myth, and popular fiction' (88).

The last of the manned NASA missions to the Moon, Apollo 17, left the surface on 14 December 1972. The Commander of that mission, Eugene Cernan, was the last human being to walk on another world, as he followed Harrison 'Jack' Schmitt back into the Lunar Module. 'Gene' Cernan died on 16 January 2017. Four of the Apollo moonwalkers remain at time of publication in 2019: Buzz Aldrin (Apollo 11), David Scott (Apollo 15), Charlie Duke (Apollo 16), and Jack Schmitt. Duke is the youngest, at age eighty-one. Soon, time and age will take the other moonwalkers, and a particular chapter in human history, the Space Age, will come to a definitive close. The Heroic age of space exploration, of Saturn V rockets and Lunar landers and Neil Armstrong, is long gone. It is difficult, therefore, to approach Apollo without falling prey to nostalgia, and this has been true for some time. Constance Penley, writing about the then twenty-fifth anniversary of the Apollo 11 landing, noted that 'there were innumerable books, journalistic retrospectives, videos, and television specials that endlessly replayed NASA's most glorious triumph. But clearly this celebration was shot through with nostalgia for what may never be again' (12). 'Nostalgia for the future' was identified by Simon Reynolds and Mark Fisher with a group of musical projects and sound artists, who attempted to recapture a certain structure of feeling associated with the 1960s. Reynolds, author of *Retromania* (2011) and Fisher, author of the *K-Punk* blog and later *Capitalist Realism* (2009) took Derrida's concept of 'hauntology' to attempt to characterize the uncanny nature of much of this music. In a *K-Punk* post from 2006, Fisher suggests:

> [T]he period since 1979 in Britain has seen the gradual but remorseless destruction of the very concept of the public. Public space has been consumed and replaced b[y] something like the 'third place' exemplified by franchise coffee bars. Here, you are transported into the queasily inviting quasi-domesticated interior of one of SF Capital's space-ships: deterritorialization (you could be anywhere) and reterritorialization (you are in surroundings whose every nuance is shinily familiar). [...] [I]nside the pod, it's possible to literally forget what city you are in. What I have called nomadalgia is the sense of unease that these anonymous environments [...] provoke; the travel sickness produced by moving through spaces that could be anywhere.

The Space Age and the Apollo programme are an antidote to what Fisher identifies as the commodified spaces of contemporary life, the world as the 'interior of one of SF Capital's space-ships'. The future proposed by Apollo is one of possibility, of change, of optimism, of a different understanding of human beings and their place in the cosmos.

Ian Sales' 'Apollo Quartet' of texts – three novellas, a novel, and a coda – constitute a very different set of responses to NASA and the Moon missions. Published from 2012 to 2016, the novellas are: *Adrift on the Sea of Rains* (2012), *The Eye With Which the Universe Beholds Itself* (2013), *Then Will The Great Ocean Wash Deep Above* (2013), and the longer novel *All That Outer Space Allows* (2015), with a *Coda: A Visit to the Air and Space Museum* (2016). Taken as a sequence, they constitute an alternate history of the Apollo programme; or rather, a sequence of different alternate histories, which re-imagine the Space Age, then science fiction, and then finally the Quartet itself, to bring to the surface its ideological underpinnings and in particular its gender codings. The texts become increasingly experimental in form, and while they begin with an overt critique of technocratic, belligerent Cold War masculinity in *Adrift on the Sea of Rains*, they move to a re-imagination of the space programme and then science fiction itself which places women at the centre of the narrative.

Adrift on the Sea of Rains won the British Science Fiction Association short story award in 2012 and was a finalist in that year's Sidewise Award. It imagines a NASA programme (eventually part-funded by the Pentagon) that extended to twenty-five missions, encompasses the building of a lunar base, and is ongoing in 1979 when the novella is set (the year that Skylab fell from orbit). A timeline of missions is given in extensive detail at the back of the novella, lending authenticity to its extrapolation of the Apollo programme. A glossary follows, additional documentation that attests to the novella's hard-sf credentials. The milieu is resolutely homosocial, and the novella deftly articulates the personal dynamics between members of this masculine group, mainly from the point of view of its 'leader', Colonel Vance Peterson. Peterson is an ex-US Air Force pilot (like many of the early astronauts, drawn from the ranks of test pilots in the Air Force and Navy) who seems to be conceptually limited to the horizons of his own institutional embedding and of continuing Cold War antipathies, a set of prejudices which ultimately leads to destruction.

In investigating this gendered geopolitics, the text combines formal with narrative and thematic elements to trace the origins of the historical timeline which leads to nuclear war on Earth, and the terminal stranding of the American astronauts on the Moon. The Moon base (named Falcon, a reference perhaps to Captain Robert Falcon Scott, who famously died in Imperial 'exploration' of the Antarctic) is the repository for the novella's main novum, the 'Bell', a remnant of Nazi *'wunderwaffe'* (meaning 'wonder weapon'). The Moonbase is a research station for investigation of these wonder weapons, and the 'Bell' is a means by which alternate realities can be reached. This is vital, as a nuclear war has stranded the men on the moon, and they activate the 'Bell' to search for an Earth in which Armageddon has not taken place. The men work the 'Bell' until a blue, unharmed Earth is seen in the Moon's sky. Essentially, the men search for what the text calls a 'decision node' (*Adrift* 13), a point of divergence which will allow the astronauts to shift into an alternative historical continuum in order for them to be rescued. While not travelling in time, their use of 'the Bell' to switch into a different timeline requires that they seek a 'decision node' further and further back in time. Interleaved with this narrative are italicized sections which narrate Petersen's former career as a USAF pilot, which are presented in reverse chronology, and it becomes apparent that these constitute the 'decision nodes'. The final section narrates the moment when Petersen decides to shoot down a Soviet supersonic bomber which intrudes onto

Canadian airspace. The narration of the italicized sections much more
closely approximates Petersen's macho fighter-pilot discourse (although
the entire novella is focalized by his point of view):

> *He saw the impact, the sudden blossoming of flame on the T-4s flank, the*
> *enemy bomber shedding shattered panels which spun mirror-bright in the*
> *sun as they fell, the curving smoke trails of debris as the aircraft broke*
> *apart; and his wizzo said, Jesus Christ, you sure as shit shouldn't've done*
> *that. He was right, of course, and back at the base the colonel chewed him*
> *a new one though they both knew it was a righteous kill, but relations*
> *were hair-trigger and neither side wanted to give the other provocation.*
> (*Adrift* 51, original emphasis)

The word 'righteous' is key to decoding Petersen's macho discourse:
he entirely believes in the rightness of his own ideological position,
the rightness of the use of military force by the USA against the Soviet
Union, and the rightness of his own decision. This world view leads
to disaster. After the Bell delivers them to a timeline closer to our
timeline's 1979, in which the Soviet space station Mir is in low Earth
orbit (and in which, as I have noted, Skylab has fallen to Earth), the
astronauts engineer a lunar module to enable Petersen to take off from
the Moon's surface, cross space and hope to contact or dock with the
orbiting space station. As he approaches Mir, thinking the presence
of the Soviet space station must mean they have 'won' the Cold War,
Petersen is consumed by 'sour hate-filled rage': this 'is not the world
he knows, nor any he wants to know' (*Adrift* 54). He targets Mir with
the module and bails out in a spacesuit, consigning himself, his fellow
astronauts on the Moon, and the cosmonauts on Mir to death; but his
last realization is that the Russian word Mir means 'Peace'. The irony
is all too apparent: the Cold Warrior, achieving a self-righteous 'peace'
of mind following his 'revenge', only perpetuates conflict. Petersen will
burn up in the atmosphere unlamented. His 'heroic' masculine ethos is
the very cause of his, and his world's, destruction.

All the Quartet have glossaries following the narrative, and *Adrift
on the Sea of Rains* and *The Eye With Which the Universe Beholds Itself* also
contain appendices. The appendices and bibliography work as part of
the apparatus of the text itself, part of a world of documentation, a
textual world: the astronaut's library of scientific reports, NASA manuals,
technical files. Much of the historical backstory and framing contexts
for the novellas are given in 'Glossary' sections, which ostensibly
concentrate on the technical details of the story (Apollo missions,
names for craft and suits) but act as a kind of *parallel text*, a textual

device with a strong tradition within speculative fiction. The appendices are organized alphabetically, a kind of glossary or mini-encyclopaedia, re-articulating chronology in a textual form that opens up the novellas in interesting ways. The appendices are at once a supplement (the narratives can be enjoyed without them) but are also central to Sales' extrapolative method. The encyclopaedic form is a kind of extrapolation/ legitimation, working to deepen or expand the narrative world but also to make it more concrete as a *historical* extrapolation; at the same time, of course, as with all formal play with this kind of apparatus, the effect is also self-reflexive, to foreground the text *as* a text. More artfully, the *parallel texts* within each of the novellas formally present the motif of the alternate historical continuum that is central to the mode of the alternate history.

In *Adrift*, the extended Moon programme is a direct extension of the historical Apollo; in *The Eye With Which The Universe Beholds Itself*, the second novella in the sequence, the 'decision node' is the moment in the descent of Apollo 11's LM (Lunar Module) when Neil Armstrong, in our timeline, piloted the module manually to a safe landing. *The Eye With Which* predicates NASA's Mars programme (named Ares) on Armstrong's decision to abort the landing, which then gives the opportunity for the Soviet Zond programme to land Cosmonaut Alexei Leonov on the Moon first. (In our timeline, the catastrophic failure of the 3 July 1969 test of the N1 rocket delayed the Soviet programme for two years, and no Cosmonaut ever walked upon the Moon.) This failure drives the US to land a human being on Mars, which is the Ares programme; this first man is the protagonist of *The Eye With Which*, Major (later Brigadier General) Bradley Emerson Elliott. *The Eye With Which* is a narrative with a double timeframe; in 1979, Major Elliott lands upon Mars, and makes a discovery that will alter the possibilities of human exploration of the galaxy; in 1999, Brigadier General Elliott (long since absent from NASA) is invited to travel to a distant star aboard a craft powered by the technology that is a result of his Mars landing. Sales connects the second mission with Elliott's growing estrangement from his wife, a consequence of his career as an astronaut (and the kind of desires and gratifications that career entails).

In the second novella, however, the shift into personal and emotional territory deepens Sales' portrayal of the male astronaut. Rather than Petersen's somewhat limited Cold Warrior, Elliott is presented as a man whose long journeys (to Mars and to an exo-planet somewhere far from Earth) are spatial analogues of his own emotional dislocation. His voyage out, unlike that of Petersen, is not followed by the consoling thought that 'he is coming home, and he will never leave' (*Adrift* 54); although

Elliott just about makes it back to the craft on Mars after an accident during an EVA (Extra-Vehicular Activity), his journey to the exo-planet is a one-way trip: the novella ends 'This time, he is not going home' (*The Eye With Which* 56). For Elliott, this is a wished-for outcome: 'I knew what I was doing. [...] I knew I'd be stuck down here' he tells the crew on the orbital craft who are unable to rescue him (*The Eye With Which* 55), and connects with the book's opening sentence: 'This time, when he returns home, he knows she will have left him for good' (*The Eye With Which* 11). The interleaved dual narrative is then circular: Elliott's self-willed marooning is both an escape and a completion of the emotional trajectory of the astronaut. As Andrew Smith notes in *Moondust*, 'the huge divorce rate in the Astronaut Corps [meant that by] the end of the 1970s [...] the highest rates in the nation settl[ed] on the Cape Kennedy area of Florida' (58). The cost of the space programme in *The Eye With Which* is not strictly geopolitical or financial: it is also personal and emotional.

Where the first and second books of the Quartet interrogate masculinity, the third and fourth books, through their projected alternate histories, focus on the experience of women. *Then Will The Great Ocean Wash Deep Above* (2013) has another dual narrative, split between the 'Up' experiences of Geraldine 'Jerrie' Cobb, one of the 'Mercury 13' female astronauts that, in our timeline, undertook the same physiological testing as the male NASA astronauts in a privately funded programme but never flew, but in the novella goes into space as all the male USAF and Navy pilots are bound up in an ongoing Korean War; and the 'Down' narrative of Lt Commander John McIntyre, a submariner who pilots a submersible to recover a spy-satellite film 'bucket' from the bottom of the ocean, a canister which contains photographs of Sino-Soviet military build-up on the North Korean border. At the end of the novella, Sales gives us the *real* (our timeline) histories of the 'Mercury 13' women who were excluded from NASA; the thirteen women passed 'Phase I' of the testing, and the only one to pass 'Phase III', Jerrie Cobb, becomes a kind of 'everywoman' astronaut in *Then Will The Great Ocean*.

Rather than the military man or career pilot (the two masculine avenues into the astronaut programme), both implicated in an institutional and philosophical narrowness of mind, Cobb is religious as well as ambitious, full of wonder for the universe as well as inhabiting a burning will to succeed. For Cobb spaceflight is an encounter with God's creation. On an EVA, Cobb is so intoxicated by the freedom of spacewalking and her sense that she is completing God's purpose (as well as NASA's mission) that she barely finds the will to re-enter the capsule:

> Someone is talking to her. Cobb blinks and tries to focus.
> It is Hixson: Jerrie, they want you to come back in now.
> Back in?
> Back in.
> A minute longer, Cobb replies, please.
> Mission Control say you have to come in now, Jerrie.
> [...] Now I can enter, Says Cobb. This is the saddest moment of my
> life. (*Then Will The Great Ocean* 31–32)

This directly repeats the moment when Ed White became the first American astronaut to spacewalk on the Gemini 4 mission in 1965 (and who was to die, with his 'Capcom' colleague Gus Grissom, in the Apollo 1 launchpad fire in 1967), as recounted by Andrew Smith:

> Grissom: Gemini 4 – get back in!
> (White pretends he hasn't heard. He's looking at the Earth.)
> White: What are we over now, Jim?
> McDivitt [Command Pilot]: I don't know, we're coming over the west now, and they want you to come back in.
> White: Aw, Cape, let me find a few pictures.
> McDivitt: No, *back in*. Come on.
> (pause)
> White: Coming in. Listen, you could almost not drag me in, but I'm coming ...
> (a few more minutes stalling by the reluctant spacewalker, who finally relents)
> White: This is the saddest moment of my life. (203)

Sales politicizes this sense of freedom by referring to Rosie the Riveter as Cobb struggles to get back into the craft, and this admixture of a sublime sensibility *and* feminist politics lends Cobb a particular interest. McIntyre, the commander of the bathyscaphe, is, by contrast, a rather shrunken figure, who is immensely relieved to return to the surface. Even though he imagines himself as Orpheus, descending into the underworld (misremembering the myth), it is Cobb, through her perception of the sublimity of even low Earth orbit, that ascends to an 'epic' grandeur of vision.

In *Then Will The Great Ocean*, the relation between narrative and 'appendix' (non-fictional) material that 'explains' the extrapolative method is different: more directly historical and *not* bracketed off as a supplementary 'appendix', but rather following directly from the narrative. The section on the female 'astronauts' is clearly polemical; at

the very end, Sales notes that it was not until 1983 that NASA sent a
woman crew-member into space (Dr Sally Ride), and not until 1999 that
a NASA mission had a female commander (Eileen Collins). The exclusion
of women from the NASA programme is revealed to be purely ideological,
if a woman such as Jerrie Cobb is as physiologically, psychologically, and
technically capable of enduring the rigours of spaceflight as their male
counterparts. Here, the alternate history is not an extrapolation from
our own history, but a critique of it. Sales' next move is to critique the
gender bias of the history of science fiction itself.

The main character in the final book of the Quartet, *All That Outer
Space Allows* (2015) is Ginny Eckhardt, the wife of Walden Eckhardt
who is, as the novel opens, a test pilot at Edwards Air Force Base
(AFB) in the mid-1960s. Ginny is not only a pilot's (and then, when
Eckhardt is accepted into NASA, an astronaut's) wife, but is also a
science fiction author, writing under the name V. G. Parker (Virginia
Parker, her birth name). The conceit of *All That Outer Space Allows* is that
sf is a genre written and read by women: its most famous authors are
women (Ginny is pen-pals with 'Ursula, Judith and Doris'), the editors
of *Galaxy* and *Astounding* are women, its readers and correspondents are
mainly women. The gender politics of this alternate scenario mean that
sf had still less cultural capital in the 1950s and 1960s than it had in
our world: disregarded as a 'women's genre' (like romance fiction, or
the melodrama that the novel's title overtly refers to) sf is something of
a social secret for Ginny. Frowned upon by her 'flyboy' husband, who
inhabits a typically retrograde patriarchal machismo, her writing is kept
hidden, like the copies of sf magazines she stashes in her cupboard.
Throughout the narrative, it is suggested that Ginny writes sf in part
because the patriarchal structures of the postwar USA means that she
cannot and *will not* be allowed to go into space herself; it is a kind of
displacement activity that stands in for all the exclusions suffered by
women in a patriarchal social and cultural circumstance.

This allows Sales to present the idea of performance and role-playing;
we first see Ginny in 'slacks and her favourite plaid shirt' (*All That Outer
Space Allows* 11), which is both her writing attire and a symbol of the
'real' Ginny masked by the enacting of the role of 'wife' that she must
do to support Walden's career. Later in the novel, Sales suggests that
Ginny no longer needs that hidden persona symbolized by the clothes,
that Ginny is able to bring public and private personas together, but the
details of her career – after some success in the late 60s and early 70s,
she drifts away from sf – indicate otherwise. The importance of clothes
is connected to a crucial theme in the novel, to do with gender and
women's lives under patriarchy: that of seeing and being seen.

At the beginning of the novel, Ginny watches a plume of smoke hanging over Edwards AFB, and fears that it is her husband who has crashed, perhaps fatally. This isn't so; an officer comes to seek out Ginny's neighbour with the news that the pilot has been injured, but is in the hospital. She invites him in for an iced tea while he waits, and after an awkward interlude, wonders whether she has overstepped the bounds of social propriety, but he soon leaves, wanting to wait outside in the car for the neighbour 'so I don't miss her' (*All That Outer Space Allows* 14). In an unassuming way, this introduces a recurrent motif in the narrative: men *not seeing* women, both physically and literally. When Walden takes Ginny on a tour around the Houston Manned Space Center, he runs off to check on a missed appointment. Abandoned to her own devices (another recurrent motif) Ginny is taken into the suiting room by Dee, a female technician. Searching for her, Walden pokes his head around the door, scans the room, scowls, and departs, only later coming back to locate her. He has physically *not seen* his wife (*All That Outer Space Allows* 140). Other details compound this motif: when she has lost an item in the house, he 'happily' joins in the search, but 'never' finds it, and Ginny often comes across the object in a place he has already looked.

This idea is literalized through a short story Ginny publishes, given in full in the novel, called 'The Spaceships Men Don't See' (*All That Outer Space Allows* 64–73). Like the title of the novel itself, this is a playful intertextual allusion, this time to James Tiptree Jr/ Alice B. Sheldon's famous story 'The Women Men Don't See' (1973); in a mocked up *Encyclopaedia of Science Fiction* entry for V. G. Parker (*All That Outer Space Allows* 143), it is suggested that Ginny's story gains more visibility retrospectively, after readers make the intertextual connection to the Tiptree story. There is a curious and playful tampering with chronology here, where Ginny's story anticipates the more famous (and 'real') Tiptree's, which then refers back to and legitimates it in some way. This playfulness has the effect of stitching Ginny's story into the history of actual science fiction written by women throughout the twentieth century, and in that sense, we can see *All That Outer Space Allows* as a parallel project to Sales' *SF Mistressworks* project, which explicitly challenges the gendered language of Gollancz's sf Masterworks series, a kind of critical recuperation. In both, Sales attempts to make visible the *unseen* history of sf by women.

All That Outer Space Allows does not only rewrite, through an alternate history scenario, the gendered history of science fiction; it also rewrites the gendered history of the Apollo Quartet itself. It becomes ever clearer, in each successive book, how an underlying tension between Sales' admiration for and investment in the Apollo programme and a critique of the patriarchal masculinity and codes of 'heroic' endeavour are being worked out. *All That Outer Space Allows* explicitly rewrites this in gender terms, as when Ginny begins writing the novella 'Hard Vacuum', her last significant sf publication, the opening paragraphs are given in the text itself: 'Some days, when it feels like the end of the world yet again, Vanessa Peterson goes out onto the surface and gazes up at what they have lost' (*All That Outer Space Allows* 140). This is the opening of *Adrift on the Sea of Rains*, with 'Vanessa' substituted for 'Vance'. Several other moments in *All That Outer Space Allows* suggest that Ginny is the 'author' of narratives that approximate *The Eye With Which The Universe Beholds Itself* and *Then Will The Great Ocean Wash Deep Above*.

All of the novellas in the Quartet offer a formal extension to the political and thematic revisions offered in each text. In *All That Outer Space Allows* Sales goes further still, and begins to deconstruct the narrative *from within*. The first such moment takes place in chapter one. Ginny muses that it was 'so strange that his parents should name [Walden Eckhardt] after a book subtitle "Life in the Woods"'. And then we have this:

> They didn't, of course; I did. I named him Walden for Henry David Thoreau's 1854 polemic. There is a scene in Douglas Sirk's 1955 movie *All That Heaven Allows* – the title of this novel is not a coincidence: the movie is a favourite, and in broad stroke, both *All That Heaven Allows* and *All That Outer Space Allows* tell similar stories: an unconventional woman who attempts to break free of conventional life. (*All That Outer Space Allows* 17)

After a paragraph and a half, we segue back into Ginny's point of view. This technique recurs throughout the novel, wrenching the reader out of the immersive experience of reading Ginny's story into something else entirely. The syntax and flow become halting, as though unsure of itself, jumping from Thoreau to Douglas Sirk, interrupted by dashes, by colons (twice), by ellipsis marks. As well as Sales demonstrating that *this is a fiction*, it is a kind of crisis in the parameters of Sales' own project, a point at which narrative can no longer be written, where the cultural work of revision and re-scripting comes to a halt *because it is narrative.* As Sales points out, partly through these 'authorial' disruptions, Apollo was always embedded in a range of different narratives, from official documents, jargon and acronyms (some of which are directly reproduced in *All That Outer Space Allows*) to the *Life* magazine's news-management of NASA's image to the memoirs of astronauts and their wives, many of which appear in the novel's bibliography. To rewrite Apollo, particularly in the way Sales does so (through exhaustive research and citation) is, in part, to be complicit in Apollo and its narratives.

The *Coda* to the Quartet, published in late 2016, folds Sales' personal investment in Apollo back into the sequence explicitly. Titled *A Visit to the National Air and Space Museum*, the first-person narrative presents Sales making a trip to the museum in Washington, DC, sometime in the mid-1990s. This appears to be in our timeline until, after looking at a Mercury capsule and then an Apollo Command Module, he encounters a photograph with a board bearing the words: 'The Last American Spacecraft'. The narrative then tells the story of the fatal flight of Skylab 4, in which the crew began to hear strange communications while in orbit, and then perish when a pressure valve opens on their descent back to Earth, asphyxiating the crew. 'There is something in the American psyche which reacts badly to public tragedy, particularly when fatal', Sales writes (*A Visit* 17); the consequence of the disaster was that crewed NASA spaceflights were abandoned, but American writers and filmmakers began to create a fantasy space programme that compensated for this trauma:

> In literature and the cinema, the USA launched an all-out offensive to take back high orbit and the planets of the solar system. In popular fiction, the US maintained a vigorous space programme, with space stations in low earth orbit, bases on the Moon, and even an outpost on the surface of Mars. Hollywood studios produced big budget space movies: murder mysteries set in lunar bases, disasters in orbit, asteroids due to impact the earth but only the US can save the planet. (*A Visit* 17)

Of course, there was no Skylab 4 disaster in 'our' history. The crew returned to Earth safely. The 'Glossary' to the text implicitly reveals the source of this alternate, imaginary history of the end of the space programme: the deaths of the three cosmonauts aboard the Soyuz 11 craft in 1971, in which the crew were asphyxiated when a pressure valve opened on their descent. In a kind of auto-critique which echoes the terms of my own approach in this chapter, Sales then notes that:

> [T]here is also that aspect of the American character in which the imaginary is occasionally privileged over the reality – the Space Race may have continued to exist only in the minds of Americans, but it did allow them to live with their abrupt retreat from space, despite having put twelve men on the surface of the Moon between 1969 and 1972. The country created a mythology

of progress based on what might have been, a future they used
to have. Perhaps when US troops finally pull out of Vietnam, the
same will happen. (*A Visit* 17)

In another divergence, which repeats that in *Then Will The Great Ocean
Wash Deep Above*, the Vietnam War had not ended by the mid-1990s.
This switching and interleaving finally affects the Quartet itself, when
Sales declares that he had had enough of this imaginary space race,
and on reading a narrative about US ocean exploration, wrote his own
'Poseidon Quartet': '*Adrift in the Gulf Stream*, *The Eye With Which The
Universe Beholds Itself*, *Then Will the Great Ocean Wash Deep Above*, and *All
That The Ocean Depths Allow*, which I eventually published through my
own small press, Benthic Books' (*A Visit* 20).

There is one more reversal. Before the Glossary which, like the other
four texts, provides a supplement and revision to the main narrative, the
text of *A Visit to the Air and Space Museum* takes the form of a screenplay.
It describes shots of the Saturn V rocket lifting off on 16 July 1969 for
the Apollo 11 mission, over which runs a voiceover:

> Given my interest in space exploration, especially the US space
> programme of the mid-twentieth-century, my desire to visit the
> Smithsonian Institute's National Air and Space Museum came as
> no surprise to the friends I was visiting in Maryland. I had, after
> all, written a quartet of books – three novellas and a novel – based
> on alternate visions of NASA's Apollo programme. (*A Visit* 24)

This repeats, word for word, the beginning of *A Visit to the Air and Space
Museum* itself. The text becomes a film, implicated in the 'theatre' of
Apollo, its dominant spectacularity, and its heroic masculine adventurism
as the enormous rocket lifts from the Earth and into the sky. The
circularity I have noted as a formal motif throughout the Quartet
tightens to a recapitulation, the ending repeating the beginning but
in an alternate medium – or perhaps, the textual simulacrum of an
alternate medium. At the very end of the Quartet, in its (paradoxical)
fifth text, the *Visit* points to the limitations of fiction itself: not just
science fiction, not just NASA, not just the Apollo missions, but the
capacities of literary narrative to present the meanings of Apollo, of
the astronauts and their stories, and its role in post-Second World War
popular culture and fiction.

In Sales' Apollo Quartet, then, alternate history is turned to specific
purposes. Not simply a means by which to investigate socio-cultural or
political developments in our timeline through alternate history, Sales

uses the form to critique the ways in which gender was constructed and encoded in key institutions in the post-Second World War United States, from NASA to science fiction itself. Ultimately, though, there is no exterior, 'neutral' space of critique, in the Quartet; in its multiple enfoldings and extrapolations, the texts' (and their author's) own implication in the allure of Apollo and the Space Race is placed before us. If Apollo is still a source for the Quartet's 'cultural dreaming', it is one that disrupts the fabric of the texts themselves, deliberately and necessarily.

References

Carter, Dale. *The Final Frontier: The Rise and Fall of the American Rocket State.* Verso, 1987.

Fisher, Mark. 'Nostalgic Modernism'. *K-Punk*, 26 October 2006. Accessed 20 January 2017. <k-punk.abstractdynamics.org/archives/008552.html>

Penley, Constance. *NASA/TREK: Popular Science in America*. Verso, 1997.

Sales, Ian. *Adrift on the Sea of Rains*. Whippleshield, 2012.

—. *All That Outer Space Allows*. Whippleshield, 2015.

—. *Coda: A Visit to the Air and Space Museum*. Whippleshield, 2016.

—. *The Eye With Which The Universe Beholds Itself*. Whippleshield, 2013.

—. *Then Will The Great Ocean Wash Deep Above*. Whippleshield, 2013.

Smith, Andrew. *Moondust: In Search of the Men Who Fell to Earth*. Bloomsbury, 2005.

Time and Affect After 9/11
Lavie Tidhar's Osama: A Novel

Anna McFarlane

In 2002, Barbara H. Rosenwein wrote 'Worrying About Emotions in History', which called for historians to include emotions in their historiography. She traces the history of such an idea from Lucien Febvre in 1941, who saw emotional history as an important means of recognizing the emotional dimension of political situations, an important task if fascism was to be faced and understood. Emotional historiography and its aim to recognize the political impact of emotion had a significant resonance in the aftermath of the Twin Tower Attacks in New York on 11 September 2001 and the military and political response, described as the 'War on Terror'. While Rosenwein suggests a move towards an emotional historiography, Lavie Tidhar's *Osama: A Novel* (2011) foregrounds the emotional charge and the subjectivity of the alternate history. In their introduction to this volume, C. Palmer-Patel and Glyn Morgan explain that alternate history and counterfactuals have traditionally been met with a wary reception from historians; for those accustomed to rigorous historiographical practices, the genre deviates too far from established causes, leading to unscientific extrapolations. However, Tidhar finds the emotional subjectivity of the form perfect for dealing with terrorism and the 'War on Terror'.

Through the use of alternate history's modes, *Osama* excellently captures the confusion and fear that terrorism inspires and uses as its weaponry. It does so by showing a parallel reality, precariously inhabited by a character named Joe who finds himself in this reality as the result of a trauma that took place in our own world, his involvement in an unspecified terrorist attack. Joe's trauma interrupts the passage of time, damning him to live in an endless present, a traumatic experience of time that Sigmund Freud described as *Nachträglichkeit*, or 'afterwardsness'; this concept refers to the deferred nature of trauma, as an event can happen which only reveals its traumatic nature at a later date, forcing the subject to experience the trauma as an atemporal anomaly, something that disrupts his or her experience of linear time.[1]

In the language of the novel, the division between the past and the present imposed by the trauma is represented as a veil between Joe's present consciousness and the 'secret inscriptions on the mind' (151) so that Joe's story is told through these secret inscriptions, the emotions and affects which are all that is left of his life before the trauma. The facts of our world – the terrorist atrocities committed by Osama bin Laden and the wars against the Arab world – are encountered by Joe at a distance, through the *Osama bin Laden: Vigilante* series of pulp fiction novels set in the reality that readers recognize as their own, and that Joe studies in his role as a private detective in search of their author. This interrogation of traumatic time is expressed in *Osama* as a renegotiation of what alternate history can be, as the novel maintains some familiar characteristics of the genre while adapting them to convey an emotional historiography rather than a linear retelling of history with a difference. Rather than write a conventional alternate history, *Osama* uses the genre as a discourse to express the affect of the post-9/11 atmosphere.

The 'secret inscriptions of the mind' captured in Tidhar's text invite the reader to consider the importance of emotion and affect to our understanding of post-9/11 politics and how this affective approach impacts our understanding of time, history, and memory. Tidhar not only draws attention to such concerns in the content of his novel, as he describes the affects Joe experiences, but through the form which borrows from various popular genres of literature and film. The pulp narratives on which he draws are sensation texts, designed to appeal to the reader on the basis of affect, and the confluence between the terror and violence of the attacks and the affective media of pulp fiction and classic film suggests that the former might sometimes be the most appropriate means of approaching difficult topics, including war. In exploring the emotions raised by 9/11 and their depiction in Tidhar's pulp-influenced novel, I will turn to affect theory which aims to consider subconscious feelings, emotions, tangible sensations, and other non-linguistic forms of understanding within the framework of literary theory and cultural studies.[2] Through this reading I contribute to the

---

[1] The term is a Freudian neologism, and Friedrich-Wilhelm Eickhoff points out that this renders diverse and inconsistent translations (including *'après-coup'*, 'afterwardsness' and 'deferred action' [1454]) which have made the consistency of the term difficult to divine in translation. Eickhoff finds the first use of the term in Freud's 'Project for a Scientific Psychology' (1895) and points to its significance in the case of the Wolf Man.

[2] There is some debate among affect theorists about the role that 'emotion'

ongoing discussion about the importance of affect in post-9/11 literature while giving one of the first scholarly readings of Tidhar's work.

We are not given Joe's nationality, though the hardboiled genre suggests his origin is American and his name evokes a Western rootlessness, reminiscent of the 'John Doe' label used by American law enforcement to describe unidentified and unclaimed bodies. His name is certainly not Laotian, although he lives and works in Laos as a private investigator and the novel begins as he takes on a new case. Joe has a quiet life in Laos living above a second-hand bookshop until, in the style of hardboiled detective fiction, a mysterious woman tasks him with finding the pulp fiction writer, Mike Longshott, the author of a series of novels called *Osama bin Laden: Vigilante* which appear to depict our world and the terrorist atrocities of the late twentieth century in forensic detail. Armed with a credit card that seems to have no limit, Joe's investigation takes him from his office in Laos to a seedy pulp publisher in Paris, on to London and then to New York where Osama bin Laden fans are holding the world's first convention in his honour, OsamaCon. He then finds himself kidnapped by a shadowy governmental organization, the Committee on the Present Danger, or CPD, who interrogate him before he mysteriously arrives in Afghanistan, at the home of Longshott.

Throughout his journey, Joe encounters shadowy figures known as 'refugees', or by the pejorative, racialized term, 'Fuzzy-Wuzzies', that others find difficult to see unless under the influence of opium. It dawns on Joe that these refugees may have arrived in his world from that of the *Vigilante* novels, and that he may be one of them. When he discovers Longshott he does not resolve the mystery, as it turns out that the author has written the novels based on dreams inspired by his opium addiction. The mysterious woman who gave Joe the mission reappears and knows intimate details about his life, details that he has suppressed beneath his identity as a detective. However, rather than join the woman, the end of the novel sees him back in his office in Laos living a solitary life, a return that suggests that we have not been reading an alternate history at all, but a novel in which the protagonist has been paralyzed and comatose all along, or trapped in a kind of purgatory, unable to move forward in time. This interpretation is reinforced by a section

should play in affect theory. Certainly the two should not be conflated, or treated as synonyms, but I find it useful to join Robert Seyfert in arguing that emotion should be considered here a part of the affective environment. Seyfert makes the distinction by arguing that '"emotion" usually refers to the particular human configurations' while affect should be read as 'a general term that defines relations among all kinds of bodies, of which emotion is but one particular form' (Seyfert 31).

towards the novel's end, entitled 'Ghost Stories' which gives voice to victims of the terrorist attacks, and of the military retaliation, relating their situations and their final living moments. The chapter is made up of single-paragraph vignettes, all told in the first person and in the past tense. These snapshots give the everyday context of the victims, reporting from the other side. One of them recalls what seems to be his last moments, when he remembers, 'the ceiling was collapsing, and I remember looking up. That's what I remember. Looking up and suddenly not seeing anything' (251). Another recounts, 'that was the last thing I remember thinking – what did I want to have for dinner that evening with my wife' (252). These accounts, taking place towards the end of the novel, lead the reader to think that perhaps Joe, too, has been a victim and is in a no-man's-land where he can no longer remember his own 'ghost story'.

There are nonetheless some ways in which *Osama* invites the reader to approach the novel as an alternate history while, at the same time, the novel acts as a commentary on the genre of alternate history itself through suggesting what the genre might have to offer in the post-9/11 environment. *Osama* has some identifiable nexus points, points of deviation from our historical reality; in Vientiane Joe sees propaganda for the Asian Co-Prosperity Sphere, a political alliance between Laos and the Japanese empire that does not exist in our world. The Greater East Asian Co-Prosperity Sphere was indeed a concept used in Japanese imperial propaganda during the Second World War as an alternative to European colonialism, but it was shown to be a wishful fiction in 1945 when Japan surrendered to the allies. However, in Joe's world this alliance lasted long enough to significantly affect Vientiane's architecture, which shows a Japanese influence that continues to the time period of the novel's setting with the construction of the Japanese Kobayashi Bank Building, and overshadows the city's French-colonialist architecture. Another difference is represented by the French presidency: Joe sees a plaque commemorating De Gaulle's death in Algiers in 1940, meaning that he never lived to become the President of France, whilst Antoine de Saint-Exupéry survives his time as a pilot in the Second World War and becomes president instead (57–58); in one version of the story of Saint-Exupéry's disappearance put forward since his plane was identified in 2004, De Gaulle had played a part in blackening Saint-Exupéry's name as a collaborator during the Second World War which may have contributed to the pilot's suicide by crashing his plane, so perhaps De Gaulle's early death and Saint-Exupéry's survival are linked here (Buckley 2004). At one point Joe gets off a train in order to board a ferry across the English Channel, implying that the Channel Tunnel has not been built. Collectively, these differences and many others imply a realignment of the alliances with which we are familiar, but the effect is subtle, left to the reader to decipher, and does not depend on more significant recent events (such as the outcome of the Second World War) with which the majority of readers could be assumed to be familiar.

The complexity of the nexus points is reinforced by the lack of opportunity to understand the reasons for Joe's different world. The reader is never given the year in which Joe's story takes place and this lack of context can make it difficult to understand whether changes are due to time period or to nexus points; for example, the Channel Tunnel was not opened until 1994 so it is difficult to tell whether its absence here is due to historical differences, timing, or both. The same goes for the lack of reference to great men of history. No historical figures play a significant role in the narrative, save the fictionalized Osama bin Laden, and there are none of the 'cameo' appearances often made by famous historical figures to anchor an alternate history text. This lack of context leaves the reader uncertain and forced to take the narrative as it comes through Joe's focalization. There is uncertainty over whether the novel portrays an alternate history of our own world, a parallel universe, or a dream universe – maybe even a kind of limbo, or afterlife. In his chapter in this volume Adam Roberts describes alternate history as 'the deaf sub-genre' (following Tolstoy's opinion that history is 'like a deaf person who is in the habit of answering questions that no one has put to them') as alternate history:

> can only think of history as a succession of 'great' (that is, significant) individuals, of moments around which everything might hinge. We could say that alternate history necessarily styles history as fundamentally fragile; or we might prefer to put the emphasis the other way about and argue that it styles 'man' as possessing the sublime power to bend history and society around him. (39)

In showing only 'weak' nexus points for the majority of the novel and building his plot around the impotence of a man whose ineffectiveness is contrasted by his detective man-of-action persona, Tidhar heralds his interest in subverting the alternate history.

The uncertainty evoked by the text's subtle nexus points and lack of historical markers do not stop it from engaging with the pleasures of alternate history, primarily the enjoyment of repetition with a difference. It allows history's contingency to be approached and examined, a reason that has kept the genre popular among historians in the form of the counterfactual, by using history as an original text and writing a new version. *Osama* brings this kind of enjoyment into the text through the enthusiasm of an amateur detective at OsamaCon who explains the attraction of the *Vigilante* novels and, by implication, the alternate history genre more broadly while also highlighting some nexus points that have remained unclear until this late point in the novel:

> The question of *what if*. Right? What if the Cairo Conference of 1921 went ahead as planned, with Churchill and T.E. Lawrence and Gertrude Bell dividing up the Middle East for the British? What if they chose a Hashemite king to rule Iraq, and would that have led to a revolution in the nineteen fifties? Or, what if the French war in Indochina somehow led to American involvement in Vietnam? Or if the British held on to their colonies in Africa after the Second World War? You see ... the *Vigilante* series is full of this sort of thing. A series of simple decisions made in hotel rooms and offices that led to a completely different world. (223)

Osama uses the repetition of alternate history in order to explore the role played by narrative in historiography itself. To the reader of science fiction, the first instance of repetition immediately evoked by the novel is through its relationship with Philip K Dick's *The Man in the High Castle* (1963). Rather than using our own history as the original version to rewrite, as is the case with most other alternate histories, Tidhar takes Dick's classic alternate history novel as a model for *Osama*, so that his novel becomes a palimpsestuous rewriting of a novel that was already a rewriting of history to begin with. Just as Joe searches for Mike Longshott, the characters in *The Man in the High Castle* search for the author of the mysterious novel *The Grasshopper Lies Heavy*. There are other references to Dick's novel throughout the text to reinforce this point: Joe looks for Mike Longshott at a private members' club in London called the Castle, and when he finally finds Longshott's home it is described as 'a ruined castle' (281). Through these allusions to alternate history as a genre, and *The Man in the High Castle* particularly, *Osama* suggests that the novel should not be read as a pure alternate history, but as a novel in conversation with alternate history as a discourse for understanding historiography.

The circular nature of time in the novel reinforces its deviation from alternate history. Alternate histories tend to find a moment in the past from which to extrapolate, representing history as a linear process that emerges from the outcome of significant events; as Karen Hellekson points out, this relies on a 'genetic model' (2) of history, an interest in the historical conditions that give rise to contemporary outcomes. By creating a character trapped within cyclical time and a novel with a cyclical structure, Tidhar suggests that the importance of affect after 9/11 – the importance of terror, and the emotional impact of the attacks – means that events are not experienced in linear time but inflict a traumatic break with the past that demands a repeated return to the traumatic site and prevents historical progress. Joe is drawn towards an infinite present that demands neither historical understanding nor confrontation with the future. This leaves him defined by his affective influences; the affect of love, which offers a future, and the affect of terror which marks the future as a realm of fear that would be better left unexplored. The present is often experienced by Joe as infinite and the story arc, taken as a whole, emphasizes this impression. Beginning with Joe's life in Vientiane, the main body of the text marks a departure from this routine as he investigates the identity of Longshott, and the epilogue finds him back in Vientiane, back in his repetitive routine, with the suggestion that he will live in that present infinitely. Joe finds this infinite present comforting, significantly during the chapters entitled 'In Transit' when he travels between countries and between time zones, in an imaginary realization of a globalized homogenous time.[3] 'Passengers in an airport lounge, going nowhere, he thought. There were no clocks in the room. It felt as if time had stopped and been preserved there' (191). Joe experiences this infinite present as an equilibrium between forces, as though the haunting of the past and the threat of the future briefly balance each other:

> For Joe [...] there was a kind of peace in the moment. The point of transit was like the epicentre of two opposing forces, like the equilibrium found when an equal pull is exerted on a body from all directions, creating the moment of stillness that is free-fall. For Joe those were the moments of exquisite calm, a perfect present with no future and no past. He loved the waiting times, the empty times, the endless moments that came in-between the going and the gone. (99)

The possibility of an infinite present offers comfort to Joe as he can simply exist in the moment, rather than attempting to understand the past or confront the future. The dominance of the present moment in

---

[3] Historian Harry Harootunian points out the political nature of this move towards a 'boundless present' (471) and the political advantages to be gained by framing historical time in this way in the aftermath of 9/11.

Joe's experience means that historical time is relegated to the realm of fantasy, represented here by the *Osama bin Laden: Vigilante* novels. The books provide a historical context for their plots and a long history of the War on Terror for the reader. The bombing of Baghdad in 2005 in the name of the War on Terror is compared to its sacking in 1258, invoking a long history of conflict that gives context to the war described in the novels. The context given is political as well as historical; for example, the *Vigilante* excerpts describe the CIA's actions during the Chilean coup of 11 September 1973 (highlighting the resonance of that date) and American intervention in Cuba. While Joe longs to be lost in a homogeneous, infinite present, Longshott's historical accounts refuse this narrative, even whilst failing to provide Joe with a clear, linear account of how the War on Terror came to be. The form of the 9/11 attacks lent itself to the symbolism that they 'came out of the blue', but Longshott's accounts show that this was not the case historically or politically, and that the war emerged from a chaotic network of circumstances. As Joe's investigation deepens he begins to realize that the world around him is embedded in these circumstances, for example as he looks at exhibits in the British Museum, many of them plundered from foreign countries during the era of empire:

> It was as if the British had gone out into the world, stripped it of its heritage, and returned, laden with their cargo, to decorate their city with it. It was a terribly arrogant building, it seemed to him. Joe thought again about the books he'd read, about their secret war. Why did they fight? He thought, there at the peaceful museum, that he could see just a hint of that, the fingers of antiquity crawling into the present day and shaking it. (162)

Joe's journey in the novel is as much temporal as it is spatial, and Joe experiences it as such, as he thinks that 'going from London to New York was a sort of time travel, racing back into the night' (209). Here temporality is aligned with ideology; Laos represents a third world that has not been fully industrialized, London depicts the time of empire while New York marks the site of the 9/11 attacks and the inauguration of the new historical present and of the globalization of capital. When Joe finds himself in Afghanistan at the home of Mike Longshott it is a landscape that incorporates all of these times: a third world country marked by American drones and bombs, symbols of globalization and neo-colonialism.

While the changes in setting give the narrative a structure that seems future-oriented Joe ends up right back where he started, in

Vientiane, so that spatially and emotionally he has come full circle and the future is rendered inaccessible; affectively he remains in the same state. Despite finding Mike Longshott, Joe does not find any answers, and despite being found by the woman there is no romantic or emotional progress for him either. The lack of progress on either front means that Joe ends the novel almost exactly as he started it, erasing the illusion of futurity that was briefly introduced to his existence through the mysteries of Longshott and the woman. The woman, and the possibility of love that she represents, is connected to the future in Joe's mind explicitly at one point during the novel when he finds himself a prisoner: 'The girl was as barred from the prisoner's cell as the future is inexorably barred from the past' (244). Joe never realizes that future. Rather, he returns to the 'historical present' of his Vientiane office, he returns to his routine and 'sometimes […] he thought he saw a girl standing there, in the place where sunlight pierces rain, looking up at his window, but then the clouds would close again high above and she would be gone' (287). The affective experience of love's possibility is the only tendency that draws Joe towards a future, while the affect of terror closes it off, rendering it a realm of fear that Joe refuses to enter.

While affect is at the heart of Joe's paralysis, his inability to understand the past or to face the future, he uses 'facts' as a means of keeping himself trapped in the present. Joe's environment does not conform to the linear rationality of the detective story narrative, and yet he consistently attempts to make reality comply in the hope that he can continue to cope with his circumstances:

> But what was the trail? These were the facts: his name was Joe. He was a private investigator. He had been hired to find a man, and given more-than-adequate funds to do so. Everything else …
>
> These were the facts. Facts were important. They separated fiction from reality, the tawdry world of Mike Longshott from the concrete spaces of Joe's world. Everything else … (96; ellipsis in original)

The so-called 'facts' that Joe repeats to himself as a means of locating himself in the world hold him back from understanding the real relationship between Mike Longshott's books, his own experience of reality and his own identity, as the separation of fiction and reality prevent him from understanding the connections between the two. Joe exists between the 'fiction' of Longshott's books (which describe the facts of our world) and the 'facts' of his world (which contain his nonconscious experiences and their construction of a world). Melissa Gregg and Gregory J. Seigworth describe affect as arising 'in the midst of *inbetween-ness*, in the capacities to act and be acted upon' (1), the space that Joe struggles to understand in his desperation to think of only the 'facts' which remain outside of his direct experience. Gregg and Seigworth go on to define affect as referring to the 'intensities' that pass between bodies (whether those bodies are human, animal or inanimate) and which 'can serve to drive us toward movement, toward thought and extension, that can likewise suspend us (as if in neutral) across a barely registering accretion of force-relations' (1). In Joe we find someone who is certainly suspended in the affects around him, unable to move beyond the novel's circular structure. Joe's situation is also best understood via affect as it is one in which the cause-and-effect relationship is disturbed, something that affect theory allows for and takes into account, but one that is anathema to alternate history proper. Gregg and Seigworth explain that 'because affect emerges out of muddy, unmediated relatedness and not in some dialectical reconciliation of cleanly oppositional elements or primary units, it makes easy compartmentalisms give way to thresholds and tensions, blends and blurs' (4). The dominant social and political narratives in the aftermath of the 11 September attacks are well described by terms such as 'blurry' as ordinary citizens find themselves caught up in the 'unmediated relatedness' of terror attacks and the fear they inspire.

Terrorism exists at the juncture between affect and trauma, described effectively by key affect theorist Lauren Berlant in her book *Cruel Optimism* (2011) as an assault on the subject's experience of temporal linearity. At its roots, affect theory is related to trauma theory in that it tries to focus on nonconscious responses and emphasizes the importance of the body and bodily reactions in navigating extreme circumstances, like the fear of terrorism or other bodily violence. By forcing the subject to be ruled by nonconscious impulses, trauma also bars the subject from experiencing time as linear. Berlant describes trauma using Freud's term, *Nachträglichkeit* ('afterwardsness'). She describes the concept as evoking a complex 'temporal whiplash' one that creates a bridge between the subject and the traumatic event, evoking 'a sense of belatedness from having to catch up to the event':

> [A] sense of the double-take in relation to what happened in the event [...] a sense of being saturated by it in the present [...] a sense of being frozen out of the future (now defined by the past); and, because ordinary life goes on, a sense of the present that makes no sense with the rest of it. (Berlant 80–81)

Once again, the failure of the cause-and-effect model results in temporal disruption caused by the saturation of affect – in this case, the saturation of fear. These connections between affect theory and terrorism have been explored by Brian Massumi who points out that terrorism works by threatening the populace – an appeal to affective, visceral reactions – and feeling this level of threat has an impact on how we experience time: 'If we feel a threat, such that there was a threat, then there always will have been a threat. Threat is once and for all, in the nonlinear time of its own causing [...] the affect-driven logic of the would-have/could-have is what discursively ensures that the actual facts will always remain an open case' (54–55). The juxtaposition of this affective landscape where 'the actual facts remain an open case' and the genre of the hardboiled detective novel in which the clues build to the climax, or the genre of the alternate history where the pleasure derives from the clear points of comparison with the implied reader's own timeline, is what gives Tidhar's novel its narrative tension in a text where the plot and the mystery must remain unresolved, at least in the diegesis.

The tension of terrorism that Massumi highlights, a case that must remain open thanks to the affect-driven nature of the situation, is highlighted in *Osama* through the stylistic contrast between Joe's affective experience of the world and the excerpts from Longshott's *Osama Bin Laden: Vigilante* books. These excerpts pepper the narrative, set apart by their font which is reminiscent of cheap typewriters and cheap publishers, the ones who distribute disposable pulp fiction to the masses. Even the name of the writer seeks to highlight the unlikely nature of the events described in the pages of the books as the outlandish tactics of the terrorist atrocities are re-imagined as pulp fiction. These excerpts describe events that the reader will recognize from their own timeline: the attacks by Al-Qaeda on a Nairobi hotel, the American embassy to Tanzania, in London on 7 July 2003 and the World Trade Centre attacks of 11 September 2001. The style is clipped and factual, giving times for the movements of the terrorists with military precision and basic descriptions of the environments through which they move, not dissimilar to the plot-focused narration of pulp thrillers:

> Mohamed Rashed Daoud Al-Owhali was dressed that morning in black shoes, a white short-sleeved shirt, blue jeans and jacket. He carried a 9mm Beretta. He also carried four stun grenades. At 9:20am he made a phone call. (12)

The accounts of the atrocities carried out by the terrorists are told in a similar, factual manner with the interiority of the victims left to the reader's imagination. For example, one passage tells the story of Rose Wanjiku, a Kenyan tea-lady trapped after the bombings. Her situation is described in detail without offering any interiority: 'Rescuers, including marines and an Israeli special rescue unit, tried to reach her. She communicated with them constantly. She had been buried for five days. She died several hours before they finally reached her' (13–14). Joe observes the gruesome, clinical descriptions of the books, which he thinks 'read like the lab reports of a morgue, full of facts and figures all concerned with death. He did not understand them' (53). Joe, living in an affective milieu beyond rational facts, cannot relate to these cold, exterior descriptions of the terrorists' actions and the suffering of their victims. The fact-driven narratives of the *Vigilante* novels are contrasted with the tone of the main body of the text when the action is focalized through Joe. The description of Ventiane, Joe's office, and the characterization of Joe himself are not in the style of the pulp thriller: and while it contains plot markers associated with the hardboiled detective novel, the writing is ambling, descriptive, and melancholy. Vientiane is described with an evocative expressionism in stark contrast to the clipped reportage of *Osama Bin Laden: Vigilante*:

> Peddlers move sluggishly along the road with their wares of bamboo baskets, fruit and red-pork baguettes. The whole city seems to pause, its skin shining, and wait for the rains to come and bring with them some coolness. (17)

Meanwhile, Joe's characterization brings the interiority (and the affect) to the novel that was missing from the description of Rose Wanjiku's death. He drinks his coffee with two sugars, 'which was overdoing it, he knew, but that was the way he liked it' (17) and he lives the solitary life of a detective before the intrusion of a case:

> A long time ago Joe had learned that it was sometimes easiest to feel alone amongst people. He no longer let it disturb him, but as he sat there, isolated from the outside by the transparent glass windows, he felt for a moment disconnected from time, all contact between him and the rest of humanity removed, cauterized, his connection to the people outside no more than an amputee's ghost-limb, still aching though it was no longer there. (18)

The chapter titles also reflect this contrast between the basic plot-driven writing of the *Osama bin Laden* stories and the interiority evident in the narrative of Joe's investigation. While the excerpts from the Mike Longshott novels bear simple, descriptive titles like 'second bomb' (27) the titles of Joe's chapters are taken from metaphors and similes used within the chapter, to give the titles a surreal tone, like a line from a haiku: for example, 'an otherworldly map, like the surface of the moon' (32) describes a desk marred with coffee stains and provides the title of the chapter in which it appears. In addition to the Mike Longshott excerpts and the main narrative that follows Joe's investigations there is the aforementioned section entitled 'Ghost Stories' that gives first-person accounts from victims of the various bombings committed by Al-Qaeda or by Western governments ostensibly reacting to terrorist attacks (248–253). Contrasting the 'facts' of the case, ungraspable to Joe, with his impressionistic, affective experience of his reality shows the problem identified by Rosenwein of leaving affect out of historiography. The facts of the case are hampered by their affective impact and cannot be understood without taking the emotional realm into account. However, for Joe the tension between affect and the 'facts' leaves him paralyzed, the future hinted at only through the novel's evocation of love.

Love is that which crosses the boundary between the worlds, and this is represented in fleeting moments throughout the text. In London, Joe stands under the statue of Anteros (often referred to as the Angel of Christian Charity), the god of requited love and the avenger of unrequited love. He also sees loving couples periodically throughout the novel and their impression on him is one of unnamed loss because 'it seemed to him he had once been like that, too, somehow completed' (274). The object of Joe's love appears to him as his 'client', the woman who initially hires him to find Mike Longshott and appears periodically in the novel. It is a love that remains unarticulated, but is described through its affects on Joe's senses and his sense of self, primarily through the physical touch of the unnamed woman's hands. When she hires him she touches his hand and Joe experiences the gesture as 'terribly intimate ... intimate and familiar' (27). Joe finds himself dependent on ritual and repetition to sustain an identity and the disruptive power of love represents both a danger to his sense of self (as it threatens to destroy the routine that sustains his identity), and the only chance he has of breaking out of the world in which he finds himself and making his way back into his own reality. The prospect of such a break is too much for Joe and he turns away from the thought of reliving his trauma so that the final pages of the novel find him back in Vientiane, occupying the same routine he followed before the woman hired him. The danger of the quest the woman sends him on is even a part of this love. As Sara Ahmed identifies, 'fear is *that which keeps alive the fantasy of love as the preservation of life*, but paradoxically only by announcing the possibility of death' (68; emphasis in original).

The evocation of affect in *Osama* forces it to deviate from the genre of the alternate history, but the decision to use the genre as a discourse with a fantastical twist is no coincidence. The conviction that fantasy offers more honesty than a jaded realism is a core concern in *Osama* and one that guides the novel towards pulp genres that are juxtaposed with the sensitive subject matter. The use of fantasy allows the affective environment to be core to historical understanding, rather than something that must be put aside in order to settle on an 'objective' interpretation of the historical events. In turning to hardboiled detective fiction, film noir and alternate history to depict post-9/11 reality Lavie Tidhar highlights the drawbacks of reality itself. While realism can well capture affect, the creation of alternate worlds provides a space to draw out the fears and affects between bodies that structure our political spaces as much as the 'facts of the case'. Tidhar's distrust of realism and his faith in sensation literature and fantastika are influenced by his Israeli background and his resultant political convictions, and can be seen in his use of alternate history through several of his novels, including *The Bookman Histories* (2012), *The Violent Century* (2013), and *A Man Lies Dreaming* (2014).

Tidhar sees Israeli realism as a kind of fantasy, one that acts as propaganda for the Israeli state in their continuing conflict against the Palestinians. He describes the situation of Israelis and Palestinians as one of living 'in two parallel histories, each fighting for dominance – with the caveat, of course, that one does dominate over the other'. In bourgeois Israeli 'faux-realism', Tidhar argues, 'reality' is represented as a society without Palestinians, while there is a dearth of fantasy writing in Israel. Tidhar argues that Israeli writers, 'ape American modes, American tropes, rather than address the inherent paradox in which they live. There is no Israeli fantasy. There is nothing but Israeli fantasy'. Tidhar explains that this use of faux-realism in Israel has influenced him to turn to fantasy because the fantastic is 'inherently more honest – and honesty, I find, is a thing in short supply' (Tidhar, 'Masada'). Fantasy becomes a key aspect of addressing political situations that we might now describe as 'post-truth'. Tidhar's use of fantasy evokes the affective environments produced by the post-truth landscape and also offers the affective as a site for resistance, suggesting that an affective 'truth' might be the only way to combat the fear played upon by terrorism and propaganda, while an affective time might offer a way out of the War on Terror's boundless present.

References

Ahmed, Sarah. *The Cultural Politics of Emotion*, Second Edition. Routledge, 2014.

Berlant, Lauren. *Cruel Optimism*. Duke University Press, 2011.

Buckley, Martin. 'The Other Side of the Story', *The Daily Telegraph*, 20 July 2004. Accessed 5 April 2017. <http://www.telegraph.co.uk/culture/3621040/The-other-side-of-the-story.html>

Dick, Philip, K. *The Man in the High Castle*. Penguin, 1963.

Eickhoff, Friedrich-Wilhelm. 'On Nachträglichkeit: The Modernity of an Old Concept'. *International Journal of Psychoanalysis*, vol. 87, December 2006, pp. 1453–1469.

Ferguson, Niall. *Virtual History: Alternatives and Counterfactuals*. Penguin, 2011.

Gregg, Melissa and Gregory J. Seigworth (eds). *The Affect Theory Reader*. Duke University Press, 2010.

Harootunian, Harry. 'Remembering Historical Time'. *Critical Inquiry*, vol. 33, Spring 2007, pp. 471–494.

Hellekson, Karen. *The Alternate History: Refiguring Historical Time*. Kent State University Press, 2001.

Massumi, Brian. 'The Future Birth of the Affective Fact: The Political Ontology of Threat', in Melissa Gregg and Gregory J. Seigworth (eds), *The Affect Theory Reader*. Duke University Press, 2010.

Rosenwein, Barbara H. 'Worrying About Emotions in History'. *The American Historical Review*, vol. 107, no. 3, June 2002, pp. 821–845.

Seyfert, Robert. 'Beyond Personal Feelings and Collective Emotions: Toward a Theory of Social Affect', *Theory, Culture and Society*, vol. 29, no. 6, 2012, pp. 27–46.

Tidhar, Lavie. *The Bookman Histories*. Angry Robot, 2012.

—. *A Man Lies Dreaming*. Hodder & Stoughton, 2014.

—. '"Masada Shall Not Fall Again": Faux Realism, Parallel Histories and the Fantastic'. *Goodreads*, 2012. Accessed 25 October 2016. <www.goodreads.com/author_blog_posts/2436971-masada-shall-not-fall-again-faux-realism-parallel-histories-and-the-f>

—. *Osama: A Novel*. PS Publishing, 2011.

—. *The Violent Century*. Hodder & Stoughton, 2013.

Part II

Manipulating the Genre

The Subjective Nature of Time and the Individual's (In)Ability to Inflict Social Change

Molly Cobb

The individual's position within society is an important aspect of Alfred Bester's works of the early Cold War era. Mainly focusing on one's sense of self and the destructive influence of aspects of Cold War culture, his texts are often concerned with the impact that sociological issues such as conformity or consumerism can have on personal identity. In various short stories between the 1940s and the 1960s especially, Bester explores these contemporary concerns via the individual's place in time. These stories demonstrate Bester's examination of time as a social force and the similarities between time and society as concepts within which the individual exists but to which they remain subservient. With the 1950s being a key period in American history regarding the impact of conformity on the individual, Bester's works concerning time within this period aim to reflect the relationship between social conformity and temporal conformity.

This focus on time meant Bester wrote a number of works utilizing time travel as a means of exploring how time affects the individual, but he also examined time by writing the occasional alternate history narrative. By using alternate history rather than just time travel as a vehicle to examine the self in time, Bester was better able to examine just how much agency the individual has over time. Most depictions of alternate history require input, whether intentional or not, from an individual, whereas time travel not resulting in an alternate history requires a passive individual who observes rather than acts. However, Bester presents individuals unable to purposefully alter history regardless of their input, causing them to be passive via external forces rather than through their own actions. Even when their input does affect the course of history, it is depicted as predestined rather than a true alteration. As such, alternate history becomes the key means, especially for Bester, in which to explore how, and whether, an individual has the (in)ability to affect time and society.

Bester's approach to time within his works is frequently through the lens of satire and his alternate history stories often rely on subverting social understandings of how history works. As such, his narratives that employ time travel or alternate history rarely do so as a means of creating or determining history but rather present them as aspects which merely exist within a predetermined construction of time and history. Therefore, Bester's approach to the typical tropes of the alternate history genre consequently subverts expectations of history as readily changed or affected. To Bester, history is unlikely to be altered by individuals but individuals will certainly be altered by history. As such, he presents historical figures as only being subjectively significant by exploring the refusal of history to succumb to the whims of the individual. Bester's alternate histories are thus often created through subjective understandings or conceptions of history rather than through an actual altering of history itself. Even when given the chance to alter history, individuals are thwarted by society, reinforcing Bester's recurrent theme of individual agency versus social force.

The effect of the individual on time, or time on the individual, is of course not the exclusive remit of Alfred Bester, but his particular approach to the subjective experience of time and the relationship between the individual and society within this temporal space affords an avenue of insight which will here be focused on specifically. Bester's fiction works in a particular way to demonstrate his ideas regarding the individual's place in time and society, and, more specifically, his alternate histories position the individual in such a way that they appear to have autonomous agency but are in fact restricted by society and/or time. By focusing on the individual's perceived inability to concretely create change, Bester implies a lack of genuine free will in the face of temporal and social constructs. Norman O. Brown indicates that the individual has no choice but to be a part of history as it is collectively understood as the individual's 'essence is not united with his existence as with other animals, but is developed in the dialectic of historical time' (101–102). As such, Brown indicates that the 'essence' of an individual can only be connected to their existence through historical time and any separation of the individual from this form of time would lead to a dissolution of the self.

A number of works by Bester which utilize variations on the alternate history narrative demonstrate his subversive approach to concepts of time and history by undermining notions of linear time, socially accepted concepts of history, and individual agency. 'Adam and No Eve' (1941), for example, suggests the cyclical nature of existence as its ending implies that the events that take place, in which the hubris of an individual ends mankind, happened a hundred million centuries before life existed on Earth as we know it. Bester is therefore not necessarily suggesting an alternate history to the one we know, but rather an extension of history beyond our current understanding, thereby altering historical perception. By implying this cyclical nature of history, the ending also indicates that any number of cycles may occur after contemporary society, further reinforcing both the idea of historical cycles as well as the destructive nature of mankind.

'Adam and No Eve' further implies the ability of mankind both to destroy subjective time and create it, as Bester has his protagonist erase mankind and then become the building blocks of the next version of humanity. As such, the individual still remains subject to the collective, as his individual death will allow for the existence of future society. Not only does this subvert the traditional 'Adam and Eve' myth often seen in sf of the time, it removes the protagonist's agency of choosing whether he wishes to be the source of future life; a lack of choice which demonstrates the unending nature of history regardless of attempts at human intervention.

Another of Bester's stories which reflects his evolving textual interaction with the social and individual experience of time is 'The Push of a Finger' (1942). This narrative further indicates that no matter the perceived agency an individual may have over time, they are still subject to society. In the story, the protagonist has the ability to massively change 'history' (from a future perspective, thereby creating an alternate future history) but society prevents him from doing so. Granted, the protagonist's actions would have ended the universe so society would seem justified in its response. The actions of the protagonist within this narrative would seem to rationalize why individuals should not be able to affect time and history and indicates that there is something inherently unfair about the one affecting the many. Though both 'Adam and No Eve' and 'The Push of a Finger' were written prior to the use of the first nuclear weapon, they were written at a time when advancements were being made in nuclear fission. Thus, Bester can be seen to associate the potential of this technology with the end of humanity and the impact the actions of a single individual can have on the collective. Even the title of 'The Push of a Finger' indicates the ease, and individual nature, of launching such weapons.

Bester's later stories, such as 'Out of this World' (1964), having been written further removed from the advent of nuclear fission, eschew this destructive approach in favour of examining the individual's lack of

control as history alters itself. 'Out of this World' centres around two
individuals who, via crossed telephone wires, end up speaking to each
other across alternate realities: one that echoes Bester's contemporary
society and one in which America lost the Second World War after
being attacked with nuclear weapons. As one of the protagonists puts
it, 'Your history isn't my history' (Bester, 'Out of this World' 270). This
text thus positions alternate history as parallel to contemporary history,
rather than an actual alteration to it. Again focusing on the subjective
experience of time and the individual's place in history, Bester here still
suggests the theme of the destructive nature of nuclear weapons but has
it exist in a reality separate to that of the protagonist and therefore an
inactive plot point as compared to the previous two stories mentioned.
By doing so, he acknowledges that the potential destruction of these
weapons remains but places it unequivocally outside the realm of the
protagonist's agency, in a similar manner to his placement of time as
outside individual control.

With none of the aforementioned texts being particularly straightforward in their use of alternate history (alternate historical perception,
alternate future history, and an alternate history parallel reality, respectively), it should be no surprise then that Bester's most significant
alternate history narrative considers alternate history to be collectively
unobtainable.

The story which offers the greatest insight to Bester's use of alternate
history is 'The Men Who Murdered Mohammed' (1958). It is a prime
example of Bester's exploration of society, conformity, and time, and
their impact on the individual, as well as a key demonstration of Bester's
use of alternate history as an individual concept rather than collective.
Bester's utilization of time – as an unalterable force which acts upon
the individual – demonstrates that the position of the individual is
both within and without the collective temporal experience. Bester's
proposal within 'The Men Who Murdered Mohammed' of the isolated
nature of the individual's timeline can be seen as a representation of
the perceived inability of the individual to exhibit any agency over
their social environment. Any attempts to change wider history would
seem only to result in erasing yourself from it, indicating that collective
history will continue despite the destruction of individual timelines.
Equally, the construction of historical 'truth' and the way in which the
individual is subsumed within the collective (and so disempowered) is
demonstrated by Bester via his portrayal of time as a force that has the
capacity to dehumanize the individual by making them insignificant.
This insignificance is then confirmed by Bester's examination of the
individual's inability to exact concrete change on history or by them

having their changes circumvented or corrected by social or temporal forces beyond their control. As such, Bester strongly links the destructive nature of society as portrayed throughout his works with his repeated use of time as equally unyielding.

Having been published prior to 'Out of this World', 'The Men Who Murdered Mohammed' is the transitional narrative between the individual's perceived ability to change history, even if actually enacted without the individual's consent, as in 'Adam and No Eve', the individual's inability to alter history either socially or individually, as in 'The Push of a Finger', and the individual's exclusion from a history and reality of which they have no part, as in 'Out of this World'. As an example of this transitional period in Bester's writing from purely nuclear concerns to more socio-cultural concerns, 'The Men Who Murdered Mohammed' is of particular interest in regard to Bester's consideration of the individual in society and the 'individual's perception of time and his fantasies about it' (Wendell 48). The protagonist of the work attempts to alter history for personal reasons only to discover he has no agency to do so as Bester postulates that every individual exists within their own time stream, separate from collective time.

The discovery of how the individual exists in time comes about after the protagonist, Henry Hassel, finds his wife, Greta, having an affair. Out of anger, he builds a time machine so he can kill her grandparents and erase her existence, hoping to consequently create an alternate history in order to favourably alter his future. Finding the death of her ancestors to have no effect on her continued existence, Hassel travels up and down the timeline murdering various historical figures in an attempt to change the future by altering the past, though nothing he does appears to have any impact. As a result, Hassel subsequently erases himself from history by altering his own timeline to the point of dissolution. Through this particular approach to temporal existence, the story explores individual identity by separating the personal from the social not only physically but temporally. By privatizing temporal experience, individual reality becomes divorced from social reality, representing a repression of the individual self which mirrors the potential effect of social conformity on personal identity.

An individual's place in time and space, especially socially, would help shape individual identity. Thus, the destruction of one's place in time and space would consequently affect that identity in response to its altered external state. Brown considers the twentieth century to have 'seen the disintegration of the universality and, with the universality, the rationality also, of the time-schema' (95). The separation of objective and subjective experiences of time within 'The Men Who Murdered

Mohammed' echoes this disintegration as well as the dissolution of the main characters' rational responses to their situation.

These themes of social repression and individual dissolution play out in the story through Hassel's discovery of the apparently unalterable state of history as a result of his own altered microhistory and eventual temporal extinction. Hassel's altering of time ultimately only affects history as it exists within his personal timeline, due to Bester's extrapolation of the lack of a universal continuum. However, this does cement Hassel's identity as intrinsically tied to his place in time. Israel Lennox, another man made extinct as a result of his altering his own timeline, explains to Hassel that 'There are [...] billions of individuals, each with his own continuum; and one continuum cannot affect the other' (Bester, 'The Men' 171). By existing in their own continuum apart from, but within, society, both identity and time, as linked aspects of the self, can be seen as being socially influenced but ultimately a personal creation. Despite the collective experience of time and society, Bester's proposition of the personal nature of temporal existence deems that each individual can only affect their own timeline and thus only alter their own history.

This solipsistic approach to time is reflected in Hassel's solipsistic approach to time travel. More focused on erasing his wife than any impact his actions may have on others, Hassel's compulsion for revenge causes him to behave irresponsibly; luckily for mass society, Bester disallows time travel from being a deciding factor on the course of history. Lennox's admission that he accidentally killed a small Pleistocene insect echoes Ray Bradbury's 'A Sound of Thunder' (1952), in which the alterations in the future may have been subtle, but still, alterations they were. Lennox's incident has no repercussions except for himself and his subsequent rampage through time and space in an attempt to alter the present serves only to dismantle his own position in reality.

Hassel's focus on his personal relationship is similar to 'The Push of a Finger' and the protagonist's selfish approach to time in that story wherein he puts his personal need over the collective effect of his actions. Though the protagonist of 'The Push of a Finger' is aware his actions would end the universe, he becomes fixated on instigating the events that would lead to this end in his desire to be with a woman. The relatively minor importance of this relationship being placed above the stability of the universe is similar to Hassel's selfish reactions regarding his wife's affair. Both protagonists of 'The Push of a Finger' and 'The Men Who Murdered Mohammed' attempt to alter history for selfish reasons but regardless of the intent behind these attempted temporal adjustments, it does not change the fact that individuals lack this agency in the first place, either by passive or aggressive interference by society at large.

Bester's interest in Freudian psychology would have informed his presentation of the relationship between individual desires and the ability to alter history. His protagonists' myopic focus on personal passion reflects the power of the id over the individual and implies the reason behind these protagonists' attempts to change time is in order to appease the desires of the id. The id, as the seat of passion, is deemed not to be subject to time as its position in the unconscious means it has no 'recognition of the passage of time' (Freud, 'Ego and the Id' 450, 'The Dissection' 501, 499). As such, ruled by their id as these protagonists appear to be, they would be unable to comprehend the connection between their actions and their effect on the timeline.

Hassel does attempt to understand the interconnected dichotomy of individual and social historical time in terms of the level of significance needed in order to alter the future. However, he fails to fully grasp the concept as a result of misunderstanding the difference between what is socially significant and what is personally significant. The death of Greta's grandparents, which turn out to have no effect on Greta, are deemed trivial by the AI of the Simplex-and-Multiplex Computer (an encyclopaedic computer known as Sam, which Hassel consults for information on time) and instead becomes the starting point for Hassel's temporal disintegration and loss of identity.

Sam tells Hassel that time is a continuum and mass-action effects are needed to 'divert existing phenomena streams', causing Hassel to ask, 'But how trivial is a grandmother?' (Bester, 'The Men' 163). This desire for significant events causes Hassel to go so far as to teach Marie Curie about nuclear fission, thus giving her all the tools needed to start a nuclear war in the nineteenth century. This incident underscores Hassel's misunderstanding of the difference between social and personal trivialities. To Greta, her grandparents' existence is surely crucial. To mass society, two individuals would hardly make a difference.

Lennox and Hassel's decision to murder famous historical figures, through the assumption that their deaths would preclude their historic achievements, underscores this difference between social and individual importance. Christopher Columbus, for example, may be an American icon socially, but ultimately, even without him, the story acknowledges that the New World would still have been discovered. Edward James writes that the 'very act of labelling some events or some individuals as "crucial" or "significant" implies that, without them, the outcome would have been different' (7). The label 'great' could be added to that list. For Lennox and Hassel, the only outcome that differs is their continued existence. Writing in 1955, Herbert Marcuse refers to 'the notion of the autonomous individual' as one of the 'strongest ideological fortifications of modern culture' but considers this to be undermined by 'the power of the universal in and over the individuals' (57). Though Lennox and Hassel consider themselves autonomous, the overwhelming nature of the universal renders their altered histories irrelevant beyond their own selves. As such, due to Bester's proposed lack of a universal continuum, only the individual to whom an altered timeline belongs will experience those alterations, regardless of how significant they may be deemed socially. Thus, it might be said that this separation between the social and the personal causes each individual to live in their own alternate history, with Hassel and Lennox altering their own history to the point where collective time can no longer accommodate them and they are written out of mass time altogether.

Lennox and Hassel, by destroying their timelines and themselves, have become 'insubstantial'. Hassel is described as a 'man who mutilated history' (Bester, 'The Men' 159). Mutilation, as denoting physical trauma, foreshadows Hassel's physical disintegration resulting from his historical destruction. Removal from society has cemented the men as 'other' but also removed them as 'other', since, according to the rest of society, they no longer exist anyway. Hassel's slow dissolution from time is revealed via an unhinging from time and space in which he can now move without a time machine and finds himself unable to be seen or heard. Even he becomes unaware of himself when he watches himself murder George Washington and finds he cannot recognize the man he sees committing the murder. The expected position of the self as an internal construct means an inability to reconcile that with an external manifestation.

Allowing the self to be constructed by society results in a self only perceived and recognized externally by that society, leading to an identity crisis as the internal and external selves are perceived as separate entities rather than aspects of the same individual. It is this splintering of the self which leads to Hassel's ignorance of his own identity. Without an anchor to ground him, in this case, a solid position in his own time stream, Hassel's self continues to exist, but in a divorced state from reality, representing the potentially repressed state of his personal identity in collective society. Brown states that 'repression and the repetition-compulsion generate historical time'. Hassel's repressed individual self, coupled with his repetitive attempts to alter the future, only cements his existence as external to collective time and in fact reinforces historical time as more concrete and realistic than his own time. Brown asserts that a 'life not repressed [...] is not in historical time' (93), which, when taken in relation to Bester's narrative, indicates that if Hassel's self were unrepressed by society, his temporal changes would have the ability to

create the alternate history he aimed to achieve, by overriding historical
– and thus socially constructed – time.

This dissolved existence is reaffirmed by Sam, who insists Lennox is
dead, despite Lennox's subjective experience of his continued existence.
Lennox's reference to himself as a 'ghost' indicates his acknowledgement
of his place in temporal limbo but demonstrates a continued assertion
of his own idea of self, regardless of society's assumptions regarding
his existence. Priscilla Wald refers to this concept as an exclusion from
history, similar to Orlando Patterson's idea of 'social death', in which
individuals are not accepted as human by society (Wald 190). Lennox
refers to it as 'chronocide', but the ideas are the same. The individual
removal from society, and thus from the collective experience of time,
results in the death of the individual by their becoming something not
quite human, thereby changing one's identity to the 'other' – in this
case, a 'ghost'.

Lennox argues that this interconnectedness of time and existence
relates to time's association with memory: 'When you erase a man's
memory, you wipe him out, but you don't wipe out anybody else's'
(Bester, 'The Men' 171). Reaffirming the link between a person's place in
time and their identity, Lennox further indicates a connection between
mental and physical identity. A similar idea can be seen in Robert
Heinlein's 'By His Bootstraps' (1941) regarding the protagonist's multiple
selves: 'The only thing that bound them together into a feeling of identity
was continuity of memory' (107). The destruction of time, as related to
memory, equates to a destruction of the mental self, while the dissolution
of Hassel into a ghost equates to a destruction of the physical self. The
inability to experience anyone else's timeline emphasizes the nature of
individual self-destruction as resulting from attempting to identify the
self solely through external means – in this case, identification based
on the time streams of others. Memory, as an inherently personal and
subjective concept, aligned with history, implies the past to be personal
and subjective as well, hence Lennox's assertion that there is no such
thing as objective time for an individual and that the concept of objective
time can only be experienced via the collective.

By existing both in time and out of it, Hassel embodies a state of
quantum superposition similar to that of 1950s' America. The suspended
stasis in which the United States existed during the early Cold War,
always under the shadow of the atom bomb but not yet being destroyed
by it, meant that collective historical time would have simultaneously
flowed and ceased in a perpetual state of quantum superposition.
Concisely, quantum superposition consists of two states which are valid
depending on the position of a subjective observer, but when considered

to be existing simultaneously indicate that either state is an objective possibility in time and reality. By existing simultaneously, these states may also potentially produce a third valid state, separate from the initial two.[1] Hassel's self could be seen as both alive and dead since, mentally, his consciousness continues to exist, but physically, he would be considered destroyed. Hassel is only able to interact with Lennox, who also occupies this dual reality, after he himself has entered this quantum state, indicating a collapse of reality for the rest of society into a state where Hassel is concretely dead but a convergence of states for Hassel in which his dual identity is reaffirmed. By being both an individual and a member of a collective, the collapse of one reality or another enables us to see which state we inhabit but, in lieu of this, an indeterminate limbo is more likely the result. Existing as Hassel and Lennox do in this literal and figurative state of limbo, between their perceptions of themselves and society's perception of them, they are also existing in an identity crisis which rests not on the psychological self but on its physical location in time and space. If time were in fact personally objective, Hassel's historical alterations would have altered time collectively and his death would have been unequivocal.

The destruction of Hassel's individual identity in 'The Men Who Murdered Mohammed' can be seen as a reflection of wider Cold War anxieties regarding mass nuclear destruction. In an attempt to control this destruction and influence the flow of history – by emerging victorious in the Cold War and ensuring the ability to propagate a specific version of history – both the United States and the Soviet Union utilized propaganda, domestically and abroad. Creating their own contemporaneous history in which they subjectively existed, they removed themselves from the collective, relatively objective, history of the rest of the world, essentially creating an alternate ongoing history within which only their society existed. Karen Hellekson writes that 'history might be its own kind of fiction, one meant to be "true" even though it is created using the same strategies as a fiction text might be created' (249). If the recording of history is reliant on subjective remembrance, then the need for official documents to understand history of which one was not personally present means a certain level of trust that those events have been accurately recorded. Bester repeatedly returns to this in 'The Men Who Murdered Mohammed' by demonstrating the individual struggle to reconcile one's place in time when the 'official' records do not match personal knowledge. Sam's insistence that Lennox is dead, for example,

[1] See Merzbacher, especially chapter 2, section 1, 'The Principle of Superposition', for a further discussion of superposition as it is used here.

does more than place his individual timeline outside collective time; it also acts to falsify his experience.

In comparing murders, Hassel finds that he and Lennox killed many of the same individuals, due to their separate timelines, but despite these compounding deaths, these men continued to survive in the history books. Hassel's murdering of historical figures such as Washington, Columbus, Napoleon, and Mohammed, among others, makes these deaths true for him but not historically. The AI in the Library insists they not only survived but performed their prescribed historical role, which can be seen as the individual's predetermined level of social significance regardless of personal desire or action. Brown refers to history as 'subordinating the life of the individual to the historical quest of the species. History is made not by individuals but by groups' (105). Brown's comments on history can be applied not only to historical figures but to Lennox and Hassel as well, as their individual attempts at altering history fail, reinforcing Bester's subversive approach to the 'great men' of history.

The Library's insistence that there is no record of any of Hassel's actions denies Hassel's historical alterations and disregards his personal experience in favour of recorded history. Though it could be argued that, in respect of subjective time, the individual experiencing that time exists in a solipsistic world, meaning their effect on others is irrelevant, the accepted existence of objective time essentially creates forced objectivity of subjective experience. Granted, in this case, Hassel's history is altered from the history of others due to the story's proposed subjective nature of time but Hassel's continued appeals to the Library for validation speaks to the social comfort and belief in the idea of official records holding collective historical truths. Hassel visits Enrico Fermi and asks him whether Marie Curie discovered nuclear fission in 1900. His question causes Fermi to exclaim 'We are the first' (Bester, 'The Men' 167), indicating an assertion in the way time is meant to progress and a denial of Hassel's ability to create an alternate history. James refers to the opinions of professional historians in stating that 'historical change is not a matter of individual decisions but the result of impersonal social and economic developments which cannot be changed or set in a different direction by individuals' (9). Favouring collective history over individual history, this view perhaps explains why Bester may consider individual experience to be overlooked in favour of mass experience. Regarding postwar America, Robert J. Corber comments that 'potentially disruptive stories [...] have been marginalized and repressed because they contradict official representations of the nation's past' (155). The erasure of Hassel's experiences which do not fit the national narrative reflects Corber's assertion and further indicates the individual's inability to enact actual change by reinforcing the social need to ignore subjective experiences which do not fit the objective 'truth'.

Being included in history can be seen as a prerequisite to being included in the history books, or else risk exclusion from social memory. As Lennox states, being wiped from memory, akin to being wiped from the past, means ceasing to exist. This sequence of events is acknowledged when Hassel shoots Fermi and 'awaited arrest and immolation in newspaper files'. Hassel's decision to 'go on record' examines how history functions differently for society than it does for the individual by underscoring the disregard Bester perceives is shown for individual temporal experience in the face of a social construction of history (Bester, 'The Men' 167). In recording history, James acknowledges that 'there cannot be sources for things that never happened' (9). However, the absence of a source does not necessitate the absence of an event, for its source could have been destroyed or forgotten, thereby expunging the event through erasure of associated memory. Pending invention of a time machine or collective omniscience, anything that happens outside one's personal experience could be seen as an existing and continually altering history. History's existence thus depends on the memory of those who experienced it. Even those told about history would only experience it second-hand and would therefore suffer the natural degradation of information through repeated communication. Thus, the further removed one is from the origin point, the more alternate the sense of history. Each step removed from the event itself is therefore destined to be changed in some minute way, making each person's understanding altered. This chain reaction of historical alterations, intentional or otherwise, reflects Bradbury's vision of a subtly altered future in which minor details are changed just enough to establish differing realities. With 'The Men Who Murdered Mohammed' having been written at a time when nuclear annihilation was a possibility, this obsession over being included in the history books reflects the fear of complete erasure from history due to nuclear destruction, as seen in 'Adam and No Eve'. The subsequent creation of a hidden history known only by a select few or none at all reflects the exclusive nature of a collective history which omits individual experience in favour of society as a whole.

With this, individuals are not only separated by their respective timelines, as the story contends, but by history itself. Misremembering past events or forgetting them altogether creates an alternate history of one's memorial past in which they then exist and believe, causing each individual to exist in their own alternate history. With each alternate history being real to the person who exists within it, this can perhaps be seen as a more individual experience of Hugh Everett's 'many-worlds interpretation'. This is indicated within the story by Hassel's memory of the alterations he has committed in his timeline, making them irreversibly true in his reality. Equating memory with history, the story explores ideas of how history is created and the often unintentional, but easily capitalized upon, reliance of the individual's need to be told history in lieu of directly experiencing it.[2]

Bester's approach to time and the individual's place within it in 'The Men Who Murdered Mohammed' argues a natural, partial overlap of the social and the personal but cautions the destructive results of attempting to unite the two as a single entity. The lack of understanding regarding this relationship, according to Bester, would seem to stem from a perceived social ignorance of the beneficial nature of maintaining an individualized, and thus authentic, self. For Bester, the alternate history format demonstrates to the individual (and by extension, the reader) that there is often a need to compromise between individuality – as historically insignificant – and the social/external self – which may not be directly linked to one's personal *self*. Though both selves are required, one should not be sacrificed for the other nor united into a single all-encompassing self. The separation of temporal continuums thus shows the innate nature of the self as operating within, but still individually from, mass society. Since changes in one timeline will not affect another, these changes remain internal and can only be affected by the self, meaning changes of the self and its place in time must be self-mediated. As the narrative tells us, 'Time is a private matter' (Bester, 'The Men' 165). As such, attempts to create an alternate history therefore only lead to altering an individual's personal history. Each person can thus be said to live in a hermetic history of their own creation, unalterable by others and inherently alternate to others, thus exemplifying the separation between individual understanding and social understanding of one's place in time and society.

The increasingly repressive nature of society as Bester saw it throughout the period in which the stories mentioned here were written indicates that even if an individual were allowed to affect history, they would be unable. Bester's protagonists are arguably repressed in some nature by aspects over which they have no control. There then arises the potential correlation between attempts to alter time and this repression. If not repressed, perhaps the protagonist would not feel the overwhelming

---

[2] For additional discussion on the fictionality of history, hidden histories, and how history is socially constructed and consumed, see Derek J. Thiess' chapter in this book on Juan Miguel Aguilera's *La locura de Dios*.

need to change their lot in life. Brown asserts that '[r]epression generates the instinctual compulsion to change [...] the external world' (105). Bester's works contend that, by being repressed in contemporary time, the individual remains repressed in their agency throughout all of time, indicating that this repression is not immediately lifted upon leaving or altering the historical time which itself is repressive. The individual's lack of understanding regarding their place in time and the pressures of conformity perhaps explain why this repression travels with them, as it is internalized via this misunderstanding. As such, no matter when in time an individual may travel, the similarities between time and society as concepts within which the individual exists but remains subservient to is consistently reasserted. This connection further indicates the impact which society has on the individual and reflects how the state of society changes the individual's (in)ability to affect time.

Overall, it is the intertwined nature of the individual and society which Bester is examining and how this relationship impacts the individual's existence in time, often via ideas of conformity. Alternate history in 'The Men Who Murdered Mohammad' thus works by using time to demonstrate just how much agency (or how little) the individual has regarding this relationship. By attempting to break out of historical time, Hassel goes against the social narrative and, instead of managing to assert his individuality, finds himself excluded from, and destroyed by, this very same social narrative. 'The Men Who Murdered Mohammed' is thus, essentially, a failed alternate history. Though Hassel utilizes all of the typical sf tropes to create what should be an alternate history or altered present reality, his ultimate failure reinforces what Bester presents as the repression of individual agency by society. By using the framework of alternate history to examine and expose the individual/social dynamic, Bester is able to portray the unmalleable nature of society by aligning it with the unmalleable nature of time. Despite increasingly extreme attempts, Hassel's failure to enact objective temporal change ultimately depicts the creation of an alternate history as being much harder to accomplish than many of Bester's contemporaries would have readers believe.

References

Bester, Alfred. 'Adam and No Eve'. 1941. *Virtual Unrealities: The Short Fiction of Alfred Bester*. Vintage, 1997, pp. 273–286.
—. 'The Men Who Murdered Mohammed'. 1958. *Virtual Unrealities: The Short Fiction of Alfred Bester*. Vintage, 1997, pp. 159–172.

—. 'Out of this World'. 1964. *Redemolished*. Ed. Richard Raucci. ibooks, 2000, pp. 259–272.

—. 'The Push of a Finger'. 1942. *Redemolished*. Ed. Richard Raucci. ibooks, 2000, pp. 181–237.

Bradbury, Ray. 'A Sound of Thunder'. 1952. *The Golden Apples of the Sun*. Greenwood Press, 1971, pp. 135–50.

Brown, Norman, O. *Life Against Death: The Psychoanalytical Meaning of History*. Wesleyan University Press, 1985.

Corber, Robert, J. *In the Name of National Security: Hitchcock, Homophobia, and the Political Construction of Gender in Postwar America*. Duke University Press, 1993.

Everett, Hugh. '"Relative State" Formulation of Quantum Mechanics'. *Reviews of Modern Physics*, vol. 29, no. 3, 1957, pp. 454–462.

Freud, Sigmund. 'The Dissection of the Psychical Personality'. *The Essentials of Psycho-Analysis*. Trans. James Strachey. Vintage Books, 2005, pp. 484–504.

—. 'The Ego and the Id'. *The Essentials of Psycho-Analysis*, Trans. James Strachey. Vintage Books, 2005, pp. 439–478.

Heinlein, Robert. 'By His Bootstraps'. 1941. *The Menace From Earth*. Corgi, 1973, pp. 49–115.

Hellekson, Karen. 'Towards a Taxonomy of the Alternate History Genre'. *Extrapolation*, vol. 41, no. 3, 2000, pp. 248–255.

James, Edward. 'The Limits of Alternate History'. *Vector: The Critical Journal of the British Science Fiction Association*, no. 254, 2007, pp. 7–10.

Marcuse, Herbert. *Eros and Civilization: A Philosophical Inquiry into Freud*. Routledge, 1998.

Merzbacher, Eugen. *Quantum Mechanics*. 3rd ed. John Wiley & Sons, 1998.

Patterson, Orlando. *Slavery and Social Death: A Comparative Study*. Harvard University Press, 1982.

Wald, Priscilla. 'Science, Technology, and the Environment'. *The Cambridge Companion to American Science Fiction*. Eds. Eric Carl Link and Gerry Canavan. Cambridge University Press, 2015, pp. 179–193.

Wendell, Carolyn. *Alfred Bester*. Wildside Press, 2006.

Between the Alternate and the Apocryphal
Religion and Historic Place in Aguilera's
La locura de Dios

Derek J. Thiess

The typical starting point for theoretical considerations of history and literature, particularly in sf, might best be summed up by Arthur B. Evans in his entry on 'Histories' for *The Oxford Handbook of Science Fiction*:

> History is fiction. Not the events, but the telling of them. From Herodotus to Jules Michelet to Howard Zinn, historians not only chronicle the past, they also invent its meaning. Writing history is not a scientific enterprise ... History, as the word itself implies, always tells a story. (47)

Much of this approach is valid – the process of history making is in fact one of 'making sense' of events and of telling a story. And the linguistic connection between history and story is even starker in the Spanish language where the term for either is the same: *la historia*. But this starting point is arbitrary. An alternate critical timeline of historical theory itself might just as easily begin by asking *why* instead of *if*: why we find it necessary to fictionalize history. What do we make of the impulse to demand the fictional, narrative nature of the past? This is not a popular line of questioning – even less so when one suggests, as this essay will do via a reading of Spanish writer Juan Miguel Aguilera's *La locura de Dios*, that religion plays a significant role in this problematic consensus.

Browsing the racks in a popular bookstore chain (which will remain unnamed) in the southern US reveals an interesting taxonomy. Sections are devoted to literature, to genres such as science fiction and fantasy, and of course a whole range of non-fiction topics. However, the section titled 'History and Religion' might be most striking to the literary critic. It seems this chain has decided not that history is fiction but that history is religion. Ironically, several instances bear this latter claim out – from the first council of Nicaea, to the backlash against the life of Jesus movements in the nineteenth century, and even in the reactions to Dan Brown's *The Da Vinci Code*, there have been clear guidelines, enforced by orthodox consensus, for the writing of certain aspects of history.[1] Yet this equation of history and religion is problematic, particularly when it confronts the theorist's claim that history is also fiction – was not Dan Brown's offence that he fictionalized a very dogmatic history? Within science fiction criticism, too, religion is generally viewed as at least a highly important component of the science fictional landscape and at most as synonymous with sf. Farah Mendlesohn concludes that '[i]n a genre predicated on the thought experiment, theological discourse comes naturally. In a genre dedicated to world-building, recognizing the significance of faith has proven crucial in generating the critical density of the "full" science fiction text' (274–275). Stephen R. L. Clark further examines the relationship between religion and sf noting that '[s]cience fiction, as a religious movement, sometimes exalts just that intellectual conceit, rootless ambition, and contempt for ordinary life and morals that tradition has associated with the Devil' (109). Taken together the idea of these treatments appears to be that science fiction and religion are inextricably linked, in stark contrast to the overt materialism that, in the estimation of such critics, science fiction presupposes.

The nature of this materialism, however, is typically a reference to a simplified secularism, European Enlightenment in the nineteenth century or various movements in the US of the twentieth century. In this formula, scientific explanation lampoons the superstition of religion and treats the religious institution or individual like an alien Other. Elizabeth Small, for example, laments that 'science fiction seems to find Christians as alien as Martians' because the works of Spanish sf writers "come with a great deal of baggage relative to these Spanish authors" cultural experience, which inextricably links the idea of organized religion with Imperial Spain's colonial history, from the Reconquest through the medieval Crusades to the Conquest of the Americas' (33–34). For Small this baggage also applies to Spanish science fiction, including Aguilera's *La locura de Dios*. This novel presents a layered narrative, the frame story beginning in 1348 when a young friar Nicolau Eimeric (based on a historical figure) visits his mentor friar Gerónimo, a former General Inquisitor for the Crown of Aragon, who bestows on Eimeric a scroll containing the testimony of Ramón Llull (also a historical figure) years before the Inquisition. Llull, the so-called Doctor Illuminado who

---

[1] For more on this, see my *Relativism, Alternate History, and the Forgetful Reader* (2014).

has spent his life searching for a scientific demonstration of faith, was once suspected of a 'desviación herética' or a heretical deviation. The terminology here is important. Like the alternate history taking the reader sideways in time – suggesting a spatial element to history much like Wells' fourth dimension – the accusation is of going off (des) the way (via) that is preordained by dogma.

But as Small and other critics displeased with the treatment of religion in sf would point out, this novel complicates matters significantly. The main narrative of the story follows Llull as he is summoned by Roger de Flor (another loosely based historical figure) a powerful nobleman in the court of Constantinople. There Llull discovers a scientific lab left behind by mysterious visitors who came at a crucial moment in history to introduce advanced weaponry that thwarted an invasion of the city. De Flor believes these people were from a distant place, the mythical Ciudad de Preste Juan, a city of gold settled by Christians centuries before (a twist on the Prester John legend), and he charges Llull with leading a group of his warriors on a search for this city. The journey leads them to a city called Apeiron, in a salt desert and made entirely of crystal, with an advanced technological society dedicated to rationalism. In finding the city, however, they also inadvertently alert El Mal, an antagonistic entity attempting to take over the world and whose origins the Apeironitas do not know, to the presence of the city. What ensues is a battle between the warriors and the Apeironitas on one side and the minions of this mysterious evil on the other, which ultimately results in the destruction of both. Llull is one of the few survivors. The novel draws on many subgenres of sf from all over the world, from a rather typical adventure story, or *reiseabenteuer*, to the lost-race fictions of H. Rider Haggard. In its mixture of fiction and actual historical persons and places, however, it draws especially on the apocryphal or 'secret history' and alternate history, creating a space for itself poised somewhere between these genres.

The reason for the novel's hybrid nature has everything to do with its treatment of material and cosmic history. The novel is clearly an adventure story brought about by otherwise undiscovered, apocryphal historical material – from the scroll in the frame narrative to the laboratory in Constantinople to the city of Apeiron itself. That most of this material bears the trappings of scientific rationalism suggests critics are correct about sf's historical ties to deterministic materialism. As Mariano Martín Rodriguez notes regarding such traditional lost-race fictions in the Spanish tradition, they 'tend to emphasize cognitive rather than adventure elements. These narratives focus on what the lost world and its people can teach us about the way evolution and history have *determined* our world' (464, my emphasis). While, again, the novel does not fit neatly into this category, it certainly hints at this kind of materialism. But it also offers an interesting alternate history, in this case a cosmic history in the tradition of alien master-race fictions. When Llull finally confronts El Mal, the creature explains that he is from an older alien race who came to Earth to populate it with the slave species he created. But this alien race is at war and some of its siblings conspired against it, taking one of its slave species and engineering it to multiply and evolve on its own, destroying the other species of El Mal. According to this being's story, humans are this engineered weapon. One might expect critics to focus on this detail, which might have earned its author a charge of heresy two centuries ago, but in our present the inherent materialism of sf draws more attention than this seemingly absurd alternate creation narrative. *La locura* exploits this tension, highlighting the very fragility of materialism in history and its treatment at the hands of religious institution.

Poised between the apocryphal and the alternate, then, a hybrid book such as Aguilera's demands a reconsideration of the relationship between materialism and religion in either history or sf. For all the critic's insistence on religion as an *'open* system' (Clark 96), in contrast to the rigid determinism of the Enlightenment and its inheritors, such criticism often has no problem reifying its own approach. Thus Smart notes an anti-clericalist tendency in sf, inspired by the story of Galileo and the Church, which 'equat[es] organized religion with organized ignorance' (35). To this she responds decisively: 'However, the *real* attitude toward scientific developments was more complex' (35, my emphasis). There is a reality to history, only not this particular one.[2] Which history, then? Who decides what is orthodox? There is an acceptable materialism to history, but there is also clearly unacceptable historical material and it is the latter that must be fictionalized. Dale Knickerbocker has concluded that this novel's 'invocation of and ultimate digression from the classic heroic model, along with the work's mixture of the conventions of various genres and its defamiliarization of recognizable historical, mythological, technological, and biblical elements makes [*La locura*'s] message concerning the conflict between materialist and religious interpretations of reality ambiguous, indeterminate' (45).

The novel is in fact highly complex in its treatment of materialism and religion. As Chloé Germaine Buckley reminds us in the next

---

[2] Of course, with their focus on 'systems' and 'complexity' here, Clarke and Small are operating in a vein of criticism very common among historians of science and religion. For more on this, again please see my prior work.

chapter, an emphasis on materialism does not necessarily indicate a rigid determinism. In fact, the absurd cosmic history of this novel shares a critical kinship with the Lovecraftian tradition of the weird. But perhaps the complexity of Aguilera's novel is precisely the problem for some critics in that it reveals the false dichotomy that is the divide between materialism and religion. When it serves a supposedly higher, transcendent purpose, materialism and religion may coincide. It is only when historical material does not serve this purpose that it must be redacted, must become apocryphal.

Thus, history is fiction when it is unorthodox. But the writer of apocryphal histories and alternate histories, with their didactic tendencies, may reverse this trajectory as Aguilera has done. *La locura* overtly pits historical materialism against religious orthodoxy, and demonstrates the fragility of the former at the hands of the latter, a movement that requires the dissolution of the thin line between materialism and religion. The crystal city of Apeiron, destroyed by the hordes of El Mal's slaves and disappearing into the desert is the very crystalline nature of historical material that must either remain apocryphal itself or face destruction.

La locura is situated from the very first line of the frame narrative in a very clear temporal environment. Thus on 'El cuatro de abril del año de nuestro Señor de mil trescientos cuarenta y ocho, fray Nicolau Eimeric visitó a su maestro, fray Gerónimo, que había enfermado de la Peste' [The fourth of April of our Lord of 1348, friar Nicolau Eimeric visited his master, friar Gerónimo, who had taken ill with the plague] (19). Even if the date means little to the casual reader, there are clear signals regarding the time period. References to the plague, as well as to the *Tribunal de la Santa Inquisición de la Corona de Aragon*, offer temporal landmarks, although it is noteworthy that references to the Crusades are minimal throughout the book – there is much political intrigue and infighting, but organized attempts at the holy land are almost never mentioned. The story is thus situated in a turbulent time of change, poised between the Crusades (which seem to be a distant memory) and the coming power of the more localized Inquisition that would sweep over Spain a century later, as well as the imminent threat of the Black Death. In the midst of this seemingly chaotic time, however, the level of detail perhaps stands out the most, the fact that there are such precise historical records. This is an initial reference to material history as next to Gerónimo's bed lies a chest 'lleno de rollos de pergamino y un montón de legajos' [full of rolls of parchment and a mountain of files] that he had been reading on his death bed (19). Almost the entirety of the book is the relation of one of these scrolls, the meticulous recording of the testimony of Ramón Llull before the Inquisition of Aragon.

However, it is also important that this particular scroll is clearly apocryphal. Although Nicolau has just completed a two-year study of the life and works of Ramón Llull, he 'desconocía que tal investigación hubiese sido nunca llevada' [did not know that such an investigation had ever been carried out] (23). Not only does this situation place the story within the apocryphal or 'secret history' genre, but also complicates the simple equation of sf with materialism against the 'open process' of religion. The Church in this story is very much in control of the flow of history, forward or sideways, and it exerts this control through not merely the physical recording of history, but also the redaction of this history. This text issues a direct challenge in the first few pages: how can an 'open system', opposed to deterministic materialism, exert so much control in keeping certain physical and intellectual materials apokryphos, that is 'secret' or 'non-canonical'? The covert irony of the situation is that the institution aligned with the transcendent and ethereal should travel so much with what amounts to gall ink scrolled on stretched animal skins. But as Susan Spencer reminds us, the power to direct received wisdom, essentially to control history, in the Middle Ages 'comes down to a situation of who has the vellum' (339). For this reason, the Church carefully directs the material of history, and it is likewise for this reason that this story really begins on a stretched animal hide in a chest at Gerónimo's bedside. But time and history collide with physical objects within distinct physical spaces in this novel in ways that defy the control of the transcendent.

In fact, this novel greatly emphasizes the alignment of historical place – that is, of physical buildings –and the material creation of history beyond the parchment. Llull's narration begins in a haze as 'El Palacio de Constantinopla tenia la brutal suntuosidad de una alucinación' [The Palace of Constantinople had the brutal sumptuousness of a hallucination] (29). However, it also very quickly comes into focus as Llull is led into a secret chamber, hidden in the bowels of the palace, where he will meet Roger de Flor. On his way down, however, the novel offers some insight into the connection for Llull between time, physical place and history as he notes an inscription carved into the stone above an arch: 'Tú has respondido a los que te han llamado [...] Y ellos conocen bien la utilidad de tus cálculos' [You have responded to those who have called you [...] And they know well the usefulness of your calculations] (31). But Llull's reaction is even more important: 'Sentí un estremecimiento que recorría todo mi cuerpo; como si aquellas palabras tocaran alguna profunda fibra de mi alma [...] como si el desconocido autor de aquellas frases, muerto quizá siglos atrás, me hablara desde la distancia del tiempo' [I felt a shiver run over my entire body; as if those words touched some deep fibre of my soul [...] as if the unknown author of those sentences, dead perhaps centuries ago, spoke to me from the distance of time] (31). This passage also speaks to the physical effects of this place-history on the body of the individual who encounters it, who lives it; the following sections will examine that connection in more detail. For now, it is important that, unlike the parchment within its chest, written history and the physical container that enfolds it in this case are one and the same. Ramón feels the inscription is speaking to him, but as he discovers the laboratory erected by the mysterious saviours of Constantinople led by one named Calínico, the inscription may just as easily indicate these prior scientists. History is literally inscribed on the walls of the palace – the parchment is the chest.

This connection of physical place and history is upheld again in the laboratory itself, where Llull first meets Roger de Flor, who commands him to lead an expedition to find the lost city of Preste Juan. The history of Calínico is again inscribed on the lab equipment left behind, all except for the location of his origin. This location Llull must discern from what he knows about the routes travelled in ancient history and using his considerable deductive rationalism. In all of these travels, which continue to take the group east, the narrative forges an ever-stronger connection between place, whether landscape or building, and history and memory. First, travelling through Artaki in eastern Greece the domesticated landscape reminds Llull that 'La Historia se repetía' [History repeats itself] (52). The group continues east, Llull narrating the cities of historical and biblical importance. He concludes that 'Aquellas tierras nos recordarían durante muchos años' [Those lands would remember us for many years] (79). The linkage of memory, history and physical space in these passages is evident and serves to indicate a materialism every bit as ironic as the apocryphal scroll that began the story. These biblical sites (such as Mt Ararat) are acceptable histories, acceptable memories for Llull whose philosophy he repeatedly reminds us is that 'Dios es la primera razón de todas las cosas ... pero se sirve de los mecanismos de la naturaleza para ejecutar sus obras' [God is the first principle of all things ... but he makes use of the mechanisms of the natural world in order to carry out his works] (109). There is an acceptable place-history that may be recalled, but there is also an apocryphal one, and it is the apocryphal that allows this narrative to proceed. What is up until this point a merely fictional retelling of mythic history becomes apocryphal with the discovery, once again, of secret knowledge.

In these eastern lands, the group finds themselves in continually greater danger, surrounded by hostile forces that Llull associates with the biblical Gog and Magog. At the same time, they uncover an otherwise unknown history, even in the middle of familiar landmarks. Near the biblical city of Harran, they come upon the ruins of a temple, where 'Un grupo de siete edificios de piedra en ruinas parecían contemplarnos como centinelas petrificadas' [A group of seven stone buildings in ruins seemed to contemplate us like petrified sentinels] (82). But within that temple they find another message from this mythical Callinicus (a reference to Callinicus Heliopolis, an architect from the seventh century believed to have invented Greek fire), again carved into stone. This inscription calls Callinicus the son of Aristarchus, a reference to Aristarchus of Samos, an ancient Greek normally attributed the first heliocentric theory of the universe and even in his time, according to the novel, persecuted for it. Llull sympathizes with this latter figure, though he knows heliocentrism to be false, because 'Yo también había sufrido situaciones semejantes y mis argumentos dialécticos habían sido respondidos con piedras, lo que me había obligado a correr para salvar mi vida, sobreviviendo en ocasiones con graves heridas en mi cuerpo' [I also had suffered similar situations and my dialectic arguments had been met with stones, which had forced me to run in order to save my life, surviving sometimes with grave wounds on my body] (88). The apocryphal history here gives expression to the overt materialism of history: anthropomorphized buildings that guard a history carved into its very walls, a history that again calls to mind the suffering of the material body of the one reading it.

The apocryphal in this instance refuses to remain secret and non-canonical – the essence of the apocryphal history is that the secret history will be uncovered. This novel equates this kind of history to material history, and even intimates that this materialism is related in some way to the bodies of those that consume them. But the story becomes even stranger as the travellers begin to encounter otherwise unknown peoples. The presence of other places, and especially of *competing histories*, take this novel beyond the merely apocryphal and threaten to lead the reader to aporia.

The novel takes a Manichaean turn, even as it begins to blend the apocryphal with the alternate. Just before the group finds the city of Apeiron, Llull is kidnapped by the people he takes to be the biblical Gog. In the midst of some kind of ritual, presided over by a tribal chieftain and a heretic Nestorian priest, a strange creature resembling a scorpion stings him in the neck. This wound gets gradually worse, growing a mass under the skin that causes pain and hallucinations until he eventually falls unconscious just before they are found by a steam-powered airship from Apeiron and brought to the city. Llull is therefore semi-conscious when he first views the city, but he equates it, with its fine crystalline architecture, to the City of God. This architecture stands out in distinct contrast to all that before it. It is not the hard stone of the apocryphal laboratory or temple but more delicate and refined. Llull observes that:

> Toda la ciudad parecía estar hecha de cristal ... combinando el blanco traslúcido con el cristal tan fino como encaje, pero lo suficientemente resistente como para permitir que los edificios alcanzasen la altura de las más altas catedrales que yo hubiera visto nunca. [The entire city was made of crystal ... combining translucent white with crystal as fine as lace, but strong enough to allow the buildings to reach the height of the tallest cathedrals I had ever seen]. (171)

This architecture, unlike the vulgar and apocryphal stone of even the palace of Constantinople is equated to the sacred city of God. From this moment on, the story becomes seemingly a battle between good and evil.

The city is under attack from the same forces that kidnapped Llull, led by the mysterious El Mal. When he wakes in the city, he finds they have removed the mass in his neck, or what they call a 'Rexinoos ... La piedra de la locura; aquel que corrompe el alma' [Rexinoos ... The stone of madness; that which corrupts the soul] (175, original emphasis). The stone here, again equated with the vulgar and the bodily, is aligned with the evil that threatens the city of God, and once again the story that the stone tells is what moves this narrative forward. This rexinoos is a biological weapon that allows El Mal to take control of people's minds. The Apeironitas remove the mass before it may do so to Llull, but not before it communicates the location of the crystal city to its enemies. Thus, the apocryphal again, the stone hidden inside Llull's body, leads them to yet another new land, this time in search of El Mal, whom they seek to destroy before its forces attack the city. They trace this mysterious entity to the remote north, into a deep cavern reminiscent of the tiered cave of Dante's Inferno, and it is here – again in a place carved into stone – that the reader is introduced to an alternate cosmic history. El Mal claims not to be a demon, as Llull believes, or from another planet, as the Apeironitas believe, but rather of a race from the stars and as old as creation. This warring race conspired against El Mal, confining it to earth and creating a modified race of Gog (its slaves) to revolt against it – humanity. The secret history of humankind is an evolutionary perversion of the creation of an alien master race, or as

El Mal puts it, 'Erais parte de mi carne y de mi sangre, pero al igual que un cáncer; no obedecíais mis ordenes' [You were part of my flesh and my blood, but like a cancer; you did not obey my orders] (349). El Mal is destroyed just after offering this alternate history, but not before threatening a final revenge on humanity – a plague that would kill the entire world.

The competing materialism of the stone within Llull's body – that is, the contrast that it draws to the fine architecture of Apeiron – and the history revealed in the final moments of the novel provide direct challenges to the theistic rationalism shared by Llull and the people of Apeiron. There is no apparent reason, no fulfilment of scripture, to the *rexinoos*, only an invasion of corporeal materialism. In fact, in the end Llull goes to find help for the city under siege unsuccessfully and does not learn of the fate of the city until much later, foreshadowing the very premise of the novel that it is a suppressed and secret history rather than the apotheosis of reason that Llull longs for throughout. There is a sense that some may have escaped to spread the city's advancements throughout the world and prepare for future threats (El Mal was perhaps not destroyed but only gravely injured, waiting to return for a final battle), but the narrative does not devolve into aporia after the manner of Lovecraft's fictions. However, the alternate historical elements of the novel are also somewhat undone by the return of the apocryphal in the frame narrative. At the end of the story, friar Eimeric concludes that Llull's story is a work of evil and orders it destroyed before anyone else can read it. The entirety of the testimony, the bulk of this story, it is declared, is not merely apocryphal, but evil and worthy of destruction.

What do we take from this strange interplay of the apocryphal and the alternate? The confluence that most stands out is perhaps the similar material destruction of the parchment that contains the story and the crystal city itself. Throughout the novel physical space and written history have come together to signal precisely the kind of rigid materialism that critics suggest epitomizes sf, against religious openness. Moreover, both the city of Apeiron and the cave of El Mal suggest possible alternate timelines, both the secret history of humanity already mentioned and a possible future if Apeiron starts to interact with the world. Several times throughout the novel, Llull considers a counterfactual: 'Una vez más, me pregunté cuánto dolor y sufrimiento podría evitarse la humanidad si la ciencia de Apeiron fuera conocida por todos' [Once more, I asked myself how much pain and suffering could humanity avoid if Apeiron's science were known by all] (253). In the manner of L. Sprague de Camp's *Lest Darkness Fall* (1941), Aguilera's text suggests that the discovery of this fictional city is a possible nexus point, from which the ensuing 'dark ages' might be avoided. But the city is entirely destroyed, as is the scroll that contains its story. Perhaps, the city being fictional, its destruction has no repercussions beyond this novel. But what of the scroll's destruction? Is there not a 'real world' corollary to this kind of destruction of historical documents – because, after all, histories are merely fictional – in the censorial measures taken by certain communities, particularly those acting in the name of religion?

One important lesson this novel demonstrates is that there appear to be limits upon the alternate histories that one may write or read and which must remain apocryphal. History may in fact contain elements of fiction. Likewise, the alternate history may offer 'a critique of the metaphors we use to discuss history [... and] foreground the "construct-edness" of history and the role narrative plays in this construction' (Hellekson 5). However, as has become clear in this analysis, history may be constructed, but external forces play an active role in making certain constructions normative, even orthodox. Or perhaps it is fairer to say that there is often a tendency toward a universalized perspective that will seek to maintain itself. Hence the apocryphal history stands as a stark reminder that there are competing histories, and some deemed unacceptable histories, and one is not free merely to construct as one wishes. Like Adam Roberts' chapter early in this volume, this reading complicates the notion that alternate history 'styles "man" as possessing the sublime power to bend history and society around him' (39). The apocryphal history is about the *careful control of acceptable alternatives*. Religion complicates this matter even more – it is acceptable to criticize the universalizing of, for example, a white, male, western, historian's perspective, but far less acceptable to criticize a perspective based on religion (as a protected component of intersectional identity). Thus the strands of criticism that deal with religion in sf may openly adopt an apologetic stance and suggest that 'science fiction seems well suited to the needs and fantasies of an irreligious age, easily persuaded that there are no *transcendent* purposes ... But there are other ways of thinking of science fiction, and other ways of thinking about religion' (Clark 98). What *La locura* accomplishes, however, is to bring much needed attention to the creation of apocryphal history, which is after all the censorship, sometimes the wanton destruction, of an otherwise acceptable alternate history.

The material history that supposedly 'irreligious' sf embodies is therefore not as solid as it first seemed. The linkage of physical place with written history in this novel suggests that either are subject to external control and destruction, especially the crystalline city of Apeiron and the animal hide on which its history is inscribed. This linkage presents a challenge, too, to that strand of criticism and theory that would easily liken history to fiction, from Linda Hutcheon to Beverley Southgate, in that this criticism conspicuously fails to question the redaction of that fiction.[3] What makes one alternate acceptable and the other apocryphal? In the absence of considering such questions, something that ought to give us pause has happened in this so-called 'cultural–historical turn'. Llull even cites Augustine at one point that 'La providencia divina conduce la Historia de la humanidad como si se tratara de la historia de un solo individuo que se desarrolla gradualmente desde la infancia hasta la vejez' [Divine providence drives the history of humanity as if it concerned the history of a single individual that developed gradually from infancy to old age] (204). Parts of this passage sound much like the very positive aims of cultural history – to privilege the ordinary, the everyday person, even to consider underrepresented perspectives. But there is also an interesting return to God as the prime mover of history that one might argue appears in a great deal of critical theory in history and literature as well. And this formula may justify much redaction, the making apocryphal of a parchment, a city, or even that 'single individual'.

There is a claim in the above paragraph beyond the scope of the proof offered here – that there is something Augustinian hiding within the social-cultural or narrative turns in history, a new kind of orthodoxy in a return to God as prime mover of history. This assertion is not meant to be universal, it merely suggests that counterfactual histories of many kinds are easily co-opted by a strand of criticism seeking to reinvest history with a sense of religious transcendence, to put history and religion on the same bookshelf. Aguilera's novel both reflects this tendency and offers a surprisingly self-reflective criticism, not only in the figurative destruction of the very fragile material history at the hands of religious institutions, but also in the stakes of that destruction. There are repeated references to bodies throughout this story – and one must not forget that the story itself is printed upon the dead body of an animal. Moreover, these references are almost always related in some way to historic place and written history. The novel drives home the intrinsic materiality of history in the forms not just of buildings and structures, but human bodies as well, hosts as they are to their own histories. And perhaps most demonstrative, when Llull is entering the cave of El Mal to receive the cosmic history he 'sentí como si caminara por el interior de un enorme útero, un pensamiento repugnante que me inmovilizó'

---

[3] See Hutcheons's *Poetics of Postmodernity* (1998) and Southgate's *History Meets Fiction* (2009).

[felt as if I were walking through the interior of an enormous uterus, a repugnant thought that immobilized me] (344). The connection established in this novel is not merely between place and history, but between history and those that live it, the human body itself being the vessel that carries that history forward.[4] The redaction, the making apocryphal, of history, may not be merely history's destruction but the destruction of the human body as well.

One might suggest that the control of history – that is, the limitation of alternate possibilities through the creation of the apocryphal – reflects the control of bodies themselves. Clark once again offers an interesting suggestion that certain elements of sf reflect an overt religiosity, in particular referencing posthumanists (i.e. those who dream of being uploaded into cyberspace or cryogenically frozen). He offers a warning of such people that we 'know what people who profess to despise the flesh – that is, to think the flesh unimportant – often do, unless they are very carefully educated and controlled' (108). One must wonder at the kind of control recommended in this case. How ought we to regulate the bodies of others? This 'control' is only another kind of redaction, the control of an individual history. This kind of control ought to be resisted, though the intent here is not necessarily to validate such posthuman dreaming either. What *La locura* teaches is that even history, whose interpretation appears to be so free and limitless because it is socially constructed and consumed, deals with material that defies that construction. This material may be fragile, as a crystal city or as the human body itself, but that is because that material *is* the human body itself, and for that very reason must not be dissolved in social theory that seeks to make a peaceful network of history, literature, and religion. Clark's equation of posthumanism and religion (i.e. the transcendent) might alternately be seen as a condemnation of both when '[t]echnological visions of a post-embodied future are merely fantasies about transcending the material realm of social responsibility [...] The ability to construct the body as passé is a position available only to those privileged to think of their (white, male, straight, non-working class) bodies as the norm' (Vint 8). A materialism, even a historical materialism, that links to the human body must now be central to our greater social responsibility – so that those non-normative bodies are not lost.

---

[4] Clearly, this chapter also mostly sets aside questions of colonialism, and also gender, race and other intersectional identities in this novel. That is not meant to give them short shrift, but merely to maintain a focus on religion and place. For more on relationship of embodiment (including gender and age) and material history see my 'Bodies That Remember'.

This may, once again, seem a strange argument – that the very narrative cultural–historical turn that gave rise to world history and the reconsideration of the canon of 'Western' literature has created its own exclusions. But the assertion that history is fiction, that it is narrative and socially constructed is itself a narrative construction and it is not a politically neutral assertion. What it *is*, however, is almost entirely devoid of bodies and losing a sense of embodied immediacy has consequences. To take Ta-Nehisi Coates slightly out of context:

> [A]ll our phrasing – *race relations, racial chasm, racial justice, racial profiling, white privilege,* even *white supremacy* – serves to obscure that racism is a visceral experience, that it dislodges brains, blocks airways, rips muscle, extracts organs, cracks bones, breaks teeth. You must never look away from this. You must always remember that the sociology, the history, the economics, the graphs, the charts, the regressions all land, with great violence, upon the body. (n.p.)

While the critique of religion does not currently enjoy the same popularity as that of 'race relations', the social turn in history is just as linked to the charts, and the graphs of the sociologist or the anthropologist and it is worth remembering that '[r]eligion was perhaps the most ancient organizing concept in the emergence of anthropology as a discipline' (Jameson 95). The push toward the transcendent in history or literary theory, like the push toward a universal terminology in race theory, is a push past embodied, lived experience.

This realm of pure social theory, devoid of bodies, is not a position from which to ethically approach the past, or the present or future. What science fiction has allowed us to do is to explore this realm in safety. Alternate histories have the potential to explore limitless possibilities. As Hellekson aptly reminds us, they revel in the indeterminacies of history. Apocryphal histories, on the other hand, remind us that there are external limits upon our free-play with history. They continually demonstrate that this play is, in fact, not free but constrained both by the political and the material. In a novel like Aguilera's, which combines elements of both the alternate history and the apocryphal history, one finds a reminder that the material is always present. From the parchments of written histories to the buildings and geographies that contain them and finally to the human bodies that lived those histories, the alternate and the apocryphal remind us that the clarion call to read history as fiction may also hide an apologetic for the control of that history and of those bodies.

References

Aguilera, Juan Miguel. *La locura de Dios*. Grupo Zeta, 1998.

Clark, Stephen R. L. 'Science Fiction and Religion'. *A Companion to Science Fiction*. Ed. David Seed. Blackwell, 2005, pp. 95–110.

Coates, Ta-Nehisi. 'Letter to my Son'. *The Atlantic*. 4 July 2015.

Evans, Arthur B. 'Histories'. *The Oxford Handbook of Science Fiction*. Ed. Rob Latham. Oxford University Press, 2014.

Hellekson, Karen. *The Alternate History: Refiguring Historical Time*. Kent State University Press, 2000.

Hutcheon, Linda. *A Poetics of Postmodernity: History, Theory, Fiction*. Routledge, 1998.

Jameson, Fredric. *Archaeologies of the Future: The Desire Called Utopia and Other Science Fictions*. Verso, 2005.

Knickerbocker, Dale. 'Science, Religion, and Indeterminacy in Juan Miguel Aguilera's *La locura de Dios (The Folly of God)*'. *Foundation: The International Review of Science Fiction*, no. 37, 2008, pp. 30–47.

Mendlesohn, Farah. 'Religion and Science Fiction'. *The Cambridge Companion to Science Fiction*. Eds. Edward James and Farah Mendlesohn. Cambridge University Press, 2003, pp. 264–275.

Rodríguez, Mariano Martín. 'Longing for the Empire? Modernist Lost-Race Fictions and the Dystopian Mode in Spain'. *Science Fiction Studies*, no. 40, 2013, pp. 463–479.

Small, Elizabeth. 'Religious Institutions in Spanish Science Fiction'. *Science Fiction Studies*, no. 28, 2001, pp. 33–48.

Southgate, Beverley. *History Meets Fiction*. Longman/Pearson, 2009.

Spencer, Susan. 'The Post-Apocalyptic Library: Oral and Literate Culture in *Fahrenheit 451* and *A Canticle for Leibowitz*'. *Extrapolation*, no. 32, 1991, pp. 331–342.

Thiess, Derek J. 'Bodies That Remember: Historical Revision and Embodied Age in Joan Slonczewski's *Children Star* and *Brain Plague*'. *Science Fiction Studies*, no. 44, 2017, pp. 137–158.

—. *Relativism, Alternate History, and the Forgetful Reader: Reading Science Fiction and Historiography*. Lexington Books, 2014.

Vint, Sherryl. *Bodies of Tomorrow: Technology, Subjectivity, Science Fiction*. University of Toronto Press, 2007.

Weird History / Weird Knowledge
H. P. Lovecraft versus Sherlock Holmes in Shadows Over Baker Street

Chloé Germaine Buckley

The 2003 short story collection, *Shadows Over Baker Street*, featuring eighteen stories by writers such as Neil Gaiman, Brian Stableford, and Barbara Hambly, is just one example of a postmillennial resurgence of Weird writing. This horror collection offers a selection of alternate Sherlock Holmes tales by contemporary writers, pitting the master of rational scientific enquiry against the terrifying monsters of H. P. Lovecraft's mythos. In so doing, *Shadows Over Baker Street* makes a contribution to current debates about belief and knowledge, revising dominant ideas about the relationship between human perception and the material world. The stories put forward a double alternate, or 'secret', history. First, they partake of a tradition in Weird fiction of revising the history of human civilization to reveal aeons-old monsters from beyond the stars. Second, they rewrite the fictional history of Sherlock Holmes, inserting him into this Weird ontology. The collection thus draws on two modes of writing, detective fiction and Weird horror, and the contest between the two is unsettling. Typically, Sherlock Holmes stories shore up faith in modern systems of scientific and rational enquiry. In contrast, Weird horror disrupts Enlightenment and scientific narratives about knowledge in its suggestion that everything we know about the world is wrong. In a reversal of the usual Holmesian narrative, the stories in *Shadows Over Baker Street* encourage their readers not only to suspend their disbelief, but to surrender their faith in rational systems of thought. Holmes battles with phenomena he can never hope to understand, but in which belief is undeniable. In pitting rational disbelief against Weird speculation, the collection asks its readers to surrender to a Weird ontology. This ontology is resolutely material rather than supernatural, but it refuses to be quantified or represented by scientific modes of knowledge.

The Weird is a form of fantastic horror fiction that posits the existence of indescribable alien monsters and overturns traditional histories of human civilization. It aims to produce ontological and epistemological horror in its depiction of insignificant humanity within the cosmos. The narrator of H. P. Lovecraft's short story, 'The Colour out of Space' (1927) suggests this cosmicism as he ponders 'unformed realms of infinity [...] whose mere existence stuns the brain and numbs us with the black extra-cosmic gulf it throws open before our frenzied eyes' (Lovecraft, 'The Colour Out of Space' 199). Associated with Lovecraft, the Weird crystallized in the 1920s in pulp publications such as *Weird Tales* magazine (1923–1954). Despite gaining little critical acclaim for many decades, post millennium the Weird proliferates through literature, popular culture, and critical thought. Critical interest in Weird fiction was inaugurated by S. T. Joshi's scholarly account, *The Weird Tale* (1990) and interest remains keen in a recent edited collection titled *The Age of Lovecraft* (2016), compiled by Sederholm and Weinstock. Creative writers continue to find inspiration in Lovecraft and references to the Weird abound in popular culture. From an appearance by Cthulhu in the irreverent animated comedy *South Park* (2010) to the *King in Yellow* inspired HBO series *True Detective* (2014), the Weird has emerged from the realms of pulp fiction into the mainstream. Moreover, the Weird has found a place in contemporary philosophy. The recent 'speculative turn' of thinkers such as Graham Harman take inspiration from Lovecraft's fiction.

This contemporary and postmillennial resurgence of interest in the Weird across many different modes has come about precisely because of the form's capacity to prompt epistemological horror and because of its concomitant proposal of alternative modes of knowledge to those that have dominated Western thought and culture since the Enlightenment. In this sense, the Weird is kin to the alternate history, since both are heirs to the Fantastic and aim to create moments of 'estrangement' (Hellekson 3). The principal mode of conceiving of knowledge in post-Enlightenment Western culture is a form of disbelief informed by the strategy of inductive reasoning used in scientific enquiry. Religious thinkers have long noted the post-Enlightenment shift away from belief as a mode of knowledge. Theologian William Desmond, for example, argues that 'modern thought claims to begin anew with doubting, not with believing' (12). Desmond identifies the shift in thought promoted by Enlightenment ideology, that is, from belief, which is often characterized as superstition or irrationality, to the doubt and disbelief central to Enlightenment modes of rational enquiry. Whilst challenges have been mounted against this shift, notably by the postmodern deconstruction of Enlightenment grand narratives, its influence remains powerful. In modern secular societies, deference is given to inductive scientific reasoning and to a technologically focused iteration of the Enlightenment narrative of progress. In Western culture this has voiced itself most vociferously in so-called 'New Atheism', whose proponents include Richard Dawkins, Christopher Hitchens, and Sam Harris. New Atheism is particularly dismissive of 'irrational' modes of knowledge founded on belief, from folk psychology to mainstream religions. Dawkins argues that 'we cannot, of course, disprove God, just as we cannot disprove Thor, fairies, leprechauns and the Flying Spaghetti Monster. But, like those other fantasies [...] we can say that God is very, very improbable' (Dawkins n.p.). For Dawkins there is no room for belief, which is reframed as 'delusion'. Read in this context, the postmillennial resurgence of the Weird is part of a counter reaction, a post secular 'turn', which includes the resurgence of religious belief as well as an increasing proliferation of speculative fictions that eschew Enlightenment rationality for the Gothic, the Fantastic, or the Supernatural. The current cultural moment is characterized by a conflict between works espousing rational (or 'scientific') disbelief on the one hand and works of speculation on the other.

The Weird makes a particular intervention in this dialogue about belief and knowledge since it is a speculative mode, evoking terrified awe in the creatures and 'gods' it depicts, but also a materialist mode since these 'gods' and monsters are emphatically creatures of matter and substance. As Michel Houellebecq states, Lovecraft's fiction is 'rigorously material' even if the creatures and landscapes he describes seem beyond the understanding of human perception (32). Hence, Weird fiction's appeal to contemporary philosophy's speculative realists. Meillassoux's *After Finitude* (2008), which inaugurated this strand of philosophy, seeks to account for materiality outside human perception thus to know something about the universe beyond what he characterizes as the impasse of Kantian 'correlationism' (5). That is, Meillassoux seeks to get beyond the formulation that knowledge of the world (or, even, the world itself) is only ever the human idea or perception of it. In this endeavour, he exhorts philosophy to be more like empirical science in its acceptance of objects of the material world that lie outside human perception, such as ancestral events and substances dating back to before life on earth (9). Yet, such dealings with objects are necessarily speculative in that they demand a belief in a material world that is not verifiable through human perception. Weird fiction's combination of speculation with absolute materialism provides a fertile imaginative space in which to explore these tensions in modern thought.

Graham Harman's writing on speculative realism directly engages with Lovecraft's fiction in its attempt to account for this world outside human perception. This mode of philosophy follows in the steps of the Lovecraftian protagonist seeking knowledge beyond human understanding:

> What do we know of the world and the universe about us? Our means of receiving impressions are absurdly few, and our notions of surrounding objects infinitely narrow. We see things only as we are constructed to see them, and can gain no idea of their absolute nature. (Lovecraft, 'From Beyond' n.p.)

In Lovecraft's story, searching 'beyond' reveals a sinister universe inhabited by predatory creatures. Harman's speculations reveal not monsters, but ways to know reality differently. For Harman, it is not that there is another realm beyond reality, but that reality is itself made up of 'weird substances with a taste of the uncanny about them, rather than stiff blocks of simplistic physical matter' (Harman, 'On the Horror of Phenomenology' 347). This philosophical enquiry does not represent the impossibility of knowledge, which is how Lovecraft's works have been read, but combine a spirit of enquiry engendered by the Enlightenment and empirical science with belief in aspects of reality that lie outside the purview of human perception. Reality is Weird because it 'is incommensurable with any attempt to represent or measure it' (Harman, *Weird Realism* 51). Knowledge of reality is not possible directly, but indirect contact of the kind proposed in Lovecraft's writing requires belief before it will produce knowledge.

At the popular end of the cultural spectrum, Weird fiction expresses an enthusiasm for the espousal of outlandish beliefs that fly in the face of rational science and traditional religion. Fans evoke Lovecraft's terrifying pantheon of gods and monsters in a playful and gleeful rehearsal of belief in the unbelievable. Enthusiastic depictions of Cthulhu, for example, appear in numerous adaptations of Lovecraft's mythos and in playful fan fiction homages. Examples include fake religious tract comics available online, which evangelize about the 'great old Ones' for uninitiated readers. A wide-eyed wizard in 'Why We're Here' tells an incredulous neighbour that 'everything you've been told by everybody is a lie [...] *Especially* in school' [sic] as giant tentacles reach towards the earth through space (Ellis and Van Lente n.p.). Whether philosophical or comical, the Weird in contemporary culture expresses an enthusiasm for belief and awe in forces beyond human understanding, but which are nonetheless of this world rather than of a supernatural origin. The Weird thus suggests a world beyond human understanding, outside the purview of inductive scientific reasoning, which requires belief even as it resists knowledge.

One of the ways in which Weird fiction proposes its alternative mode of knowledge, and so prompts *epistemological* horror, is by giving what critics have termed a 'secret history' of the world. Typically, secret histories tell stories that have supposedly been suppressed, forgotten, or ignored. In the case of Weird fiction, this secret history is both human and geological. As Joshi notes, the Weird suggests that '*more* things have happened in history than we suspect' (Joshi 194, emphasis in original). Lovecraft's protagonists discover events and personages expunged from accepted history, or find evidence of cataclysmic geological events not accounted for by conventional science. Both types of insertions into history reveal the insignificance of human civilization. This 'secret history' mechanism of the Weird contributes to its underlying epistemological pessimism and its materialism. Though more things have happened in history than suspected, these things are material in nature, even if man is unable to make sense of them. Thus, the Weird secret history directly counters Enlightenment ideology and scientific enquiry, which position man as central in the quest for knowledge.

The mode of revelation employed in Weird fiction likewise poses a challenge to Enlightenment narratives. Not only is *what* we know wrong, but *how* we know what we know is wrong. Knowledge is not the result of a historical accumulation of data inexorably bringing the human perceiver closer to the truth about the world, but a single moment of horrified realization that recasts all prior knowledge as delusion. In *Shadows Over Baker Street* secret histories are proposed for principal characters (as in James Lowder's 'The Weeping Masks'), or else stories retroactively place accounts within the Holmes canon (a visit to New York City, for example, in Steve Perry's 'The Case of the Wavy Black Dagger'), or reasons are given as to why events have only now come to light (as in Watson's belated recount in Barbara Hambly's 'The Adventure of the Antiquarian's Niece'). In Neil Gaiman's story, 'A Study in Emerald', the entire history of Holmes's Victorian Britain is rewritten to incorporate the emergence of Weird Gods and their rise to power in human civilization. This latter story, in particular, evokes the alternate history mode because it proposes a very different materiality as well as an alternate political history. As Karen Hellekson argues, 'instead of strictly historical events, alternate histories [...] may also play with what we consider fundamental truths: the existence of fixed physical laws or rules that govern such sciences as cosmology or physics' (50). This disruption of accepted physical laws destabilizes the detective's attempts to 'deduce' knowledge from material evidence.

Shadows Over Baker Street's secret history of Sherlock Holmes disrupts the usual operations of detective fiction, which works to shore up late Victorian readers' faith in a system of rational enquiry and the bourgeois social order that notions of rationality underwrite. Stephen Knight states that the Holmes stories in their original incarnation offered a comforting 'materialistic model' of epistemology, 'which can read off from physical data what has happened and what will happen' (74). Material causation and linear history support one another in Conan Doyle's narratives, which uncover, via Holmes' certainty that his rational deductions will prevail, and establish a clear chain of events and a criminal perpetrator. A material scientist as well as detective, Holmes epitomizes the Enlightenment ideal of man as master of knowledge. In contrast, Lovecraft's protagonists cannot make sense of the information they uncover. Though many describe themselves as men of science, they wish they had remained on their 'placid island of ignorance' (Lovecraft, 'The Call of Cthulhu' 47). In Lovecraft's narratives, epistemological horror (realizing the error in human knowledge) leads to ontological horror (the revelation of a cosmic numinous). Thus, the Weird story already contains within it the opposing tensions of the detective story on the one hand and the science fiction genre on the other. In Brian McHale's *Postmodernist Fiction* (1987), the detective story is the epistemological genre par excellence in that it takes as its theme the accessibility and circulation of knowledge (9). In contrast, the science fiction story, which posits a possible world and aims at ontological estrangement, is the ontological genre par excellence (McHale 59). The Weird partakes in a little of both, building on the Victorian detective story and anticipating the science fiction writing of the mid-twentieth century, with the investigator protagonist uncovering not the details of a crime, but the clues as to the existence of another universe. In this way, the Weird stages a horrifying disruption to the process of how we know. *Shadows Over Baker Street* thematically foregrounds this disruption, placing the Weird in dialogue with the epistemological certainty of detective fiction.

The first story in the collection is Neil Gaiman's unique contribution, 'A Study in Emerald'. This story not only rewrites the Holmes canon, but also the history of nineteenth-century Europe, imagining the ascension of the Great Old Ones 'seven hundred years before our modern times' (Gaiman 14). The story returns to the beginning of the Holmes timeline, rewriting the familiar elements of the first case for the Afghanistan war veteran with the consulting detective. Gaiman transposes familiar details into an enWeirded setting, in which the Great Old Ones have radically changed social, political, and physical landscapes. The moon, the narrator notes, is a 'comforting crimson' and Queen Victoria is a huge, indescribable, lumpen God who 'squatted in the shadows' (15, 11). Though there is a twist relating to the identity of the narrator (a medical doctor) and his consulting detective companion, many details from the original Conan Doyle 'A Study in Scarlet' (1887) remain. Holmes' methods follow the pattern familiar to readers from the original: he examines the word 'Rache' scrawled on the wall and from its position and composition 'deduces' the identity of the killer. Yet, despite these procedural similarities, 'A Study in Emerald' uses an enWeirded Victorian London to undermine the epistemological basis for the detective's rational deductive reasoning.

The Weird universe changes the premises of Holmes' 'deductions' since it offers a radically different material basis from that of the original story. Gaiman denotes this material difference by the green blood and the curiously invisible nature of the body, recalling the bulky intangibility of Lovecraft's 'Dunwich Horror' (1929). Gaiman's narrator notes, 'I saw it, but at first, somehow, I did not. What I saw instead was what had sprayed and gushed from the throat and chest of the victim: in colour it ranged from bile green to grass green' (7). This shift in material reality has the effect within the story of making Holmes' deductive manoeuvres somewhat parodic. After having knelt to examine the body, the detective concludes with confidence that:

> 'The corpse is obviously not that of a man – the colour of his blood, the number of limbs, the eyes, the position of the face – all these bespeak of the blood Royal [...] I would hazard that he is an heir – perhaps – no, second to the throne – in one of the German principalities'. (Gaiman 8)

He speaks of its number of limbs and of the 'Royal' blood as self-evident material facts from which clear deductions can be made. Such facts are only self-evident within the context of this Weird universe, though, and they invoke a lack of recognition in the reader. This description of the body is at once familiar and unfamiliar. The scene gestures to a Weird numinous, to non-traditional monsters and to ontological horror in its revelation of a radically different material reality.

There is nothing supernatural about the body or the murder, in the world of the story, but natural laws are nonetheless shattered. This undercuts the material basis for the detective's 'deductions'; the body confounds human perceptions of the material. The narrator cannot properly view, nor adequately describe, it. The mysterious body is part of the material world, but nonetheless eludes human perception and knowledge. Here Gaiman borrows the 'vertical gap' of Lovecraft's writing, the gap between the ungraspable nature of material reality (noumena) and the attempts of a narrator to access this reality (Harman, *Weird Realism* 24). Ultimately, the deductions of the detective in 'A Study in Emerald' are inconsequential in terms of the resolution of the plot, which unfolds in unexpected ways towards a final twist. The rational procedures carried out at the crime scene echo the original story, but do so in order to reveal an unfamiliar Weird universe rather than point to the killer. It is this revelation, rather than what we learn about the crime, that is key to the story's narrative trajectory and affectivity.

The parodic nature of deduction in 'A Study in Emerald' also reveals the ambiguities surrounding Holmes' methods in the original stories. As Knight affirms, Conan Doyle misidentifies Holmes' science as 'deduction' to suggest that 'it is both highly scientific and also a means of ordering the confusing data of experience' (86). However, if Holmes 'really were finding patterns in facts he would be practising "induction": in reality he has a knowledge of what certain phenomena *will* mean and [...] is drawing from a set of existent theories to explain new events' (Knight 86). This is more properly termed abductive reasoning, a methodology not as secure as deduction at producing valid arguments because its premises do not guarantee its conclusions. As Duncan Pritchard explains, neither induction nor deduction offer completely valid knowledge (particularly where the argument is not based on a true premise), but the further problem with abduction is that there is no good reason for thinking that *probable* explanations (drawing on existing theories or prior experience) are any more likely to be true than any other explanations (95–97). The act of enWeirding produces a material world that does not conform to existing scientific knowledge and theories, so probable explanations are useless. As China Miéville asserts, the Weird 'back-projects [its] radical unremembered alterity into history, to enWeird ontology itself' (113). The revelation of Weird monsters and Old Gods constitutes a rewriting of material histories and renders existing epistemological methods unsound. The irruption of the Weird in Holmes' world thus disrupts the circular justification of inductive and abductive reasoning on which rational scientific enquiry (including Holmes's science of deduction) is based. The Weird reveals that the material world is neither ordered nor uniform.

The act of enWeirding also undermines the ideological work of Conan Doyle's epistemological fiction. As Knight argues, the 'deductions' of Holmes are rarely consequential to the plot; rather they establish him as master and validate his power (86). The Weird history version of Holmes reveals this illusion of deduction and so calls into question the character's apparent mastery. In Conan Doyle's stories, that 'whimsical little incidents' are solved through neat acts of deduction 'implies that all disorders can readily enough be mastered' (Knight 95). Holmes' scientific and rational explanation of a materially known world emerges in this fiction as the expression of an ideology, and fantasy, of order maintained and England preserved for the middle classes (Knight 103). This maintenance of order is precisely what Gaiman's alternate history of Holmes' England turns on its head. Indeed, Gaiman's final revelation – that our detective is not Holmes after all, but the villain Moriarty, and that the killer he chases is our hero, Sherlock, inverts the moral order established in Conan Doyle's stories.

The upending of the Holmesian moral order is accompanied by a shift in tone running through the stories in this collection. Conan Doyle's stories are narrated by Watson in a generally objective, cold, and unemotional tone. In Gaiman's story, this coldness gives way to a more hysterical and nebulous narration style, akin to that usually associated with Lovecraft. The first line of Gaiman's story, which is the first entry in the collection, sets the tone for what will follow. The narrator notes, 'It is the immensity, I believe. The hugeness of things below. The darkness of dreams' (1). These grammatical fragments do not set out any material circumstances or important points of plot. Rather, they are nebulous wonderings that appeal to a speculative mode of enquiry; they gesture towards what remains unknown – the 'things below' - but which persists underneath human perception. In Barbara Hambly's 'The Adventure of the Antiquarian's Niece', Watson's narration overtly echoes the hysteria of the Lovecraftian protagonist attempting to give words to the horrors he witnesses. Groping in the dark, Watson notes the 'obscene aberration' to the geometry of the place wherein he is trapped; he observes that the wall is 'stained black with horrible corruption'; he hears 'inchoate stirrings' (178). The words 'corruption' and 'obscene' recall the decadent verbal style Lovecraft borrows from Edgar Allan Poe, here used by Hambly to suggest horrors beyond the comprehension of the rational detective. When Watson finally glimpses the 'things in the darkness' he can only make out 'horrible half-seen suggestions of squamous, eyeless heads [...] tentacles glistening [...] an appalling glint of teeth' (179). Watson's struggle to describe what he sees recalls the failed efforts of Lovecraftian narrators to give form to the fragments of a half-understood material reality. Weird monsters cannot be brought out into the light of understanding. In this respect, they serve the opposite function of Stapleton's dog in *The Hound of the Baskervilles* (1902). This seemingly supernatural beast is revealed not to be a 'hell-hound', but a 'curly-haired spaniel', a revelation that exorcises Dartmoor of the fears that have haunted it through the story (Conan Doyle 211). In Hambly's story, Watson cannot overcome his fear of the 'appalling' monsters as the tone of the narration descends to an emotional frenzy overriding the rational mechanisms of the plot.

Where Gaiman rewrites the history of Conan Doyle's Victorian London, the other stories in *Shadows Over Baker Street* insert supplementary secret histories into the Holmes canon. In so doing, they back-project the Weird into the Holmesian imaginary in ways that ask readers to reassess their understanding of the characters. James Lowder's 'The Weeping Masks' back-projects the Weird into Watson's personal history, imagining a series of events in Afghanistan that Watson has never related. The secret that Lowder inserts into the history of the two men's relationship suggests that there is something deficient in Holmes' understanding. Though Watson begins by posturing that Holmes' 'keen mind would have pierced the veil of strangeness surrounding those awful events', his confidence is revealed to be either naively consolatory, or a necessary self-deception aimed at preserving his sanity (94). He cannot risk telling Holmes and have the detective confirm his fears. The story tells how a remote village is stuck down by a sickness and describes strange priests with 'weeping masks' tending the sick. Suspecting the priests of spreading the disease, Watson follows them to a cave deep in the mountain and witnesses a bizarre rite and a manifestation of something he cannot explain.

Lowder's conclusion to Watson's history offers an overt critique of Holmesian epistemology. Watson cannot reconcile the things he has seen, in particular 'the thing that I saw move against that starry sky [...] all boneless limbs and writhing darkness' (113). Watson cannot reconcile this nameless thing with his scientific knowledge, nor can he find any satisfactory explanation for the events he witnesses. He infers, for example, that the masked priests are none other than the dead villagers, a conclusion that goes against all scientific reason. 'Even now, after all my lessons in deductive reasoning from that one true master of the science, I cannot claim with any confidence that, given the same evidence, I would not reach the same wrong conclusion' (113). Though his conclusion is 'wrong', there is no other available. 'Still', he asserts, 'I trust in logic' (113). Such contradictory statements suggest that logic fails Watson in every respect except that it provides a barely adequate cover for the horror he experiences. Hence, the necessary lie that there must be some 'explanation[s] of which Holmes would have approved' even if Watson's lack of talent means they elude him (113). Lowder suggests, though, that Holmes would not be able to provide such explanations and Watson's awareness of this deficiency in his mentor are reaffirmed at the close of the story: 'I can almost bring myself to believe those explanations. What I cannot describe away is that thing that I saw move against the starry sky' (113). Here, knowledge and belief come together as the story concludes that 'there are things logic cannot conquer' (115).

Lowder also suggests that there is a wider descent into chaos behind Watson's avowed crisis of faith in logic: 'The thing in the Afghan cave remains, while Holmes is gone, all hope with him' (115). Watson is not only denied an explanation, he recognizes an underlying menace in a material world inimical to human understanding, a menace that surpasses the comfort Watson derives from all Holmes's previous triumphs. Lowder's story is the savage in its critique of the Holmesian epistemological method, a method that separates belief and knowledge. In contrast, as Watson's experience in the cave attests, the Weird forces belief and knowledge together in a fashion contrary to Enlightenment rationality and logic, which dictates that one only believes where one does not know (Desmond 18). Watson's account suggests that he *knows* the truth, even if he cannot explain it. This position is affirmed by the point of view of the implied reader, whose extra textual knowledge of the Lovecraftian mythos confirms Watson's fears: there is no rational explanation. Thus, Watson must believe in what he has seen, even as he clings to a belief in logic at the same time, to avoid madness.

Both 'The Weeping Masks' and 'A Study in Emerald' close by hinting at a wider descent into chaos and madness that accompanies any revelation of Weird ontology. Many of the stories in the collection follow this pattern, rejecting the structure of the canonical tales that end with satisfactory resolution. In Brian Stableford's 'Art in the Blood', Holmes narrates a series of horrifying events to his brother, Mycroft. As he reaches the impossible dénouement of his story, Holmes breaks down and loses his grip on his mastery of knowledge and confidence in his methods:

> Reason tells me [...] that he must have imagined it, in much the same way that one imagines a portrait's gaze following one around the room – but I tell you, Mycroft, *I imagined it, too.* [...] The poison had leached into his liver and lights, but not his eyes or brain ... but the bleak eyes of those stone heads were staring at him, no matter how absurd that sounds, and ... do you have any idea what I am talking about, Mycroft? Do you understand what was happening in that cave? (Stableford 132–133, emphasis in original)

The italicized revelation echoes the final flourishes of Lovecraft's short fiction, in which some last, horrifying detail is revealed in italics for added emphasis. The ellipses and unanswered questions emphasize Holmes's failure to articulate an explanation for what he has seen.

Mycroft admits to never having seen his brother so 'desperate for reassurance', though he has no 'guarantees to offer' (135). The narrative coherence breaks down, finally, as the story trails off as Holmes mumbles to himself rather than addressing his interpolator, 'fear flooding his eyes, 'What became? Ah ..."' (136).

Elsewhere, the detective re-evaluates his methods as the certainties they once offered dissipate in the face of the emerging Weird. In Tim Lebbon's 'The Horror of the Many Faces', for example, Holmes admits to Watson that he has only been able to solve a particularly strange case (involving a shape shifting murderer) after allowing himself to 'believe that something out of this world was occurring' (264). This uncharacteristic belief in the supernatural (or else, super*normal*) leads not to transcendent understanding, but to the knowledge that human mastery is impossible. Again, the typically controlled narration expected in a Holmes story breaks down into ellipses and unfinished statements: 'I saw the truth behind the murderer, the scene of devastation. I saw ... I saw ...' (264). Holmes cannot finish his explanation of the case to Watson except to repeat the word 'Terrible'. In the silence, Watson notices that his 'friend was crying' (264, 265). After dismissing Watson with the revelation that 'Outside [...] beyond what we know or strive to know, there is a whole different place. Somewhere which, perhaps, our minds can never know', Holmes opts for a kind of retirement from detection (265). Holmes does not take on further cases, but stands each evening at the window in Baker Street 'looking intently across the rooftops as if searching for some elusive truth [...] I felt sure that his eyes, glittering and dark and so, so sad must have been seeing nothing of this world' (267). In Lebbon's melancholic ending, Holmes surrenders to the cosmicism of the Weird, his fate echoing that of Lovecraftian protagonist, Thomas Olney, from 'The Strange High House in the Mist' (1931), drained and dwarfed by his encounter with the cosmos.

At the same time as revelling in the demise of Holmes' methods, these Weird secret histories shore up a different kind of mastery to that offered by Enlightenment rationality. This privileged knowledge belongs to the Lovecraft fan, or 'geek', the implied reader of the tales, who is encouraged to know, often before the protagonists, the shape of the events unfolding. All the stories in the collection engage in overt intertextual play: they directly reference specific Lovecraft stories; they feature characters from the wider canon of Weird tales; and they often present a veritable checklist of mythos monsters. Such playfulness offers pleasure to the reader in the form of a recognition of their expertise. This suggests a different ideological function for these rewritings to that ascribed to Conan Doyle's original tales by Knight. In their original context, the Holmes stories offered a defence against encroaching chaos in London in the form of urban crime, along with an assertion that bourgeois property and economic capital would be protected by a man whose deductive flourishes offered the illusion of mastery. Instead, *Shadows Over Baker Street* offers its reader a measure of *subcultural* capital, recognizing their mastery of a fictional world and their encyclopaedic knowledge of Weird monsters. Sometimes the Lovecraft fan and Holmes are one, with Holmes demonstrating to an astounded Watson knowledge of arcane lore and bizarre cults that he surely does not keep in his famous card index. Whether Holmes is 'in the know', the reliance throughout on intertextual expertise from the reader positions them as active participant in the narrative, knowingly anticipating the Weird dénouement of the tale. Thus, the plots all find their forward trajectory in the incitation in the reader of the desire for the revelation of the Weird, a revelation that Holmesian logic dictates should be impossible.

On the one hand, these stories aim at a complete rejection of the rational epistemology offered by Enlightenment discourse. On the other hand, the more immersed in the Weird universe the reader becomes, the more mastery of a different kind they might accrue. Through reading, the fan acquires subcultural capital in the exercise of their expertise (often at the expense of the master detective). There is thus pleasure available in the surrender to a Weird ontology, despite its melancholic depiction in some of the tales. The continued popularity of Lovecraft and the Mythos, and its frequent appearance in popular culture is testament to this pleasure. I want to close by explaining this pleasure as part of the unique response Weird writing offers to the postmillennial rejection of Enlightenment thought. The pleasure of reading Weird fiction lies in the willing *surrender* of disbelief it invites. This surrender is in excess of the temporary willing suspension of disbelief normally required for the reader of fiction. Playful, the surrender rewards subcultural knowledge and fan expertise, but, at the same time, indulges in the desire to give oneself up completely to that Outside recognized by Holmes, that 'whole different place [...] our minds can never know' (Lebbon 265). This 'different place' described by Weird fiction finds its correlate in Meillassoux and Harman's speculative materialism as the 'Great Outdoors' or 'Weird' object.

The pleasurable surrender to the Weird invited by these alternate histories of Sherlock Holmes suggest a new structural relationship between belief and knowledge. The Enlightenment divorces belief from knowledge in a structural relationship that privileges the former over the latter. In *Shadows Over Baker Street* the conflict between knowledge as disbelief (doubting) and belief as knowledge (without the possibility of full human understanding) plays out in the form of a direct contest between the speculative mode of the Weird and the rational inductive enquiries of Sherlock Holmes. However, it is not the case that it has to be one (belief) *or* the other (knowledge) since other cultures and systems of thought offer alternative epistemological structures. Barry Hallen and J. Olubi Sodipo, in their work on African philosophy, note that Western, and particularly English, modes of thought doubt belief. Belief is what is not verifiable; belief begins where knowledge leaves off (6). Hallen and Olubi Sodipo's work suggests that this relationship need not be taken for granted. In its own way, the Weird offers the same challenge to this Enlightenment binary. In Weird versions of epistemology and ontology, belief and knowledge collide in strangely productive ways, allowing for belief beyond rational reason. That is, even if rational epistemology is useless, there is a kind of knowledge of the 'Outside' available. However, this knowledge only works alongside belief, because direct knowledge of material reality is not possible. The various stories in this collection mediate these contradictions, with narrators often professing rational doubt in the face of radical belief. In Hambly's tale, for example, Watson insists that 'I must have come down ill and lain delirious. There is no other explanation – I pray there is no other explanation' (176). Yet, his account of events, which he retroactively frames as the product of delirium, is detailed in such a way as to affirm its veracity. In 'The Horror of the Many Faces', too, the narrator expresses the contradictions that the encounter with the Weird creates. Holmes at first insists that it is his faith in proof that helps him solve the case: 'being the logically minded person I am, and believing that proof rather than simply belief, defines truth, I totally denied the truth of what I was seeing [...] And strange as it seemed at the time – but how clear it is now' (Lebbon 263). His circuitous and contradictory reasoning here holds belief as inimical to proof, but ends up expressing the clarity that surrendering to belief in the Weird brings.

Weird fiction and Sherlock Holmes seem opposed. One reading of *Shadows Over Baker Street* is to suggest that the sanity-blasting monsters of the Weird undo the epistemology of Conan Doyle's detective fiction. Instead, what my analysis suggests is something more productive. *Shadows Over Baker Street* brings together belief and knowledge in ways quite alien to dominant Western Enlightenment narratives. The stories deny the nihilistic rejection of knowledge suggested in Lovecraft's original tales, but move beyond the doubting limitations of Kantian correlationism and the temptations of indirect realism, which threaten to dislocate the human perceiver from the material world altogether. The Weird mediates and negotiates such philosophical difficulties, marrying belief and knowledge through the imagination of an encounter with a cosmic materialism in which the human perceiver is perhaps irrelevant, but not excluded.

References

Conan Doyle, Arthur. *The Hound of the Baskervilles.* 1902. Scholastic, 2016.

Dawkins, Richard. 'Why There is Almost Certainly No God'. *Huffington Post,* 23 October 2006. Accessed 14 November 2016. <www.huffingtonpost.com/richard-dawkins/why-there-almost-certainl_b_32164.html>

Desmond, William. 'The Confidence of Thought: Between Belief and Metaphysics'. *Belief and Metaphysics.* Eds. Peter M. Candler Jr. and Conor Cunningham. SCM Press, 2007, pp. 11–40.

Ellis, Steve and Fred Van Lente. *Why We're Here.* 2000. Accessed 9 September 2016. <www.fredvanlente.com/cthulhutract/pages/>

Gaiman, Neil. 'A Study in Emerald'. 1881. *Shadows Over Baker Street.* Eds. John Pelan and Michael Reaves. Del Rey and Random House, 2003, pp. 1–24.

Hallen, Barry and J. Olubi Sodipo. *Knowledge, Belief and Witchcraft: Analytic Experiments in African Philosophy.* 1986. Stanford University Press, 1997.

Hambly, Barbara. 'The Adventure of the Antiquarian's Niece'. 1894. *Shadows Over Baker Street.* Eds. John Pelan and Michael Reaves. Del Rey and Random House, 2003, pp. 158–188.

Harman, Graham. 'On the Horror of Phenomenology: Lovecraft and Husserl'. *Collapse,* Vol. IV, 2008, pp. 333–365.

—. *Weird Realism: Lovecraft and Philosophy.* Zero Books, 2011.

Hellekson, Karen. *The Alternate History: Refiguring Historical Time.* Kent State University Press, 2001.

Houellebecq, Michel. *H. P. Lovecraft. Against the World, Against Life.* Trans. Dorna Khazeni. Gollancz, 2005.

Joshi, S. T. *The Weird Tale.* Wildside Press, 1990.

Knight, Stephen Thomas. *Form and Ideology in Crime Fiction.* Indiana University Press, 1980.

Lebbon, Tim. 'The Horror of the Many Faces'. 1898. *Shadows Over Baker Street.* Eds. John Pelan and Michael Reaves. Del Rey and Random House, 2003, pp. 243–267.

Lovecraft, H. P. 'The Call of Cthulhu'. *The Haunter of the Dark and Other Tales.* Ed. August Derleth. Panther, 1963, pp. 47–74.

—. 'The Colour Out of Space'. *The Call of Cthulhu and Other Weird Stories.* Ed. S. T. Joshi. Penguin, 1999, pp. 139–169.

—.'The Dunwich Horror'. *The Haunter of the Dark and Other Tales.* Ed. August Derleth. Panther, 1963, pp. 75–114.

—. 'From Beyond'. *HP Lovecraft.com.* 2009. Accessed 9 September 2016. <www.hplovecraft.com/writings/texts/fiction/fb.aspx>

Lowder, James. 'The Weeping Masks'. 1890. *Shadows Over Baker Street*. Eds. John Pelan and Michael Reaves. Del Rey and Random House, 2003, pp. 94–115.

McHale, Brian. *Postmodernist Fiction*. Methuen, 1987.

Meillassoux, Quentin. *After Finitude. An Essay on the Necessity of Contingency*. Trans. Ray Brassier. Bloomsbury, 2008.

Miéville, China. 'M.R. James and the Quantum Vampire: Weird; Hauntological: Versus And/or and And/ or?' *Collapse*, IV, 2008, pp. 105–128.

Perry, Steve. 'The Case of the Wavy Black Dagger'. 1884. *Shadows Over Baker Street*. Eds. John Pelan and Michael Reeves. Del Ray and Random House, 2003, pp. 48–59.

Pritchard, Duncan. *What is This Thing Called Knowledge?* 2nd Edition. Routledge, 2013.

Reaves, Michael and John Pelan, editors. *Shadows Over Baker Street*. Del Rey and Random House, 2003.

Sederholm, Carl H. and Jeffrey Andrew Weinstock, editors. *The Age of Lovecraft*. University of Minnesota Press, 2016.

Stableford, Brian. 'Art in the Blood'. 1892. *Shadows Over Baker Street*. Eds. John Pelan and Michael Reaves. Del Rey and Random House, 2003, pp. 116–137.

Quest for Love
A Cosy Uchronia?

Andrew M. Butler

There is a moment at the end of the film *Quest for Love* (Ralph Thomas, 1971) when the protagonist Colin Trafford enters the hospital bedroom of a woman he has already seen die and has chased between and within alternate worlds. Her friend whispers something to her and he hands the patient a bunch of flowers, saying the name 'Ottilie'. She repeats this back as the credits appear. *Quest for Love* film is one of several adaptations of John Wyndham's short story 'Random Quest' (1962) and in this chapter I will discuss both texts as examples of alternate history, in the process noting how adaptation itself is also a form of alternate history. 'Random Quest' is one of a series of what Wyndham's biographer David Ketterer has called 'time-schism love stories', that explore a tension between arbitrary happenstance and inevitable predestination. These stories have largely been neglected in favour of the disaster novels that Brian Aldiss labelled 'cosy catastrophes'. It will be necessary to briefly discuss those novels and Wyndham's status, in order to consider how cosy his other work might be.

Whilst alternate histories are often means of exploring political distinctions between the empirical and fictionalized worlds, Wyndham's stories occupy a more domestic or cosy milieu. In this chapter, I have adopted the term 'uchronia', coined by Charles Renouvier in 1857 to refer to 'a utopia of past time [...] works in which some crucial turning point is given a different, and from the author's point of view better, outcome' (Alkon 115). The philosopher Paul Ricoeur used the word in relation to the imagined better world of the future (and as an alternative term to utopia – 'no-time' rather than 'no-place' (219)). According to Ricoeur, the philosophy of the Enlightenment had led to an expectation of unprecedented novelty, of accelerating societal improvements and the notion that humanity could determine history. The crises of twentieth-century modernity locate us between a dead past and a future that seems ever further away: 'the horizon of expectation recedes at a quicker pace than we advance. [... E]xpectation can longer fix itself on a determined future, outlined by discernible stages'. (219) But Wyndham seems more interested in Trafford's personal uchronia rather than the wider social shifts Ricoeur considers, even though he is aware of twentieth-century global politics.

'John Wyndham' was the most famous pseudonym of John Wyndham Parkes Lucas Beynon Harris (1903–1969). He began writing in the mid-1920s, selling sf stories such as 'Worlds to Barter' (as John B. Harris, *Wonder Stories*, May 1931) and 'The Lost Robot' (as John Beynon Harris, *Amazing Stories*, April 1932) to American pulps. As part of the nascent London scene of sf fans and writers, he was involved in the setting up of the fanzine *Nova Terrae*. After the Second World War, this became a professional magazine, *New Worlds*, under the editorship of John Carnell, and Wyndham was on the board of its publisher, Nova Publications, from 1948 until 1964.

It was in the 1950s, however, that he published the novels that cemented his critical reputation: *The Day of the Triffids* (1951); *The Kraken Wakes* (1953); *The Chrysalids* (a.k.a. *Rebirth*, 1955); *The Midwich Cuckoos* (1957); and *Trouble with Lichen* (1960); along with a collection of linked short stories, *The Outward Urge* (1959), first published in *New Worlds* and co-credited to another pseudonym, Lucas Parkes. The novels, being published in the UK by Michael Joseph in hardback and Penguin in paperback, were not positioned as generic sf. In his foreword to a collection of short stories, *The Seeds of Time* (1956), Wyndham notes the formulaic nature of much of the sf in the pulps and that 'even now, after twenty-five years, the bulk of science fiction, and its adaptations to film and broadcast serial form, has been determinedly kept in the cliff-hanger class' (7). Wyndham evidently had higher aspirations for his work and this enabled him to be taken more seriously by a wider public.

Yet shortly after Wyndham's death in 1969, his work was being dismissed just as science fiction was being taken seriously in the two new academic journals, *Foundation* and *Science Fiction Studies*, and by a history of the genre, *Billion Year Spree* (1973). Brian Aldiss, an sf author a generation younger than Wyndham, labelled these novels cosy catastrophes: 'The essence of the cosy catastrophe is that the hero should have a good time (a girl, free suites at the Savoy, automobiles for the taking) while everyone else is dying off' (294). The disasters sweep away the masses and the class system, as well as the government, leaving the luxuries of the old society for the survivors to take advantage of. The sub-genre is, essentially, wish fulfilment. Aldiss argued that *Triffids* and *Kraken* 'were totally devoid of ideas but read smoothly, and thus reached a maximum audience, who enjoyed cosy disasters' (294), whilst noting Wyndham's short stories were 'urbane and pleasing' (294).

If for Aldiss the cosy catastrophe was of a wish fulfilment nature, Christopher Priest's characterization of it had much more sense of loss:

> Wyndham is the master of the middle-class catastrophe; his characters are of the bourgeoisie, and the books lament the collapse of law and order, the failure of communications, the looting of shopping precincts and the absence of the daily newspaper. (194)

There is the sense that the characters would write a stiff letter of complaint to *The Times*, if only they could find a stamp. Priest noted that Wyndham, like Wells before him, juxtaposed 'the familiar and reassuring against the exotic and menacing' (194) in novels which were written in a British idiom and reflected British manners.

Perhaps Aldiss and Priest were too close in time to Wyndham to be more generous, but for them he had evidently gone out of fashion, despite (or perhaps because) of the catastrophe novels of J. G. Ballard, Keith Roberts, Richard Cowper, Charles Platt, and Priest himself that followed his lead. Aldiss and Priest were writing in the aftermath of the British New Wave, which challenged the cosiness of British sf with fragmented depictions of sexualized media landscapes. Carnell had given space to writers such as Ballard and Michael Moorcock in *New Worlds* editorials to attack the lack of literary merit, human character, and relevant ideas in early 1960s sf, as well as publishing stories which exemplified these preferred values. When Carnell stepped down from the editorship in 1964, Moorcock took over and transformed the magazine over a number of years to something closer to a literary review; the content shifted from science fiction to speculative fiction to purely fiction, alongside art criticism and appreciations of William S. Burroughs, Mervyn Peake, and Salvador Dalí. Wyndham's well-made science fictions were a convenient scapegoat for the producers of shock-the-bourgeoisie pop art-tinged New Wave fiction.

It might be thought that Wyndham's time-schism love stories are equally cosy, but there is more to his work than his critics imply. C. N. Manlove's reading of *The Day of the Triffids* and Rowland Wymer's account of *The Chrysalids* both offer revisionist accounts. Manlove argues that the novel 'serves to express the fragility of the modern human condition' (34), a fragility already exposed in the cauldron of the Second World War, with swathes of the country being destroyed by German bombers and rockets. Soldiers, nurses, doctors, artists, civilians, and reporters had seen the devastation of Europe and beyond – this being one of the crises of the modern world as identified by Ricoeur.

What might have been could be glimpsed in alternate worlds, through sf's estranging lens, as Wyndham imagined a Britain defenceless from carnivorous plants thanks to a generalized blinding of the population, an alien invasion via the sea, a post-nuclear world where mutants were zealously fought against by the puritanical survivors, and so on. In each of Wyndham's bestselling postwar sf novels, humanity's position was precarious, as the forces of evolution put its supremacy over the Earth at risk.

The threat was depicted more head-on in *Plan for Chaos*, an alternate world where the Nazi scientists had not been stopped (or cherry-picked by the Allies) and had then spent twenty-eight years raising a new Reich of male and female clones. This conspiracy is stumbled on by press photographer Johnny Farthing, when he notices that Doppelgängers of his fiancée and cousin, Freda, are being killed. His and Freda's similarity to the clones, to whom it turns out they are related, is somewhere between accident and 'a sort of a strong family strain' (*Plan* 135), between happenstance and predestination.

Humanity's precariousness is shown in the more famous *Triffids*, where it is not clear whether the carnivorous plants are the result of chance evolution or human intervention into existing species with unintended consequences. The threat is heightened by humanity's blindness, which might be the result of satellites destroyed by cosmic debris rather than meteorites. Manlove suggests that the 'misuse of science has hollowed out the reality people take for granted until a mere touch will overthrow it' (37). He borrows the word 'chancel', from a part of church architecture, to suggest a cause of change that is as likely to be blind chance as divine predestination. Meanwhile, Wymer traces a series of unsettling moments within the novels, before centring on the moral shift in the course of *The Chrysalids*. The novel's sympathetic mutant characters face exposure and slaughter by their enclave, but after their escape to a community in Sealand the society they leave is destroyed: 'The Sealand's woman calm invocation of the natural struggle between species to justify the mass killing of non-telepaths echoes the rationalisms offered by Hitler for his policies' (31). For Wymer, Wyndham critiques the bourgeois values that are at the heart of the cosy catastrophe. Wyndham acknowledges the blind harshness of evolution, and the nature of life 'as a ceaseless and ruthless struggle for existence' (26).

Beth Moore weighs up the two dominant readings of Wyndham, arguing that:

The cosy-catastrophists see Wyndham as responding to a particular kind of audience and creating a consolatory fiction designed specifically to appeal to them. Those seeing more value in Wyndham's work see him as challenging this audience, attacking bourgeois values with a harsh Darwinism. (6–7)

Wymer is reluctant to see Wyndham as endorsing Social Darwinism, but evolution plainly occurs whether one likes it or not and human intervention into the environment can have unintended consequences. It seems likely that a similar hermeneutic tension would be at work in 'Random Quest', even if it is part of a different sub-genre.

This short story begins with a framing narrative, as a young man Colin Trafford visits Dr Harshom as part of his quest to find Ottilie Harshom. The doctor insists that she never existed and that Trafford's quest is doomed to failure. Trafford recounts an accident he has had in a laboratory, which transferred him to an alternate universe, different from and yet reasonably close to our own, in which he was a writer rather than a scientist. There he meets and falls in love with Ottilie Harshom, who in this alternate universe is Trafford's wife. On returning to his own realm, Trafford wishes to be reunited with this woman, whom it is assumed will also love him. Trafford is not clear as to the chancel, the precise point of divergence, but it seems to be at some point during the period 1926–1927, if not before. The great trauma of our and Trafford's modernities, the Second World War, has not taken place, and in this parallel world the League of Nations is challenging the Weimar Republic's policies. Meanwhile, Rab Butler is Prime Minister and India still a British possession, with Nehru in prison. But Wyndham's interest is less in how these global consequences play out than in minor estranging details such as changes to the Café Royal, the London Passenger Transport Board still being the General Passenger Transport Board and writer, actor and singer Nöel Coward having died, leaving a daughter. The personal consequences of there having been no war is that Martin Falls, Trafford's closest friend in both realms, has not lost his hand in battle. For Trafford, the alternate world is preferable: he is rich and famous and has a beautiful wife. It is not quite at the level of the cosy catastrophe – 'the hero should have a good time (a girl, free suites at the Savoy, automobiles for the taking)' (294), as Aldiss phrased it – but he *does* have a wife and apartment. This clearly edges towards a uchronia which is cosy, in which the horizon of expectation could almost be reached for Trafford, even if it is short-lived in the parallel world.

Wyndham is careful to couch the point of divergence between alternates in scientific language: particle physics. Trafford observes:

> There must [...] have been some point where, perhaps by chance, some pivotal thing had happened, or failed to happen, and finding it could bring one closer to knowing the moment, the atom of time, that had been split by some random neutron to give two atoms of time diverging into different futures. ('Random Quest' 88)

This derives from the ideas of quantum mechanics and the ambiguity over whether light should be considered to be wave or particle. If a light source is shone through a plate with a single slit, it produces a bright pattern on a screen on the other side, consistent with light being particles. If a second, parallel, slit is opened, a striped pattern is produced, as if light were a wave. It is not clear how the particles 'know' which slit to pass through or whether somehow the particles pass through both slits, but the conclusion in quantum mechanics was that light is both wave and particle. Light is only observed in one state at once, as if the observation determines the state of the photon. Erwin Schrödinger was sceptical about the understanding of particle physics based on probability in quantum mechanics and proposed a thought experiment to demonstrate how ridiculous it was: a cat is placed in a box with a phial of poison that will break and kill the creature if a radioactive atom decays. There is a fifty-fifty chance of this happening, with no telling if the cat is dead or alive until the box is opened. Schrödinger felt it ridiculous that a cat could both be dead and alive, but various theorists went on to offer explanations about what was going on. In the Copenhagen interpretation, the probabilities collapse into a definite, actual, state when the box is opened and the situation is observed. In another interpretation, the relative state or many-worlds theory, both possibilities exist in alternate universes.

The film historian and theorist David Bordwell discusses the many-worlds theory as a means of complicating the linear or 'straight corridor' narrative he locates as central to Hollywood film production:

> Hugh Everett III posited what's come to be called the 'many-worlds' interpretation of quantum mechanics. John Wyndham's 1961 short story 'Random Quest' developed the idea in a science fiction framework; but it seems to have had few immediate successors. (186–187)

The story posits two parallel historical narratives, both navigable through causality and psychology, with only Trafford crossing over between the two. The flashback disrupts the straightforward narrativizing of events, but the key is that unknown random atom – or chancel – is sufficient for Trafford to switch cultures from science to art and for Ottilie to be alive (and married) and not alive (albeit finally located and available). The atom is the proverbial lost nail. Trafford scientist/writer, Falls having/not having a hand, Nöel Coward being dead/alive seem arbitrary happenstance rather than predestination.

Karen Hellekson includes quantum theories in her discussion of alternate histories. The parallel worlds story 'posits a universe populated by an uncountable number of worlds that exist simultaneously with our own, each the product of a different effect springing from any given cause' (47). Both the alternate history in which a character is immersed – in which they and/or the reader perceive an alternative course of events – and the parallel worlds story – in which the protagonist moves between alternate worlds – reveal the arbitrary nature of reality and history. The arbitrariness is set against a notion of agency: the protagonists are 'agents [who] cause actions to happen' (48). At the same time, the choice is often a small one, a chancel perhaps, with the protagonist not necessarily aware of the change at the moment of decision.

Ketterer describes 'Random Quest' as a 'time-schism love story':

> [A]bout a man who should have married a particular woman; she has gone on to marry someone else. The situation is rectified by some kind of time-switch transfer to an alternate world, where the 'right' relationship (a minor counterfactual from the primary-world point of view) applies. (353)

In 'Random Quest', the Ottilie located by Trafford is the daughter of a chance liaison between Dr Harshom's son, Malcolm, and young woman. They had seen a boat named 'Ottilie' and Malcolm had told her that his father had a dead sister called Ottilie who he wanted to name his daughter after. After Malcolm dies in a car accident, the pregnant mother-to-be had married Reggie Gale and the adoptive child is called Belinda instead. Ketterer reads this and the other time-schism love stories – 'The Man Who Returned' (1931 but unpublished), '[The] Chronoclasm' (*Star Science Fiction Stories*, February 1953), 'Opposite Number[s]' (*New Worlds*, April 1954), 'Stitch in Time' (*Fantasy and Science Fiction*, March 1961), and 'Modification' (1964, unpublished) – as biographical wish fulfilment on Wyndham's behalf. Wyndham is imagining a cosier alternative to his own life, where barriers delayed his marriage to Grace Wilson for twenty years. The cosy utopia of marriage is contrasted with the dystopia of star-crossed lovers whose destiny is to be together but who are kept apart by happenstance.

In 'Chronoclasm', for example, Gerald Lattery marries his great-great-grandniece Octavia, who has travelled back to see him having read a letter he has left for her. Their meeting may be predestined, but the situation is said to 'fraught with unpredictable consequences' (12). Meanwhile, in 'Opposite Number', Peter Ruddle sees his former fiancée Jean and his own counterpart from a parallel world – in his own world, she had married Freddie Tallboy instead of him. This rendezvous is both random and predestined: 'Seeing the couple when I did was simply a matter of chance. Probably I should have run across them just a little later, anyway, but the results could have been quite different' (140). The meeting is inevitable, but not the manner or timing of it. Similar to 'Random Quest', Wyndham explains the crossover between parallel worlds in terms of exposure to 'quantum radiation', which has split time. Finally, in 'Stitch in Time', Thelma Kilder was being stood up in 1913 by her fiancé Arthur Waring Batley and has since married and had children. In the story's present, scientists experimenting with time travel in a laboratory built on her land accidentally bring Batley forward in time, causing him to miss their meeting. Batley's own son, conceived with a different wife, is now engaged to Thelma's daughter. Whilst Kilder and Batley remain separate due to bad luck, their genes seem predestined to unite.

Whilst the cosy catastrophes centre on the blind harshness of evolution, these time-schism love stories feature the blind harshness of chance, even as they offer potential utopian or eucatastrophic conclusions. That optimism locates them as uchronian. In each case there is talk of relativity, particle physics, or quantum mechanics. Trafford notes that 'although the infinite point which we may call a moment in 1954 must occur throughout the continuum, it *exists* only in relation to each observer' ('Random Quest' 178). Thelma, meanwhile, accepts her situation as an accident 'though so many things seem to be accidents that one does sometimes wonder if they aren't really written somewhere' ('Stitch' 153). As with the ambiguity of light, life is both happenstance and predestination and the protagonist has little agency either way but may perceive both versions of their life.

Wyn Wachhorst discusses the film adaptation of 'Random Quest', *Quest for Love*, in his study of time travel romance films. He describes how

> the hero moves sideways in time into a parallel universe, [where] the incongruities of the alternate world still suggest the innocence of the past – a more feminine world, where Everest and the moon remain unconquered and heart surgery is unknown – a world, that is, with less compulsion to violate the heart or displace God, one

where Kennedy is still president, Vietnam still an obscure country, and the last bit of innocence was not lost in the sixties. (341)

Vietnam is where Lewis lost his arm – one of the points of estrangement for Trafford is that his friend is not injured. Wachhorst identifies 207 time travel movies, with fifty-one that he considers to be serious thematic explorations of time travel and includes parallel worlds within his corpus. He suggests the typical structure of the sub-genre: '(1) a male time traveler who encounters (2) a female inhabitant of another time. Usually the male belongs to the present and the female to the past' (341). The tendency of time travellers to be male is perhaps a result the typical Hollywood straight-corridor narrative to be focused on problems to be overcome by male protagonists, with women as the reward for success. Whilst neither Wyndham nor director Ralph Thomas and his scriptwriter Terence Feeley were working within Hollywood, the paradigm is to some extent still followed.

Wachhorst identifies the other world as feminine, innocent, and provincial – a childhood retreat that establishes the heroine as a mother figure – and also associates it with death. The protagonist is 'disillusioned with his culture, his occupation, and/or his girlfriend' (344), returning to a Paradise before the Fall where he 'seek[s] unconditional love' (345). This holds true for 'Random Quest' and the film, in which Trafford finds his alternate world to be somewhat old-fashioned, most notably in his description of the feminine sphere of the kitchen: 'A fridge, no washer, single-sink, no plate racks, no laminated tops, old-fashioned looking electric cooker, packet of soap powder, no synthetic detergents' ('Random Quest' 181). The Second World War has not caused the technological or political progress which might lead to a general rather than personal uchronia.

Wachhorst's association of the alternate world with death at the same time offers a chance rebirth, akin to the necessary catastrophe that paves the way for utopia as in *The Chrysalids*. Passing into the other world is akin to a return to the womb. The man might have the power to control time, but the woman transcends time (Wachhorst 349). This returns us to the sense of cosiness – Trafford could overcome his dissatisfaction and assert his masculine power by returning to the womb so that he gains the eternal woman. In the end, he provides an heir for Dr Harshom, who drinks a toast to 'the restoration of order, and the rout of the random element' ('Random Quest' 204). Trafford has first restored Belinda Gale to being Ottilie Harshom and has now transformed her into Mrs Colin Trafford. His agency is powered by patriarchal privilege.

Of course, the story and the film offer different versions of Trafford's quest. Changes are inevitable in adapting a text between media. Actors might not match the author's image of their characters. The casting of Denholm Elliot as Falls/Lewis or of Joan Collins as Ottilie/Tracy Fletcher will have an impact on our reactions to the 1971 adaptation. Events dealt with in brief in the written version might need spelling out at length or a series of incidents could be reduced to a montage. 'Random Quest' had already been adapted for television in 1969 as part of the *Out of the Unknown* series, but the episode is missing, believed wiped. A further adaptation followed from BBC4 in 2006. The alternate choices made by the crew create alternate versions of the same narrative. The choice of Bernard Brown/Shaun Parkes and Tracy Reed/Kate Ashfield in the leads of the 1969 and 2006 versions would have also led us to read the text in a different way. It is tempting to consider such alternates as more or less true to an authentic original and privileged texts, but they are just alternate versions.

One obvious change from 'Random Quest' to the 1971 film is the shift of action from on or around 27 January 1954 to the then present, avoiding the need for period detail. Another is the jettisoning of the frame narrative to focus on Trafford's experiences rather than the power of his potential father-in-law. But in adaptation studies, measures of 'faithfulness' and 'fidelity' – what I have referred to as the 'f-words' (86) – are frowned upon. Robert Stam notes that criticism of literary adaptations may use terms such as 'infidelity', 'betrayal', 'deformation', 'violation', 'vulgarization', 'bastardization', and 'desecration' (3), with a value judgement approving of the perfect original and rejecting an inferior copy. Any audience viewing an adaptation that has knowledge of the source will be 'haunted at all times by their adapted texts' (Hutcheon with O'Flynn 6), but this is not in itself a guarantee of quality for either alternate.

I am therefore arguing that adaptation is another form of alternate history – a narrative in which details, whether minor or major, are changed but the whole is still recognizable. This is clearer in cases where authors write their own screen adaptations – in creating another version of their narrative they are taking different decisions, possibly even returning to rejected options, for example in the different choices that Ian McEwan made in his 2017 script for *On Chesil Beach* (2007) – dramatising the female protagonist's traumatic memories in a different way, adding a more upbeat ending and so on. In fiction where characters move between parallel words, one oeuvre is no more real than the other, nor is the adaptation less authentic than its source. Martin Falls in 'Random Quest' becoming Tom Lewis in *Quest for Love* makes these texts distinct rather than creating a hierarchy of quality. However, the emphases and aesthetics of a science fiction writer – even one who to some degree had disavowed the label – are likely to differ from the production context of cinema or television.

The director of *Quest for Love*, Ralph Thomas, had been known for broad comedies with elements of farce, innuendo, and sexual materials, emphasized by his other film from 1971, *Percy*, about a man with penis transplant, and its sequel, *Percy's Progress* (1974). He had also directed the Doctor films based on Richard Gordon's novels and two Carry On films – *Carry On Regardless* (1961) and *Carry On Cruising* (1962) – and the Carry On films and *Quest* were produced by Peter Rogers Productions. What should be the theoretically emotional height of *Quest* – Trafford frantically trying to find Ottilie – comes across as a farcical chase in which he runs around Heathrow Airport and car parks and speeds down urban and suburban roads. James D. White calls it 'a ludicrous chase around Heathrow airport' (202) and he has a point. One side effect of this light touch is that the cosy side of the narrative becomes more visible.

I have already noted that Wachhorst observes the time travel romance film's alternate world is 'a more feminine world', (341) cosier than ours. It is a cosy catastrophe minus the catastrophe. Trafford is here wealthy, from his career as novelist and playwright with glittering West End premieres and interest in his work from the BBC, he has a large apartment just behind the Albert Hall in Kensington, a gentleman's club of which he is a frequenter, a sports car and a beautiful wife, even if his alcoholic counterpart has abandoned her in favour of a mistress. Trafford sees no problem in taking up with what is effectively another man's wife; she is his for the taking. The (feminine coded) innocence of the alternate is balanced by the lack of (masculine coded) scientific: 'heart surgery is unknown' (Wachhorst 341). Thus, when Ottilie has a heart attack, she dies, returning Trafford to what he takes to be reality, still very much still in love and looking for her counterpart. He finds her in the shape of air hostess Tracy Fletcher and the chivalrous knight rescues his damsel in distress. Whilst Tracy initially hides from someone who evidently appears to her to be a stalker, the film never questions that she will be his. The quest for love underscores a heteronormative narrative that in comedy usually ends with marriage.

In both story and film we have elements of happenstance – the arbitrary estranging differences between alternate worlds – and predestination – the mutual affinities between characters, continued desires at different points of a relationship. The story's title, 'Random Quest', emphasizes chance and happenstance, and is dominated by conversations between men, policing desire, whereas the film, *Quest for Love*,

emphasizes agency through the notion of the quest, although still related
to desire. The two Traffords are different men, having bifurcated into
the separate realms of science and culture – it is not at all clear what
the status of the usurped Trafford is and whether the transportation is
a purely psychological one or if there are other Traffords, convenient off
page or off screen. The gulf between Ottilie and Belinda/Tracy should
be greater, being distinguished even before their birth(s), with distinct
fathers and names, and living in different countries. Both nature and
nurture should lead to differences between the two.

The counter to this objection may lie in that strange name, 'Ottilie'.
There are two earlier Ottilies – one, in a poem by Robert Louis Stevenson,
'To Ottilie' need not detain us long. In two verses, Stevenson reminds
someone (Ottilie?) of the rising August sun shining on bird cages in
a house, and grey doves in the street. The second, although earlier,
reference is to Johann Wolfgang von Goethe's *Die Wahlverwandtschaften*
(*Elective Affinities* 1809). This is a curious, tragic novel, in which Charlotte
and Eduard are a middle-aged couple, both in second marriages, who
are creating a comfortable mansion in Weimar. Charlotte decides to fill
her time redesigning the surrounding landscape, to make a paradise
for Eduard. But this scheme is threatened by the arrival of two guests.
First, there is Eduard's old friend, the Captain, who expands the scale
of Charlotte's plans and brings in professional builders to cope with the
extra work. Then there is Ottilie, an orphan much younger than the
other three, who joins the household at the end of her education. Perhaps
inevitably, Eduard falls in love with Ottilie (and Eduard's middle name
is Otto, of which Ottilie is a feminized version). In turn, the Captain
falls in love with Charlotte. Tragedy strikes – a boy nearly drowns in
the pool created by the new dam and then Charlotte and Eduard's son
Otto (who looks uncannily like the Captain and Ottilie) drowns when
in Ottilie's care. Ottilie then stops eating, dying of grief.

The process of attraction between the characters is explained by the
novel's title and in some of its dialogue. R. J. Hollingdale explains that
'[t]he term Wahlverwandtschaft was a technical term of eighteenth-
century chemistry, the German translation of a coinage of the Swedish
chemist Torbern Olof Bergman' (13) in 1775. The Captain explains that
if two connected substances are brought into contact with two other
connected substances, then two new connections are created:

> Imagine an A intimately united with a B, so that no force is able
> to sunder them; imagine a C likewise related to a D; now bring the
> two couples into contact: A will throw itself at D, C at B, without

our being able to say which first deserted its partner, which first embraced the other's partner. (Goethe 56)

Eduard explains that he is A, Charlotte is B, the Captain is C and the soon to visit Ottilie is D. In other words, the characters' adultery is seemingly predestined, the result of an irresistible affinity; J. Hillis Miller suggests Goethe uses a 'parabolic analogy, between the natural realm of chemical reactions and the human realm of irresistible erotic attractions' (86). This is similar to the term Octavia uses in 'Chronoclasm': 'Do you believe in predestination? [...] Oh – no, well perhaps it isn't quite that at all – more a sort of affinity' (22). The affinity of counterpart Trafford with Ottilie is displaced onto the 'real' Trafford with Ottilie and then, more messily, onto the 'real' Trafford with Belinda/Tracy. The seemingly cosy relationship Trafford is gifted with is the result of both the agency of searching and the ceaseless, ruthless, and blind operations of chemistry. The conclusions to 'Random Quest' and *Quest for Love* question cosy bourgeois norms, just as Goethe welds together science, 'social criticism and his romantic plot' (Hollingdale 16) in a critique of bourgeois life.

The deaths of Goethe and Wyndham's Ottilies may also bear comparison. Bhanji, Jolles, and Jolles diagnose Goethe's Ottilie as suffering from anorexia nervosa, noting '[t]he subterfuges she resorted to are typical of those encountered [...] as is the denial of the gravity of her condition' (582). Peter M. McIsaac argues 'that Ottilie is trained to take on a role of self-denial based on an aestheticized model of saintliness' (348). Deprivation makes her more beautiful and freezes her, subduing any wilfulness and controlling her body. Her corpse is displayed in a glass-lidded coffin in a chapel that becomes the focus of pilgrimage. When Eduard dies, Charlotte buries him next to Ottilie, with the narrator declaring 'what a happy moment it will be when one day they awaken again together' (Goethe 300). This is plainly a romantic thought, but there is also something uncomfortable about it.

Quest for Love depicts an equivalent moment of awakening. Tracy/Ottilie had survived an air raid during the Second World War and has been brought up in an orphanage. After a period of time teaching, she has found a job as an air hostess for Pan AM, which contributes to the distance put between her and Trafford. Trafford has to blag his way through old memories, confidentiality, privacy, and friends' protectiveness, to get to her side at precisely the instant when she needs medical aid. Ottilie is resurrected though Trafford's agency.

In each alternate version of 'Random Quest' and *Quest for Love*, the male protagonist is given a second chance by his passage into a feminized alternate world and his subsequent rebirth along with the woman he desires. An eucatastrophic ending will lead to a personal utopia. The uchronia, despite being used for alternate histories and future utopias, was for its coiner Renouvier 'a means of speculating on lines of historical causation. Alternate history was for him primarily a way of identifying crucial turning points with potentially very different outcomes' (Alkon 116). Trafford is exposed to the blind harshness of chance in his on/off relationship with Ottilie, with different outcomes that he strives to fix, in terms drawing on theories of particle physics and echoing elective affinities. In different worlds, he finds a romantic counterpart, just as Wyndham's cosy catastrophes seemingly offered moments of joy to the surviving white, male, middle-class protagonists.

The uchronia in 'Random Quest'/*Quest for Love* is domestic, romantic, and cosy, even as other, tragic, alternatives to the narrative haunt us, especially from his other time-schism love stories, which have more of a sense of lives not lived. It might be chance or happenstance that has brought Trafford and Ottilie together, but there it seems assumed that the other Ottilie will fall in in love with Trafford. Indeed, the film concludes with both of them speaking this name, insisting on the elective affinity between them. The existential traumas of the mid-twentieth century, centred on the Second World War, have been eclipsed by the much more mundane crisis of the pain of being separated from one's own true love, lovers who seem predestined to be together in any alternate history.

References

Aldiss, Brian W. *Billion Year Spree: The History of Science Fiction*. Weidenfeld and Nicolson, 1973.

Alkon, Paul K. *Origins of Futuristic Fiction*. Georgia University Press, 1987.

Banji, S., Jolles, F. E. F. and Jolles, R. A. S. 'Goethe's Ottilie: An Early 19th Century Description of Anorexia Nervosa'. *Journal of the Royal Society of Medicine*, vol. 83, no. 9, 1990, pp. 581–585.

Bordwell, David. *Poetics of Cinema*. Routledge, 2007.

Butler, Andrew M. 'Unimportant Failures: The Fall and Rise of *The Man Who Fell to Earth*'. *Science Fiction Across Media: Adaptation/Novelisation*. Eds. Thomas van Parys and I. Q. Hunter. Gylphi, 2011, pp. 81–95.

Goethe, Johann Wolfgang von. *Elective Affinities*. Trans. R. J. Hollingdale. Penguin, 1971.

Hellekson, Karen. *The Alternate History: Refiguring Historical Time*. Kent State University Press, 2001.

Hollingdale, R. J. 'Introduction'. In Johann Wolfgang von Goethe. *Elective Affinities*. Penguin, 1971, pp. 7–16.

Hutcheon, Linda with O'Flynn, Siobhan. *A Theory of Adaptation*. Routledge, 2013.

Ketterer, David. 'John Wyndham's *Chocky* (1968): The First Covert Alternate World?' *Science Fiction Studies*, vol. 35, no. 2, 2008, pp. 352–355.

McIsaac, Peter M. 'Exhibiting Ottilie: Collecting as a Disciplinary Regime in Goethe's *Wahlverwandtschaften*'. *German Quarterly*, vol. 70, no. 4, 1997, pp. 347–357.

Manlove, C. N. 'Everything Slipping Away: John Wyndham's *The Day of the Triffids*'. *Journal of the Fantastic in the Arts*, vol. 4, no. 1, 1991, pp. 29–53.

Miller, J. Hillis. *Versions of Pygmalion*. Harvard University Press, 1990.

Moore, Beth. *A Critical Study of John Wyndham's Major Works*. PhD, University of Liverpool, 2007.

Priest, Christopher. 'British Science Fiction'. *Science Fiction: A Critical Guide*. Ed. Patrick Parrinder. Longman, 1979, pp. 187–202.

Ricoeur, Paul. *From Text to Action: Essays in Hermeneutics, II*. Trans. Kathleen Blamey and John B. Thompson. Northwestern University Press, 1991.

Stam, Robert. *Literature Through Film: Realism, Magic and the Art of Adaptation*. Blackwell, 2005.

Stevenson, Robert Louis. *Collected Poems*. Hart-Davies, 1950.

Wachhorst, Wyn. 'Time-Travel Romance on Film: Archetypes and Structures'. *Extrapolation*, vol. 25, no. 4, 1984, pp. 340–359.

White, James D. 'Quest for Love'. *Monthly Film Bulletin*, vol. 38, no. 1, 1971, p. 202.

Wymer, Rowland. 'How "Safe" is John Wyndham? A Closer Look at his Work, with Particular Reference to *The Chrysalids*'. *Foundation*, vol. 55, 1992, pp. 25–36.

Wyndham, John. 'Chronoclasm'. *The Seeds of Time*. Michael Joseph, 1956, pp. 11–37.

—. 'Foreword'. *The Seeds of Time*. Michael Joseph, 1956, pp. 7–9.

—. 'Opposite Number'. *The Seeds of Time*. Michael Joseph, 1956, pp. 140–160.

—. *Plan for Chaos*. Penguin, 2010.

—. 'Random Quest'. *Consider Her Ways and Others*. Michael Joseph, 1961, pp. 154–204.

—. 'Stitch in Time'. *Consider Her Ways and Others*. Michael Joseph, 1961, pp. 136–153.

Agency and Contingency
in Televisual Alternate History Texts

Karen Hellekson

In my previous work, *The Alternate History,* I divided the alternate history genre up into four larger sections according to the nature of the larger narrative driving the text in question: eschatological (concerned with final destiny), genetic (concerned with origin, development or cause), entropic (concerned with randomness or disorder) and teleological (concerned with design or purpose) (2). I perceive written alternate histories as querying notions of history, including its nature, its purpose, and its outcome. My divisions – the nexus story, the true alternate history, and the existence of parallel worlds, where alternate histories lie side by side rather than being exclusive – focus on the moment of the break, not on the subject's position (5). The nexus story focuses on an important moment in history, the changed outcome of which profoundly alters what we consider established history. Some alternate histories posit the creation of a kind of temporal police, which ensures that history remains on its established, 'true' course, in order to bring about a particular, desired historical result. The true alternate history focuses on a world that appears to us to be greatly changed, the result of a change in a previous point in history – an England a few hundred years after the quelling of the Protestant Reformation, for example. Parallel worlds stories let all outcomes be equally likely and equally true: each changed moment in history branches into equally valid outcomes, where the changed event both did and did not take place.

In televisual texts, however, the larger notions of history queried by the literary form of the genre are not in play. Unlike written alternate history texts, they rely not on an historical analysis of history and its ultimate purpose but rather on an examination of individual characters and their reactions to the (from our point of view altered) world around them. This is done to address larger concerns of contingency and agency, the foregrounding of which indicates the presence of a contingency–agency feedback loop that ultimately serves to privilege the individual over the turning of the wheel of history.

Before I proceed, I want to define some terms important to what follows, which are mentioned in this book's Introduction: nexus event, contingency, and agency. A nexus event is a pivotal event that is crucial to history's unfolding as it has. Examples might be the Battle of Gettysburg in the US Civil War, or the Allied victory in the Second World War. Nexus points (I borrow the term from Poul Anderson's Time Patrol series) are commonly used in the genre of alternate history to define pivotal moments where history might be altered – cases where a single event, if changed, could profoundly alter the events that follow, thus ultimately leading to a wildly different world. These changes may be large or small: turning right instead of left at an intersection, or losing or winning a battle may be equally important in an historical outcome, although the former seems trivial and the latter of some moment. Nexus points tend to be the latter. The alternate history gives special consideration to them because altering them may result in profound historical changes – the Nazi/Japanese occupation of the United States, for example, as a result of the Allies losing the Second World War, as in Philip K. Dick's *The Man in the High Castle.*

Contingency indicates an event that may be but is not certain to occur; it is something that is liable to happen as a result of something else. Crucial to the idea of contingency is the notion of cause and effect, where something that occurs (cause) will have repercussions (effect). This seems self-evident, but in the genre of the alternate history, contingency plays an oversize role, as the cause may have any number of effects; it need not be the historically true one to be a logically reasonable outcome. Like a nexus event, contingency relies on causality, with a (changed) cause radiating outward to a (new) logically reasonable effect.

Finally, agency is simply the capacity to act or exert power. This is most obviously seen in the actions of specific individuals: someone who can alter her own destiny by her actions is exerting agency. Like nexus events and contingency, agency also relies on causality. The agent can alter the world around her and bring about a change. As noted above, turning right or left at an intersection may mean one does or does not meet one's true love, but this is unlikely to profoundly alter the world around you, unless you are Adolph Hitler or Golda Meir – someone who has the power to wield agency it in such a way that contingency results in an altered nexus point. As might be expected, such people are few. History refers to them as Great Men.

Cause and effect thus links all three of these ideas. The nexus event indicates that certain causes have such overwhelming importance that effect must certainly be affected; its reach is global. Contingency shows us that cause and effect could result in any number of logical effects from a single cause; its reach is situational but may result in global-level changes. Finally, agency shows us that cause and effect can be altered by a single person's actions; its reach is individual. These three ideas work together to create what we call history, and alternate history's role here is to alter any one (or more) of these three ideas to bring about an historical change in aid of the text's theme or point.

The roster of televisual texts that focus exclusively on the genre of alternate history, using it as the focus of the text, is surprisingly sparse. For this study, I assessed the following: *Awake* (NBC, 2012), *Charlie Jade* (Space, 2005), *Continuum* (Showcase, 2012–2015), *An Englishman's Castle* (BBC mini-series, 1978), *Fringe* (Fox, 2008–2013), *The Man in the High Castle* (Amazon, 2015–, based on Philip K. Dick's 1963 novel of the same name), *Sliders* (Fox, SyFy, 1995–2000) and *Timeless* (NBC, 2016–2018).[1]

It is far more common for television programmes to have a single episode with alternate history or parallel worlds elements. For example, an episode of *The X-Files* (1993–2002, 2016), 9.04 '4-D', is about a killer who commits crimes, then retreats to a parallel world to avoid capture. The Star Trek franchise has an established alternate world, the mirror universe, that crosses different texts in the franchise, kicked off by 2.04 'Mirror Mirror' in the classic *Star Trek* (NBC, 1966–1969), where the savage, violent Terran Empire has replaced the benevolent Federation, where the only way to move up is via dead man's boots and where Spock has a beard. But even non-sf TV likes to play with the alternate history. My favourite example is 3.04 'Remedial Chaos Theory', an episode of *Community* (NBC, 2009–2015), where each member of the gang throws a die to see who has to go downstairs to pick up the pizza. The episode resets with each throw; each number comes up, resulting in a wildly different, and hilarious, outcome, depending on who goes to

---

[1] The following texts have alternate historical elements but are not addressed here, either because I could not obtain them or because they are so recent that I haven't had a chance to evaluate them: *Amerika* (ABC mini-series, 1987), *Frequency* (CW, 2016–2017), *Otherworld* (CBS mini-series, 1985) and *Spellbinder* (Nine Network, 1995; sequel, *Spellbinder: Land of the Dragon Lord,* 1997). In addition, I viewed *SS-GB* (BBC, 2017, TV mini-series based on Len Deighton's 1978 novel), but I have chosen not to address it here because it closely follows the book. Finally, HBO has announced the creation of an alternate history series, *Confederate,* set in a world where the Civil War resulted in the South's secession and creation of a new nation, where slavery is still legal. Although the proposed programme is only in its most preliminary stages, with a tentative air date of late 2018 or early 2019, it has received considerable backlash, with fears that the programme will portray slavery as somehow normalized or acceptable. See Jake Nevins's article in the *Guardian* for a nice analysis of the kerfuffle.

get the pizza. Even *Friends* (NBC, 1994–2004) has a recurrent alternate universe, including the two-parter 6.15–16 'The One That Could Have Been', which focuses on the friends' contemplations of what their lives would have been like had something happened differently. The fun of these one-off or limited-edition episodes, however, I would argue, lies not in a critique of historical discourse but in seeing favourite characters in markedly different circumstances. The alternate history trope permits character analysis in a way that, say, sf-nal tropes like alien invasion or time travel don't. Although these one-offs have much to teach us about this topic, I do not address such stories here because they do not fundamentally focus on an altered historical milieu that is foundational to the text itself but rather on character-level responses to different worlds, often to humorous effect.

Televisual alternate histories are, as I note above, not about larger historiographic concerns. They tend not to address notions of history in the larger sense. Instead they address the individual, who often has special knowledge, power, skills, or technology; agency; and (self-)contingency. In televisual alternate history, nexus points are rarely, if ever, addressed or explained – although *Sliders* does so in some episodes, and of course the two 'Hitler wins' alternate histories, *An Englishman's Castle* and *The Man in the High Castle,* rely on a clearly defined nexus point, though both take place years later. Both of these narratives are set in what we perceive as an altered milieu, but the people who inhabit these alternate realities are just regular people, not time travellers or visitors from parallel worlds, as they tend to be in the majority of televisual alternate history texts.

Such texts imbue the point-of-view protagonist with special knowledge or power. This privileged information permits the protagonist to act as a contingent agent – that is, someone who can perform an action that results in an outcome important at more than the individual level. For example, in *Sliders* 1.03 'Fever', Maximillian Arturo (John Rhys-Davies) 'invents' penicillin, using his superior knowledge, culled from his knowledge from another reality, to cure a deadly plague. He mixes his concoction, then describes the three possible (contingent) actions before he drinks down the first dose: it may do nothing; it may kill; or it may cure. Of course it does the last and he saves the day, but Arturo acts from a position of power. He comes from an alternate reality where penicillin is commonplace, and he has special knowledge of what in this other reality is an unknown wonder drug. He knows of penicillin's existence, and he knows how to make it.

Similarly, *Continuum* 1.02 'Fast Times' flashes back to Kiera Cameron (Rachel Nichols) getting the tech that permits her to do her job: to police,

or, in the parlance of her world, to protect. This early episode provides
the technological background information to explain her superhuman
powers. Cameron has inadvertently travelled back in time – to a nexus
point, she thinks, even as she embeds herself in Vancouver's policing
world of her new time, which is our present, so she can stop terrorists
from her own time from altering her past and thus changing the future.
The narrative places her in a position of power: time travel means she
has knowledge of events. But just as importantly, as we learn in 'Fast
Times', her employers have provided her with physical enhancements
and technological tools that confer an advantage over those she meets
in her past. Her guide tells her, 'You're going to want to trust your gut
out there, Cameron. Don't. Your instincts are good, but what is going
to make you a great protector is your tech'.

Both *Sliders* and *Continuum* have extraordinary people among their
protagonists. *Sliders'* Quinn Mallory (Jerry O'Connell), who invented
the technology that permits him and his companions to slide from one
parallel reality to another, and his mentor, Arturo, are brilliant physicists.
This gives them tools to craft the technological 'breakthroughs' they
use to solve a problem – but their superior knowledge comes from what
in our world is everyday knowledge (as of the existence of penicillin).
Similarly, *Continuum*'s Cameron is a highly trained protector with special
technology embedded in her body as well as in her skin-tight suit (which
she seems to wear at all times under street clothes). Her suit lets her
become invisible, and tech inside her body permits event recording and
stealthy communication. In season three of *Continuum*, an alternate
reality is created when someone time travels about two weeks into the
past and deliberately changes an outcome. In this case, Cameron, who
went along for the time travel ride, has intimate knowledge of current
events, so on top of her enhancements, she has information that permits
her to specifically intervene.

In *Timeless,* a trio of time travellers use special tech, a time travel
machine, to visit the past, where they attempt to foil the unclear
agenda of a time-travelling evildoer, Garcia Flynn (Goran Višnjić),
who uses a ship much like theirs. They track Flynn's ship whenever
it departs and then follow. Each has specialized knowledge in her or
his field, which is why they are on the team. One is a historian, one
a commando and one the ship's pilot. Because they know where and
when they are heading before they go, they are able to visit a wardrobe
to choose appropriate clothes and obtain appropriate credentials, so
in this regard their foreknowledge is valuable. After each trip, they
remember history as it was when they left, but they quickly learn to
check on events when they get home: their exploits are now recorded

as historical fact, and although the history they set out to maintain changes in details – sometimes important details, like the circumstances of Abraham Lincoln's death – the broad strokes of history remain in place. However, for historian Lucy Preston (Abigail Spencer), the details are important: after one adventure, she returned to find that her sister no longer exists. Lucy makes it a condition of her continued cooperation that the team work with her to get her sister back. Their boss, Denise Christopher (Sakina Jaffrey), finds this loss so troubling that she hands over a memory stick filled with photos and memorabilia to carry in the ship, in case circumstances change and she no longer remembers her family. Thus in season one, personal loss, not history-changing loss, results – this despite the fact that Flynn is out to change history and our heroes are out to stop him. The season finale changes this equation when finally history seems to have changed the landscape around them, but this is not dealt with, as the change is the episode's stunning reveal. Presumably we have to stay tuned for season two. In *Timeless,* the characters' expertise and foreknowledge, as well as their use of twenty-first-century technology (guns, entry cards, tiny recording devices), provide them with an edge. In particular, Lucy's deep historical knowledge permits her to make meaning of the milieus they are placed in because she is able to identify the likely nexus point that Flynn is pinpointing, so they can take countermeasures.

In contrast, in *Awake,* LA detective Michael Britten (Jason Isaacs) has nothing special about him. He is not a brilliant physicist, a highly trained commando with (or without) special tech, or a historian with foreknowledge of historical events. The show's premise is that every time Michael wakes up, he moves from one to the other of two realities: one in which his wife died but his son survived a car crash and vice versa. He has to negotiate these realities, along with their competing social needs, while solving various crimes. Although much of the show focuses on his emotional state as he moves between two realities that have diverged only recently, with the car accident, there is enough in common between the two realities to let clues learned in one reality help solve the crime of the week in the other reality. Michael's special power is knowledge of the alternate world, and he is able to bring about change because of the nature of his job. Because he is a detective, he has access to information and a kind of institutional power unavailable to the everyday person; because he moves between two realities, he can apply information learned from one reality to the other, which helps him catch bad guys. His job, combined with the circumstances of moving from one reality to the other, combine to give him the ability to bring about change.

People with extraordinary knowledge – the ability to make penicillin, use technology to become invisible, or have pre-knowledge of specific events – can then parley that know-how into action that can alter outcomes. As these examples show, knowledge may be mundane, but when placed in a new milieu, it may play a crucial role in allowing action to be performed. All it takes is for an actor to realize the importance of the information, and then apply it. Alternate histories also show how the alternate becomes imbricated in the personal, with the one informing the other. Such tight associations foreground the role that agency plays when negotiating the world by raising the stakes. In alternate histories, knowledge really can be power.

As I note above, cause and effect are important to contingency: contingency means that something is liable (but not certain) to happen as a result of something else. To this I will add another dimension: time. One must look backward and link a narrative together in order to say, 'Because x happened, y resulted, and not z'. Yet as Richard Rorty notes, such looking backward is always to construct, after the fact, something from what has been given. Rorty argues that the construction of a retrospective personal narrative is a never-completed person's life work; the impetus of this narrative is a person's 'need to come to terms with the blind impress which chance has given him, to make a self for himself by redescribing that impress in terms which are, if only marginally, his own' (43) – in short, to make meaning. In Rorty's example, this is done by retrospectively piecing together elements of one's past, ordering them and imbuing them with meaning related to constructing one's self. It is always retrospective, and it is always a construction.

In televisual alternate histories, this notion broadens out from the self to the fictive world. The narrative provides us with clues. We, the viewers, must assemble the parts into a whole from the pieces given to us: the situation, the characters, and their ability to act. Perhaps the best visual illustration of the contingency of events – a chain of events leading to a conclusion inevitable only in retrospect – is the opening sequence of *Fringe* 3.03 'The Plateau'. The existence of parallel worlds existing side by side, with different versions of the same people on each side, is the show's core concept and the main reason for watching it when studying televisual alternate history. This particular episode has contingency as its central theme, thus foregrounding the very impetus of the entire programme. The episode takes place in the alternate reality version of the *Fringe* universe, not the world congruent with our own reality.

This remarkable sequence follows Milo Stanford (Michael Eklund) as he watches a sequence of events. The video slows down in places, as if telling us that something is important – but what? Images include a woman entering a shop to buy flowers; a bus coming down the road; a four-way red light; a man sitting outside at a café table; a car hitting a pothole and splashing water onto a blue mailbox, causing the mailbox to shake; a bicycle courier in a hurry, illegally riding on the sidewalk. We don't know what to make of these elements, other than that Milo is paying attention to them.

Milo crosses the street and balances a biro pen on its end on the blue mailbox. Then it all happens: a taxi hits the pothole, thus splashing the mailbox; the pen falls when the mailbox shakes; the café patron steps over to look at it, smiling nostalgically at the old-fashioned writing utensil; the courier swerves to avoid him; the café patron knocks into the mailbox, which falls into the street, as both courier and bicycle topple into a fruit stand, scattering apples and oranges into the sidewalk; a homeless guy grabs fruit as the fruit stand owner struggles with him. The woman with the flowers steps into the street when the light changes and the WALK sign blinks on. She is unaware that a bus driver has been distracted by the ruckus. He runs the red light, striking and presumably killing the woman. But Milo is already walking away. He does not look back, although he could not have failed to hear the thump and the screech of brakes. He knows precisely what has happened.

Only after we have seen all the elements move in this Rube Goldberg-like dance of cause and effect, of contingency – one thing happening, making another thing liable to happen, except somehow x happened instead of y – can we imbue it with meaning. Retrospectively, we piece everything together. We realize what the narrative has set us up to understand: we have witnessed a murder. Milo can assess contingency, then prospectively manipulate cause and effect.

Milo is not predicting the future. Rather, he is assessing, with preternatural correctness, contingent outcomes. Milo is only unable to avert his eventual capture – the FBI-like Fringe team is onto him – because he is unable to properly predict what Olivia Dunham (Anna Torv) will do. Unbeknownst to Milo, and even to a brainwashed Olivia herself (but not to us, the viewers), the Olivias have been switched, each going to the other's world and assuming her life. Olivia fails to don a breathing mask, which is something that anyone else from this world would reflexively do in an emergency situation that Milo engineers. This breaks Milo's chain of manipulated causality. Because she is out of her own time and place, she acts in a way he cannot predict.

'The Plateau' serves as a metaphor for the entire series' causality by foregrounding the constructedness of the narratives and the work required to establish meaning, which does not necessarily inhere in the text itself. Rorty's human agent constructs her life into a narrative that tells a never-ending story by imbuing events with a retrospectively created cause-and-effect chronology, to which she assigns meaning. The nature of this narrative tells us something about that person and about that life. Similarly, the creators of a television programme wish to tell a particular story, so the pieces are presented to us in such a way that that we are likely to construct the reading they have in mind – although, of course, as all good critics know, intent has little to do with interpretation. But 'The Plateau' shows us that prospective and retrospective analyses must work together to take the pieces and create a story with meaning that resonates beyond itself.

Similarly, fake artefacts in *The Man in the High Castle* attempt to prospectively force a particular retrospective analysis. Although these artefacts play a minor role in the story line, they drew my attention because authenticity is a theme of Dick's novel. In this alternate historical world, in 1962, San Francisco-based antique dealer Robert Childan (Brennan Brown) caters to a wealthy Japanese clientele, the occupiers of the Pacific States, and their obsession with Americana. In 1.07 'Truth', Robert has dinner at a client's home and realizes two things. First, the client is surrounded by fake artefacts, notably a Colt revolver, which the client can't tell from the real thing. Second, Robert has been made a fool of: the proffered hand of what Robert perceived as friendship with someone wealthy and powerful is withdrawn. He is shown the door early. The dinner was transactional, not friendly. Angry, the incident ignites a desire for revenge in Robert's heart. He contacts Frank Frink (Rupert Evans) with a plan: Frink, a metalworker and artist, can create authentic-looking fake artefacts, and Robert can sell them from his shop.

To the defeated Americans, historical artefacts symbolize America's unoccupied past, reflecting a now-lost glory. However, to the Japanese occupiers, owning the items symbolizes their taking of that glory. To them, collectibles are costly symbols of power, emphasizing their absolute control over the former United States. By selling fakes as authentic, Robert is withholding the truth. A fake artefact reflects the past without being part of it. A fake 1847 Colt revolver has no story of its own, the way a real revolver would; that story is instead entirely constructed. It evokes nostalgia, but nothing real inheres in it. The fake is as empty of actual meaning as Robert's client dinner; it can only bear manufactured 'meaning'.

In terms of these two texts, by switching retrospective analysis with prospective analysis, *Fringe*'s 'The Plateau' shows us that we deliberately assemble the information required to construct a series of events – here *Fringe,* and by extension the entire genre of the televisual alternate history – into a narrative, which we then imbue with meaning: in a larger sense, the series' theme, and in a smaller sense a clue to Olivia that she is not who she thinks she is. Similarly, fake artefacts in *The Man in the High Castle* are prospectively created in order to force retrospective analysis: the new, made to look old, is constructed so as to deliberately confuse the issue. The narrative thus forced isn't meaningful in and of itself, but the impetus of the deliberate creation of that narrative – Robert's revenge – is.

Crucial to my discussion of nexus events and contingency is the factor that has the power to bring them about: the agent, or the person who acts. As I discussed above, those within the narrative who are aware that something is different – as in *Awake,* where Michael literally alternates realities and can carry information from one world to another – have special information that permits them to act usefully. Like *Fringe's* Milo, they can see an outcome and can attempt to construct elements to change it or to bring about a desired outcome. That is, they can, to a certain extent anyway, control contingency. In addition, they often, but not always, have special powers, like Cameron's embedded tech and suit, which permit them to effect change on more than a simply personal level.

Thus far I've discussed protagonists with special knowledge. What about agents without such knowledge? Two texts, *Charlie Jade* and *An Englishman's Castle,* present agents without foreknowledge who still manage to engage in important, global-level contingent action. Examining the role of agency in these two texts is instructive because it shows people acting as agents despite lacking certain knowledge of retrospective contingency. Perhaps not surprisingly, the moments of agency occur in the finales of the respective TV serials. One of the protagonists who acts has no special powers; the other does. Yet both manage to make the best of a terrible situation, one because of his special powers and the other despite the realization of his utter powerlessness.

In *Charlie Jade,* the eponymous private eye (Jeffrey Pierce) discovers he is able to move among three parallel universes in Cape Town, South Africa, where he lives: the Betaverse, which is our universe; the Alphaverse, which is a dystopian version of our universe but with more advanced technology; and the Gammaverse, which is a utopian version of our universe. Each of the universes has a specific colour palette so that viewers can figure out which verse they are in. An evil company, Vexcor, uses technology to try to open a stable wormhole from Alpha into Gamma so they can steal idyllic Gamma's water, but Gamma terrorists seeking to protect their home verse set off an explosion, destroying Vexcor's wormhole network and halting travel among the three verses.

Charlie, a regular guy from Alpha caught up in the explosion, finds himself in Beta. It takes a while before Charlie discovers that he can travel without technology among the three universes; he even learns to do so without water, the medium that permits both him and his nemesis, fellow verse traveller and, depending on the verse he's in, insane psychopathic killer or loving husband and father, 01 Boxer (Michael Filipowich), to move freely among verses.

In the confusing, often metaphorical series finale, during which the show runners attempted to provide closure for not just the season's story arc but the entire show, Charlie gains the upper hand over 01 as the very existence of Beta hangs in the balance.[2] Charlie leans over a tied-up 01, knife raised threateningly – and cuts him free. 'You said none of us has a choice', Charlie tells 01. 'I don't think you really believe that. You could have killed me in Gamma, but you didn't. You chose not to'. The camera cuts to Charlie's hand: he holds a large chunk of dripping ice. 'I can't do this without you', Charlie finishes. 01 flashes back to his happy family on Gamma, dead by Vexcor's hand, then puts his hand atop the ice. The two antagonists clasp hands as the block of ice drips. The water will let them move among verses, and indeed the verses flash by as they shift together, cityscape Cape Town/(alternate) Cape City skylines alternating with the unchanging landmark of Table Mountain. Next we see three windows in the Vexcor verse room. Stable wormholes have been established to each world. All three verses can now be safely navigated. But at what cost? In an unnamed grey verse, Charlie and 01 lie side by side, doomed to permanent unconsciousness, caretakers hovering over them: the newfound stability among the three verses, it seems, is a product of their extraordinary, verse-traversing minds. By combining their powers, they have provided stability, thus saving all three verses, but at the cost of their lives.

Whereas Charlie has clear agency, thanks to his verse-traversing abilities, the protagonist of *An Englishman's Castle,* TV writer Peter Ingram (Kenneth More), learns time and again, to his dismay, that he has none. Peter lives in Nazi-occupied Britain. The setting's time is not directly specified, but it appears to be contemporaneous with the show's 1978 air date. Peter's TV creation, also called *An Englishman's Castle,* a daily soap opera set during the Second World War, retells aspects of his own life, which makes him unwilling to change certain characters he creates. He goes out on a limb to keep a noble character with a clearly Jewish name

---

[2] The plot is actually far more convoluted than what I can describe here, as what occurs is metaphorical rather than literal. See R. A. Porter's 'Ouroboros' recap for a full episode description.

in the script, to honour a fallen comrade, but when the Nazis take and interrogate his son, he realizes he is in over his head and backs down. He has to call in a favour, but the quid pro quo works: Peter agrees to give the Jewish character a less objectionable name, and his son is released. Peter gets the point: his life of luxury and privilege, his own Englishman's castle, depends completely on the goodwill of England's occupying overlords. If he tests it, he will lose. He has no real power.

As Peter lives his everyday life in occupied London, growing increasingly aware of the occupying force that had previously been invisible to him, an actress on his show, Sally (Isla Blair), seduces him. A member of the resistance and a secret Jew, she wants him to help the underground take their country back. Shaken out of his deliberate blindness, his family torn apart, he agrees. In episode 3, the mini-series finale, Peter sits in his office, watching the broadcast of the latest episode of his soap opera. Sally's character will utter a code phrase, which he has inserted into the script, and everyone in the resistance will simultaneously take up arms in what they hope will be an overwhelming show of force, driving out the Nazis. However, before Sally can say her line, Peter presses a button, overriding the programme and putting himself on live TV. As the camera focuses not on Peter but on Peter's broadcast image on a nearby monitor, he says, 'My name is Peter Ingram, the author of *An Englishman's Castle*. I have a special announcement. 'Britons, strike home!' I say again, 'Britons, strike home!'' Before he can finish the repetition, the screen blacks out and a moment later the words TEMPORARY FAULT appear on the screen. He has been shut down – just as his every petty little attempt at resistance has been shut down, and just as his two sons have been shut down. As his broadcast monitor incongruously plays Mozart's elegant 'Eine kleine Nachtmusik' in the background, in a long, slow-paced take suggesting that the events are occurring in real time, Peter hears gunfire, then again louder. He peers through the blinds, takes a sip of whiskey and sits down again. It's begun. As air raid sirens begin wailing, an unseen hand hammers on the locked office door. Then the lock is shot out. We know what will happen next. They have come for him, as they would have come for Sally if he hadn't intervened. He is certainly dead, or perhaps worse than dead, as he remembers Sally's remark about concentration camps. His last words – the episode's last words, as we do not see what happens next – repeat a line we have heard before, here given new meaning: 'I shall not behave worse than one of my fictional imaginings'.

Peter acts as a contingent agent twice over. First, he agrees to the plan of broadcasting the code phrase on a certain date by putting it in a script – after all, that was why Sally had been assigned to seduce him. The show's tremendous popularity means that many members of the underground will hear the code phrase and act on it, so everyone will raise arms simultaneously. Although the text presents him as powerless in the face of Nazi-controlled bureaucracy, actually he has access to and knowledge of broadcasting technology. He may not have tech like Cameron's implants or suit in *Continuum*, but his specialized knowledge allows him to make a stand on his own terms. Second, he chooses to save Sally's life by sacrificing his own. His nobility in the plan's success, even though it will likely result in his death, redeems his previous jealous guarding of his privileges, his ridiculous belief that he was actually important, his betrayal of his wife, his failure to protect his children. The Nazis taught him better, but in the end, he was given a way to show that he could affect not only his own destiny but that of England. His position is not as powerless as he thought. He has the power to change the world, but only if he sacrifices himself. So he does.

Peter and Charlie Jade – the former realizing he's powerless but seeing a way through anyway, the latter finally understanding that he's infinitely powerful – end up in the same place. Both act on the courage of their convictions, because ultimately the only thing they can do is be true to what they believe: for Peter that the Nazis must be stopped at all costs, and for Charlie that unrestricted travel among the three verses will free the verses' inhabitants from Vexcor's profiteering agenda. Both characters use that truth to wedge open a space that permits their agency, however infinite or limited, to alter the world on a grand scale.

In the alternate history as a genre, history is used to permit displacement, which is used to highlight contemporary concerns on a national, global, or personal level. In televisual texts in particular, the genre permits alterity as a mode of displacement of self-concern, where different worlds create situations that simultaneously literally cause and metaphorically reflect characters' circumstances. For example, in *Timeless*, Lucy's time travel literally causes her sister's disappearance from the world. But it also metaphorically foregrounds both the stakes of her adventures if she can't stop Garcia (because the changes he seems to want are so vast that a missing sister would be the least of the world's problems) and the traits that inform characters at the personal level, which in turn motivate their actions (Lucy's loss, but also her boss's feared potential loss, staved off with a memory stick of family photos; and both characters' eventual decision to go rogue, the product of their understanding of the stakes). These personal connections motivate Lucy's missions; in *Charlie Jade* they result in Charlie's self-sacrifice; in

Continuum they inform Cameron's final world-altering decision even as she knows she will never get her family back because too much history has changed.

In addition to displacement of history, these texts also rely on displacement of self-concern, which often takes a backseat to the protagonists' sense of having a mission larger than the self, as all of reality as one knows it can be at stake. They set aside personal desires, often enduring crushing emotional pain, for the greater good. There is thus a moral dimension to their actions. In *An Englishman's Castle*, Peter saves his lover, with the implication that his life is the cost, performing a morally correct action that caps his fraught journey from selfish to selfless. In *Charlie Jade*, Charlie places the stability of the universes above his existence – but so does 01 Boxer, in a final moral repudiation of his past excesses, including murder. The play between good and evil that Charlie and 01 respectively represent meet in a room with them lying side by side, unconscious, attendants solicitously hovering nearby. The implication is that the two's verse-travelling bodies have been subsumed into their verse-unifying minds, a moral choice because their sacrifice provides stability for the inhabitants of three worlds.

In televisual alternate history texts, contingency is a narrative and temporal construction to frame agency. The narrative links together elements, often overtly, to let viewers construct cause and effect. This creates stakes for the protagonist. This construction is why so many of these texts rely on elements of specialness (as in *Charlie Jade*) or tech (as in *Timeless*). Such rhetorical devices foreground agency by giving characters outsize impact on the chain of causality. The message is ultimately that we are all actors, and actors have the power to change the world. As Rorty articulates, our own narratives are constructed after the fact, given impetus by a story we want to tell about ourselves. Televisual narratives, however, control the narrative to link together causal, contingent events in order to result in characters' agency. That is the story they want to tell us.

References

'4-D'. *Friends*. Writ. Steven Maeda. Dir. Tony Wharmby, Warner Bros. Television, 2001. Television.

Abrams, J. J., Alex Kurtzman and Roberto Orci, creator. *Fringe*. Perfs. Anna Torv, Joshua Jackson, John Noble. Bad Robot, 2008–2013. Television.

Anderson, Poul. *Time Patrol*. 1955–1995; repr., Baen, 2006.

Barry, Simon, creator. *Continuum*. Perfs. Rachel Nichols, Victor Webster, Erik Knudsen. Reunion Pictures, 2012–2015. Television.

Carter, Chris, creator. *The X-Files*. Perfs. David Duchovny, Gillian Anderson, Mitch Pileggi. Ten Thirteen Productions, 1993–2002, 2016–2018. Television.

Carver, Jeremy, creator. *Frequency*. Perfs. Peyton List, Riley Smith, Devin Kelley. Jeremy Carver Productions, 2016–2017. Television.

Crane, David and Marta Kauffman, creators. *Friends*. Perf. Jennifer Aniston, Courteney Cox, Lisa Kudrow. Warner Bros. Television, 1994–2004. Television.

Deighton, Len. *SS-GB: Nazi-Occupied Britain, 1941*. Jonathan Cape, 1978.

Dick, Philip K. *The Man in the High Castle*. G. P. Putnam's Sons, 1962.

'Fast Times'. *Continuum*. Writ. Jeff King. Dir. Jon Cassar. St Clare Entertainment, 2012. Television.

'Fever'. *Sliders*. Writers. Ann Powell, Rose Schacht. Dir. Mario Azzopardi. 1995. Television.

Harmon, Dan, creator. *Community*. Perfs. Joel McHale, Danny Pudi, Donald Glover. Krasnoff Foster Productions, 2009–2015. Television.

Hellekson, Karen. *The Alternate History: Refiguring Historical Time*. Kent State University Press, 2001.

Kadelbach, Philipp, creator. *SS-GB*. Perfs. Sam Riley, James Cosmo, Rainer Bock. Sid Gentle Films, 2017. Television.

Killen, Kyle, creator. *Awake*. Perfs. Jason Isaacs, Laura Allen, Steve Harris. Letter Eleven, 2012. Television.

Kripke, Eric and Shawn Ryan, creators. *Timeless*. Perfs. Abigail Spencer, Matt Lanter, Malcolm Barrett. MiddKid Productions, 2016–2018. Television.

Mackie, Philip, writer. *An Englishman's Castle*. Perfs. Kenneth More, Anthony Bate, Isla Blair. BBC, 1978. Television.

'Mirror Mirror'. *Star Trek*. Writ. Jerome Bixby. Dir. Marc Daniels. Desilu Productions, 1967. Television.

Nevins, Jake. '*Confederate:* Will a Grassroots Movement Sink the Controversial HBO Series?' *The Guardian*. 1 August 2017. Accessed 25 April 2019.

'The One That Could Have Been Part 1'. *Friends*. Writ. Greg Malins, Adam Chase. Dir. Michael Lembeck. Warner Bros. Television, 2000. Television.

'The One That Could Have Been Part 2'. *Friends*. Writ. David Crane, Marta Kauffman. Dir. Michael Lembeck. Warner Bros. Television, 2000. Television.

'The Plateau'. *Fringe*. Writ. Alison Schapker, Monica Owusu-Breen. Dir. Brad Anderson. Bad Robot, 2010. Television.

Porter, R. A. 'Charlie Jade Recap: "Ouroboros".' *CharlieJade.net*. 21 October 2008. Accessed 25 April 2019.

Price, Noel, creator. *Spellbinder: Land of the Dragon Lord*. Perf. Lauren Hewett, Ryan Kwanten, Leonard Fung. Film Australia Southern Star, 1997. Television.

'Remedial Chaos Theory'. *Community*. Writ. Chris McKenna. Dir. Jeff Melman. Krasnoff Foster Productions, 2011. Television.

Roddenberry, Gene, creator. *Star Trek*. Perf. William Shatner, Leonard Nimoy, DeForest Kelley. Desilu Productions, 1966–1969. Television.

Roland, Chris and Robert Wertheimer, creators. *Charlie Jade*. Perfs. Jeffrey Pierce, Michael Filipowich, Michele Burgers. 4142276, 2005. Television.

Rorty, Richard. *Contingency, Irony and Solidarity*. Cambridge University Press, 1989.

Shirrefs, Mark and John Thomson, creator. *Spellbinder*. Perfs. Zbych Trofimiuk, Gosia Piotrowska, Brian Rooney. Film Australia, 1995. Television.

Spotnitz, Frank, creator. *The Man in the High Castle*. Perfs. Alexa Davalos, Luke Kleintank, Rufus Sewell. Amazon Studios, 2015–. Television.

Taylor, Roderick, creator. *Otherworld*. Perfs. Sam Groom, Gretchen Corbett, Tony O'Dell. Universal Television, 1985. Television.

Tormé, Tracy and Robert K. Weiss, creators. *Sliders*. Perfs. Jerry O'Connell, Sabrina Lloyd, John Rhys-Davies, Cleavant Derricks. St Clare Entertainment, 1995–2000. Television.

Wrye, Donald, writer. *Amerika*. Perfs. Kris Kristofferson, Robert Urich, Wendy Hughes. ABC Circle Films, 1987. Television.

Afterword

C. Palmer-Patel and Glyn Morgan

In 2003, Edgar L. Chapman, in the introduction to a now out-of-print collection of alternate history essays he edited with Carl B. Yorke, stated that he wanted his collection to call attention to two important facts:

> (1) There is neither a clear understanding of the history of alternate history fiction;

> (2) Nor is there an agreed upon poetics of this genre (or sub-genre, if you wish) of fictional narrative, although some efforts in this direction have been made. (Chapman 3)

Over a decade later, whilst progress has been made, these basic points remain cogent. Excellent works of scholarship *do* exist on alternate history, but as the introduction to this collection has pointed out there are still strangely few of them. Meanwhile, alternate history fiction itself has further developed into an increasingly important field deserving of the insightful and focused studies which are beginning to emerge. Whilst this collection cannot completely make up the difference, it provides a crucial stepping stone towards it, and we hope a timely one for a genre of ever-increasing critical and cultural value.

Why does this gap exist at all? One possible explanation is in alternate history's literary lineage, with its roots in historical counterfactualism leading scholars of science fiction studies to disregard it as kin to the mainstream historical novel (perhaps explaining the absence of chapters on alternate history from many – although by no means all – texts serving as introductions to sf), whilst many historians and scholars of historical fiction regard its playfulness as too fantastical. Or, paradoxically, perhaps the small size of the field of alternate history scholarship is due to the vastness of the topic. In putting together this collection, we could not but struggle to cover the wide range of themes, nations and cultures, and historical periods that alternate history itself has tackled. Considering that alternate history begins as far back as Livy in 35 BCE and continues in the twenty-first century at a greater intensity than ever before, the immensity of the topic is difficult to contain in one book, let alone do justice to it properly. This does not even begin to address issues of translation, when one considers the number of different cultures that produce alternate history. Furthermore, as Stephen Baxter suggested in his foreword to this collection: 'The shape of our world – cosmological, geographic, biological – has played a key role in shaping our destiny. And this becomes evident when counterfactuals are considered' (3); contemplating the infinite ways that history can branch into alternate paths leaves an immense body of material to reflect on.

Although alternate history has depicted a vast amount of possible timelines, what these texts have in common is the idea that – through the depiction of a slightly different timeline – alternate history reflects on and reveals the nature of our *current* reality. Thus, the first part of the collection illustrated the ways in which alternate history texts convey a new understanding of history, society, and culture. For instance, Roberts drew connections to the 'Great Man of History' model deployed by Geoffroy with a critique of American history (as being at once empty and full) alongside the impact of Geoffroy's hero-worship of Napoleon. The 'Geoffroyan model of alternate history', Roberts argued, counters the Tolstoyan model; for Tolstoy, history is the result of millions of smaller events, rather than being driven by a single extraordinary figure. The Geoffroyan model is influential not only in later iterations of alternate history, but in science fiction as well. Roberts' ideas are re-examined in the second half of the collection, 'Manipulating the Genre', as we moved from socio-cultural understandings of events to look at individualized comprehensions. For instance, Cobb's examination of Alfred Bester's writings presented alternatives to Robert's premise that most alternate history follows a 'great man of history'. Bester's stories, Cobb argued, are concerned with personal identity and 'the individual's place in time'. Consequently, an analysis of Bester's depictions of alternate history revealed that, while many alternate histories *do* follow the model set by Geoffroy, where individual agency affects great events, Bester in contrast poses individual's actions as negligible to history. History is predestined, in this sense, and limits agency. For Bester, Cobb concluded, 'collective history will continue despite the destruction of individual timelines' (112).

Roberts' conclusion that most alternate history is Geoffroyan rather than Tolstoyan – and that science fiction follows a similar pattern – was expanded and examined throughout the collection. Pak's chapter focused

on the form and the impact on narrative cohesion which is created
through a focus on the reincarnation of a few key characters. Like
Roberts, Pak's discussion of epic form allowed him to draw conclusions
on the nature of alternate history, which he also extended to sf more
generally, bringing attention to the depiction (or lack) of non-European
civilizations in western literature. Thus, Rayner in his chapter examined
narratives from one of these non-European traditions. Likewise, Baker
examined Sales' experimental form in order to highlight a critique of
other suppressed minority voices, specifically the place of woman as
central to the narrative in both alternate history and science fiction.
In contrast, Butler's chapter considered another form of alternate
history, the uchronia, and explored how the alternate world can be
considered gendered: 'The (feminine coded) innocence of the alternate
is balanced by the lack of (masculine coded) scientific' (165). These
discussions of narrative forms all emphasized the way in which cultural
critique of minority voices is embedded in the narrative structure itself.
Alternatively, Thiess continued the discussion of alternate history's
relationship to sf by contemplating power and authority. Thiess noted
that, for secularized science fiction, religion is considered an 'Other',
whereas for more dogmatic writers, 'science fiction and religion are
inextricably linked' (125). The difference became important as Thiess
examined Aguilera's novel as a hybrid or mediation between alternate
history and apocryphal history, a work that utilizes both real and
fictional people and events. This tension is deliberate, as Thiess argued
that Aguilera's novel 'highlight[s] the very fragility of materialism in
history and its treatment at the hands of religious institution' (127).

Roberts also asserted that although there are examples of Tolstoyan
sf and alternate history, these narratives are still 'defined by its breaks
as its continuities'. The notion of breaks and continuities as central
to conceptions of time and history, and ultimately how these models
impact on the reader's comprehension of a nation's history, are integral
concepts to each chapter of the collection in different ways. Continuing
the conversation that Roberts began, Pak discussed history in terms of
a utopian break: 'Utopian break', he argued, 'is an ongoing process that
itself becomes subject to being transformed into story [...] the approach
of this utopian break is always deferred; [...] the imagination of the
future is a utopian intervention' (51). Baker, in his chapter, moved this
discussion of utopia from a break to a tension between dreaming and
nostalgia, with his reflections on the explorations of the Space Age: 'As
an emanation of "cultural dreaming", there is something utopian about
Apollo, something to do with enacting an idea of the future which in
indissoluble from science fiction itself' (79). However, as Baker points

out, there is very little science fiction that deals with Apollo directly, 'because Apollo was science fiction already, of a particular kind: a heroic, spectacular adventure narrative' (79). Apollo, Baker concluded, is at once a source of dreaming and disruption. Likewise, McFarlane also identified a tension between experiences of time as both flowing forward and disrupting the past. Referring back to Freud's *Nachträglichkeit*, or 'afterwardsness', McFarlane explored how Tidhar's character 'lives in an endless present' where trauma is deferred, forcing an endless re-living on a person. McFarlane described how the structure and language of the novel creates a division between past and present which is represented by the 'secret inscriptions on the mind' (Tidhar 151), a concept that was developed later in this second half of this collection. Here, McFarlane explicitly drew out examples of the importance of break and continuities in the narrative by highlighting the character's actions of 'breaking out of the world' in order to return to the reality he is familiar with.

As McFarlane suggested, alternate history offers a commentary on history through the repetition of narrative retelling in historiography itself. Pak similarly concluded that the act of storytelling allows individuals to re-shape both the past and the future as alternate history can bring new meaning into the actions of marginalized individuals or groups who are normally silenced or omitted. Rayner expanded on Pak's conclusions with a survey of films and anime which deal with Japan's military history. Rayner's investigation of a number of different alternate histories suggested that re-interpretations of this past are problematic, as filmmakers struggle to come to terms with Japan's position in historical wars while simultaneously attempting to redeem the nation and convey a sense of national pride. Rayner showed us how alternate history allows re-reading and rewritings of history, and, '[i]n this nationally-specific context, alternate history has moved from peripheral, hypothetic debate to didactic, institutionalized re-inscription' (65). Rayner's discussion of war motifs, which expresses an 'ambivalent current of patriotic celebration and national mourning' highlighted the emotional impact of retelling history. Baker continued this discussion with Sales' Quartet with an interrogation of masculinity: 'The cost of the space programme [...] is not strictly geopolitical or financial: it is also personal and emotional' (84). The importance of the emotional impact of these re-interpretations comes to a crescendo in McFarlane's chapter on Tidhar's *Osama: A Novel*, where the political response to 9/11 and the 'War on Terror' incorporate an emotional one which risks sliding towards fascism. While Rayner discussed war history in terms of rewriting cultural guilt, McFarlane approached it from a manner of interrogating our cultural responses in order to prevent its reoccurrence.

McFarlane's discussion of how Tidhar's novel is divided between the 'secret inscriptions of the mind' foreshadowed the discussion of 'secret history' in both Thiess's and Germaine Buckley's chapters. Thiess began his chapter with a reflection on the words of Arthur B. Evans: 'History is fiction. Not the events, but the telling of them' (Evans 47). As this collection has argued, history involves a constant retelling and interpretations of events. Thiess's response to this idea that 'An alternate critical timeline of historical theory itself might just as easily begin by asking *why* instead of if: why we find it necessary to fictionalize history' can, on one hand, be answered by McFarlane's observation that one of the 'pleasures' of alternate history is the 'enjoyment of repetition with a difference' (96). There is indeed a Barthesian pleasure in re-interpreting and retelling history. However, as Pak and Baker have demonstrated, these re-interpretations also serve to give voices to those traditionally suppressed by history's narratives. If history is generally written by victors, alternate history offers a path for other narratives to emerge. Thus, Rayner's chapter, in turn, exemplified how alternate history can be used to reinterpret moral dilemmas. Thiess expanded on these premises, observing that while a popular bookstore has 'decided not that history is fiction but that history is religion', such an observation is problematic when considering the malleable nature of history (124). By focusing his discussion on materialism, Thiess explored the difficulties of fictionalizing dogmatic events: 'The apocryphal history here gives expression to the overt materialism of history' (131). The problems become apparent with the blending of apocryphal with alternate, as Thiess argues, '[t]he presence of other places, and especially of *competing histories*, take this novel beyond the merely apocryphal and threaten to lead the reader to aporia' (131).

Theiss' analysis was expanded in a different form by Germaine Buckley in the next chapter. For Germaine Buckley, the dogmas of secret history focused on the nature of the 'true' or 'original' text as Germaine Buckley examined an alternate rewriting of canonical texts. This rewriting, she argued, is 'a double alternate, or "secret", history', as it not only rewrites a fictional history, but it takes part in the Weird tradition of 'revising the history of human civilization to reveal aeons-old monsters' (139). Thus, Germaine Buckley's discussion of form in connection to ontological significance continued the conversation of alternate history forms begun by Roberts, Pak, and Baker in the first half of this collection. But whereas these earlier authors brought a science fictional understanding to alternate history, Germaine Buckley examined the relationship to fantastic horror, and specifically to that of the Weird. Like McFarlane, Germaine Buckley discussed the rewriting of human history as a 'pleasurable surrender', but here, Germaine Buckley focused this pleasure on 'a new structural relationship between belief and knowledge' (151). Unlike Thiess, who saw a tension between the real and unreal (or fiction and dogma) due to a tension between secularism and religion deriving from Enlightenment values, Germaine Buckley's chapter explored a successful intercession of these same values: 'This ontology is resolutely material rather than supernatural, but it refuses to be quantified or represented by scientific modes of knowledge' (139).

Further developing Germaine Buckley's arguments that the retelling of canonical fiction is a form of alternate history itself, Butler in his chapter asserted that adaptation should also be viewed as a form of alternate history. Butler's exploration of Wyndham's short story 'Random Quest' considered a number of different film and television adaptations: 'in adaptation studies measures of "faithfulness" and "fidelity" [...] are frowned upon'. However, Butler continued, '[i]n fiction where characters move between parallel words, one oeuvre is no more real than the other, nor is the adaptation less authentic than its source' (164). Butler's discussion on adaptations anticipated Hellekson's final chapter in this collection as Hellekson examined examples of televisual alternate history in further detail. Although the majority of this collection has focused on textual outputs, there has been an astonishing outpouring of texts, both literary and visual, in recent decades. Popular consciousness of the genre has risen accordingly, aided by such high-profile examples as the *Fallout* video games series (1997–present), Quentin Tarantino's *Inglorious Basterds* (2009), the comic book multiverses of mega-franchises like DC and Marvel, Amazon Prime's adaptation of Philip K. Dick's *The Man in the High Castle* (2015–present), and the BBC's adaptation of Len Deighton's *SS-GB* (2016). Hellekson's own chapter focused on a select range of these popular examples, specifically that of television series.

Hellekson's chapter on televisual adaptations brought us full circle to where we began the collection, with Roberts examination of the 'first' alternate history novel, and the discussion of both human agency with regards to 'breaks' and 'continuums' as a result of a new form. Hellekson asserted that the form of the genre expressed in a different medium produces a change in focus when considering contingency and agency, as television series emphasize cause and effect:

> Unlike written alternate history texts, they rely not on an historical analysis of history and its ultimate purpose but rather on an examination of individual characters and their reactions to the (from our point of view altered) world around them. This is done to address larger concerns of contingency and agency, the

foregrounding of which indicates the presence of a contingency–
agency feedback loop that ultimately serves to privilege the
individual over the turning of the wheel of history. (170)

Thus, Hellekson concluded that for the televisual alternate history,
individual agency is emphasized as protagonists, provided with special
knowledge or technology, are able to see cause and effect of events and
thereby directly impact on them. Even in those examples where the
character has no knowledge of events, the protagonist still demonstrates
a type of agency, and 'engage[s] in important, global-level contingent
action'. Her discussion, like the rest of this collection, emphasized the
ways in which individuals have direct agency over momentous events.

   This collection has focused on a number of different ideas that must
be considered when examining alternate history. How are the tensions
between the past and the future represented? What form does the
alternate history take, and what is the significance of these seemingly
disparate structures? Does humanity have agency over historical events?
And, if so, does the impact of an individual lead to a break in a timeline,
a continuum to a parallel world? And ultimately, what does these
changes, these points of divergences, the jonbar hinge, tell us about
our current reality?

   These questions represent some of the most prominent issues with
which the chapters in this collection have attempted to engage. Yet
they of course cannot provide definitive answers. They build upon the
discussions of alternate history in pre-existing scholarship, presenting
new ways for us to think about what alternate history is, and what the
genre does. We hope that these discussions will continue as scholars
engage with the increasingly vital and ubiquitous genre of alternate
history fiction, and that these chapters will form an important part of
that conversation going forward.

References

Chapman, Edgar L. 'Introduction: Three Stages of Alternate History Fiction
    and the "Metaphysical If"' *Classic and Iconoclastic Alternate History Science
    Fiction*. Eds. Edgar L. Chapman and Carl B. Yoke. Edwin Mellen Press,
    2003, pp. 1–28.
Evans, Arthur B. 'Histories.' *The Oxford Handbook of Science Fiction*. Ed. Rob
    Latham. Oxford University Press, 2014.
Tidhar, Lavie. *Osama: A Novel*. PS Publishing, 2011.

Notes on Contributors

Brian Baker is a Senior Lecturer in English and Creative Writing at Lancaster University. He works on science fiction, masculinities and postwar British and American fiction, having published monographs on *Masculinities in Fiction and Film 1945–2000* (Continuum, 2006), *Iain Sinclair* (Manchester, 2007), *Contemporary Masculinities in Fiction, Film and TV* (Bloomsbury, 2015) and also *The Reader's Guide to Essential Criticism in Science Fiction* (Palgrave, 2014). He is currently working on the science fiction of the 1960s, and a project that considers the relation between sound, subjectivity and narrative in contemporary culture.

Stephen Baxter has published over fifty novels, including alternate history titles from *Anti-Ice* (1993) to the *Northland* trilogy (2010–2012). He has also served as a judge of the Sidewise Award, given annually for best alternate-history fiction.

Chloé Germaine Buckley is Senior Lecturer at Manchester Metropolitan University. She writes about and teaches children's literature and culture. Her publications include articles on children's Gothic, Weird fiction, witches, and the postcolonial Gothic. She is co-editor of the edited collection, *Telling it Slant: Critical Approaches on Helen Oyeyemi* (Sussex Academic Press, 2017) with Sarah Ilott and author of *Twenty-First-Century Children's Gothic* (Edinburgh University Press, 2017).

Andrew M. Butler is the author of *Solar Flares: Science Fiction in the 1970s*, as well as books on Philip K. Dick, cyberpunk, Terry Pratchett, postmodernism, film studies, and *Eternal Sunshine of the Spotless Mind*. Recently he has published chapters on *Star Wars* and *Star Trek*. He is a co-editor of *Extrapolation* and the Chair of Judges for the Arthur C. Clarke Award. Thanks to one point of divergence, he could have been born in Belgium or not at all.

Molly Cobb is a University Teacher at the University of Liverpool. Her research focuses on mid-twentieth-century American science fiction and representations of Cold War identity, specializing in the works of Alfred Bester and his use of Freudian psychology. She also regularly contributes reviews to various publications, including *Foundation, Fantastika Journal* and *SFRA Review*, and has articles published in *Vector*.

Karen Hellekson has published books and articles about science fiction, alternate history, and fan studies. She is an independent scholar based in Maine, USA.

Anna McFarlane is a British Academy Postdoctoral Fellow at the University of Glasgow with a project entitled 'Products of Conception: Science Fiction and Pregnancy, 1968–2015'. Previously she worked on the Wellcome Trust-funded Science Fiction and the Medical Humanities project. She is the editor of *Adam Roberts: Critical Essays* (Gylphi, 2016), and blog editor for the journal *BMJ Medical Humanities*.

Glyn Morgan is a Project Curator at The Science Museum, London. He earned his PhD from the University of Liverpool and is the author of *Imagining the Unimaginable: Speculative Fiction and the Holocaust* (Bloomsbury, 2020). He is the co-founder of the annual Current Research in Speculative Fiction (CRSF) conference and a former editor of *Vector: The Critical Journal of the British Science Fiction Association*.

Chris Pak is Lecturer in Contemporary Writing and Digital Cultures at Swansea University and the author of *Terraforming: Ecopolitical Transformations and Environmentalism in Science Fiction* (Liverpool University Press, 2016). More information and links to articles can be found on his website at chrispak.wix.com/chrispak.

C. Palmer-Patel received a doctorate from Lancaster University, UK in 2017. Her research focuses on epic fantasy. She is currently working on publishing her first monograph, *The Shape of Fantasy*, which examines structures in post-1990 American literature, and has begun writing her second, with a focus on mothers and matriarchy in the genre. Palmer-Patel is head editor of *Fantastika Journal*, a journal that brings together the genres of fantasy, science fiction, gothic/horror and alternate history, among others. She currently resides in Edmonton, Alberta, Canada.

Jonathan Rayner is Reader in Film Studies at the University of Sheffield, School of English. His research interests and publications span Australasian cinema, auteur studies, genre films, naval history on film and television, and the interplay of landscapes and moving images. With Prof Julia Dobson he is co-director of SCRIF, the Sheffield Centre for Research in Film. He is the author of *The Naval War Film: Genre, History, National Cinema* (2007), *The Cinema of Michael Mann* (2013), *The Films of Peter Weir* (1998/2003) and *Contemporary Australian Cinema* (2000). He is co-editor of *Filmurbia* (2017), *Mapping Cinematic Norths* (2016), Film Landscapes (2013) and *Cinema and Landscape* (2010).

Adam Roberts is a British writer and academic. His most recent publications are the novels *The Real Time Murders* (Gollancz 2017) and *By The Pricking of Her Thumbs* (Gollancz 2018) and *The Palgrave History of Science Fiction* (2nd edition, 2016). He is presently working on a literary biography of H G Wells. He has, on occasion, written alternate history.

Derek J. Thiess is an Assistant Professor of English at the University of North Georgia, USA. His work focuses on embodiment in science fiction and horror literature. He is the author of *Embodying Gender and Age in Speculative Fiction: A Biopsychosocial Approach* (Routledge 2015) and *Relativism, Alternate History, and the Forgetful Reader: Reading Science Fiction and Historiography* (Lexington 2014).

Index